Microsoft®
Business Intelligence Tools
for Excel® Analysts

Microsoft®
Business Intelligence Tools for Excel® Analysts

by Michael Alexander, Jared Decker,
Bernard Wehbe

WILEY

Microsoft® Business Intelligence Tools for Excel® Analysts

Published by:
John Wiley & Sons, Inc.,
111 River Street,
Hoboken, NJ 07030-5774,
www.wiley.com

Copyright © 2014 by John Wiley & Sons, Inc., Hoboken, New Jersey

Published simultaneously in Canada

About the Authors

Mike Alexander is a Microsoft Certified Application Developer (MCAD) and author of several books on advanced business analysis with Microsoft Access and Excel. He has more than 16 years' experience consulting and developing Office solutions. Mike has been named a Microsoft MVP for his ongoing contributions to the Excel community. You can visit Mike at `www.datapigtechnologies.com`, where he regularly shares Excel and Access tips and techniques.

Jared Decker has over fourteen years of experience in the IT industry and ten years of consulting experience focused exclusively on data warehousing and business intelligence. In addition to playing an architect or lead role on dozens of projects, he has spent more than five hundred hours in-house with corporations training their development teams on the Microsoft SQL Server, Tableau, and QlikView BI platforms. His breadth of experience entails everything from architecture and design to system implementation, with particular focus on business analytics and data visualization. Jared holds technical certifications in Microsoft (MCITP Business Intelligence Developer and certified trainer), Tableau Developer, and QlikView Developer and Trainer.

Bernard Wehbe has over 14 years of consulting experience focused exclusively on data warehousing, analytics, and business intelligence. His experience includes data warehousing architecture, OLAP, data modeling, ETL, reporting, business analysis, team leadership, and project management. Prior to founding StatSlice Systems, Bernard served as a technical architect for Hitachi Consulting in the Dallas, TX area.

Publisher's Acknowlegments

Sr. Acquisitions Editor: Katie Mohr

Project Editor: Rebecca Senninger

Copy Editor: Lynn Northrup

Technical Editor: Mike Talley

Editorial Assistant: Anne Sullivan

Sr. Editorial Assistant: Cherie Case

Project Coordinator: Patrick Redmond

Contents at a Glance

▶ Table of Contents

Part II: Leveraging SQL for Business Intelligence

Part III: Delivering Business Intelligence with SharePoint and Excel Services

Part IV: Appendixes

INTRODUCTION

Over the last few years, the concept of self-service business intelligence (BI) has taken over the corporate world. Self-service BI is a form of business intelligence in which end-users can independently generate their own reports, run their own queries, and conduct their own analyses, without the need to engage the IT department.

The demand for self-service BI is a direct result of several factors:

> **More power users:** Organizations are realizing that no single enterprise reporting system or BI tool can accommodate all of their users. Pre-defined reports and high-level dashboards may be sufficient for some casual users, but a large portion of today's users are savvy enough to be considered power users. Power users have a greater understanding data analysis and prefer to perform their own analysis, often within Excel.

> **Changing analytical needs:** In the past, business intelligence primarily consisted of IT-managed dashboards showing historic data on an agreed upon set of key performance metric. Managers today are demanding more dynamic predictive analysis, the ability to iteratively perform data discovery, and the freedom to take the hard left and right turns on data presentation. These managers often turn to Excel to provide the needed analytics and visualization tools.

> **Speed of BI:** Users are increasingly dissatisfied with the inability of IT to quickly deliver new reporting and metrics. Most traditional BI implementations fail specifically because the need for changes and answers to new questions overwhelmingly outpace the IT department's ability to deliver them. As a result, users often find ways to work around the perceived IT bottleneck and ultimately build their own shadow BI solutions in Excel.

Recognizing the importance of the self-service BI revolution and the role Excel plays in it, Microsoft has made substantial investments in making Excel the cornerstone of its self-service BI offering. These investments have appeared starting with Excel 2007; to name a few: the ability to handle over a million rows, tighter integration to SQL Server, pivot table slicers, and the Power Pivot Add-in.

With the release of Excel 2013 and the Power BI suite of tools (Power Pivot, Power Query, Power Map, and Power View), Microsoft has aggressively moved to make Excel a player in the self-service BI arena.

The Power BI suite of tools ushers in a new age for Excel. For the first time, Excel is an integral part of the Microsoft BI stack. You can integrate multiple data sources, define relationships between data sources, process analysis services cubes, and develop interactive dashboards that can be shared on the web. Indeed, the new Microsoft BI tools blur the line between Excel analysis and what is traditionally IT enterprise-level data management and reporting capabilities.

With these new tools in the Excel wheelhouse, it's becoming important for business analysts to expand their skillset to new territory, including database management, query design, data integration, multidimensional reporting, and a host of other skills. Excel analysts have to expand their skillset knowledge base from the one dimensional spreadsheets to relational databases, data integration, and multidimensional reporting,

Microsoft Business Intelligence Tools for Excel Analysts is aimed squarely at business analysts and managers who find it increasingly necessary to become more efficient at working with big data tools traditionally reserved for IT professionals. This book guides you through the mysterious world of PowerPivot, SQL Server, and SharePoint reporting. You find out how to leverage the rich set of tools and reporting capabilities to more effectively source and incorporate business intelligence and dashboard reports. Not only can these tools allow you to save time and simplify your processes, they can also enable you to substantially enhance your data analysis and reporting capabilities.

What You Need to Know

The goal of this book is to give you a solid review of the business intelligence functionally that is offered in the Microsoft BI suite of tools. These tools include: Power Pivot, Power View, Power Map, Power Query, SQL Server Analysis Services, SharePoint, and PerformancePoint.

Throughout the book, we discuss the each particular topic in terms and analogies with which business analysts would be familiar. After reading this book, you will be able to:

➤ Use Power Pivot to create powerful reporting mechanisms

➤ Automate data integration with Power Query

➤ Use SQL Server's built-in Functions to analyze large amounts of data

➤ Use Excel pivot tables to access and analyze SQL Server Analysis Services data

➤ Create eye-catching visualizations and Dashboards with Power View

➤ Gain insight and analytical power with Data Mining tools

➤ Publish dashboards and reports to the web

What the Icons Mean

Throughout the book, icons appear to call your attention to points that are particularly important.

Note

We use Note icons to tell you that something is important— perhaps a concept that may help you master the task at hand or something fundamental for understanding subsequent material.

Tip icons indicate a more efficient way of doing something or a technique that may not be obvious. These will often impress your officemates.

We use Caution icons when the operation that we're describing can cause problems if you're not careful.

How This Book Is Organized

The chapters in this book are organized into four parts. Although each part is an integral part of the book as a whole, you can read each part in any order you want, skipping from topic to topic.

Part I: Leveraging Excel for Business Intelligence

Part I is all the business intelligence tools found in Excel. Chapter 1 starts you off with the fundamental database management concepts needed to work with the Microsoft BI tools. Chapter 2 provides an overview of PivotTables — the cornerstone of Microsoft BI analysis and presentation. In Chapters 3 and 4, you discover how to develop powerful integrated reporting mechanisms with Power Pivot. Chapters 5 and 6 shows you the basics of using Power View and Power Map to develop interactive visualizations and dashboards. Chapter 7 rounds out Part 1 with an exploration of data integration and transformation using Power Query.

Part II: Leveraging SQL Server for Business Intelligence

Part II focuses on leveraging Microsoft's SQL Server database tools to enhance your ability to develop business intelligence solutions. Chapters 8, 9, and 10 provide the fundamentals you need to manage data, create queries, and develop stored procedures in Microsoft SQL Server. Chapter 11 picks up from there, showing you how to incorporate SQL Server analyses into your Excel reporting models. Chapter 12 introduces you to SQL Reporting Services, showing you an alternative to Excel reports. In Chapter 13, you discover how to browse and analyze Microsoft SQL Analysis Services OLAP cubes. You wrap up Part II with Chapter 14 where you get a look at the Data Mining Add-In for Excel.

Part III: Delivering Business Intelligence with SharePoint and Excel Services

In Part III, you gain some insights on the role SharePoint plays in the Microsoft business intelligence strategy. Chapter 15 demonstrates how to leverage SharePoint and Excel Services to publish your reporting solutions to the Web. Chapter 16 wraps up your tour of the Microsoft business intelligence tools with a look at the PerformancePoint dashboard development solution for SharePoint.

Part IV: Appendixes

Part IV includes some peripheral material that completes the overall look at the business intelligence landscape. Appendix A provides a comparison of the currently available big data toolsets on the market today. Appendix B details some of the considerations for moving business intelligence solutions to mobile devices.

About the Companion Web Site

This book contains example files available on the companion Web site that is arranged in directories that correspond to the chapters. You can download example files for this book at the Web site:

```
www.wiley.com/go/bitools
```

Leveraging Excel for Business Intelligence

Important Database Concepts

In This Chapter

- Using a database to get past Excel limitations
- Getting familiar with database terminology
- Understanding relational databases
- How databases are designed

Although Excel is traditionally considered the premier tool for data analysis and reporting, it has some inherent characteristics that often lead to issues revolving around scalability, transparency of analytic processes, and confusion between data and presentation. Over the last several years, Microsoft has recognized this and created tools that allow you to develop reporting and business intelligence by connecting to various external databases. Microsoft has gone a step further with Excel 2013, offering business intelligence (BI) tools like Power Pivot natively; it effectively allows you to build robust relational data models within Excel.

With the introduction of these BI tools, it's becoming increasingly important for you to understand core database fundamentals. Unlike traditional Excel concepts, where the approach to developing solutions is relatively intuitive, good database-driven development requires a bit of prior knowledge. There are a handful of fundamentals you should know before jumping into the BI tools. These include database terminology, basic database concepts, and database best practices.

The topics covered in this chapter explain the concepts and techniques necessary to successfully use database environments and give you the skills needed to normalize data and plan and implement effective tables.

If you're already familiar with the concepts involved in database design, you may want to skim this chapter. If you're new to the world of databases, spend some time in this chapter gaining a thorough understanding of these important topics.

Traditional Limits of Excel and How Databases Help

Managers, accountants, and analysts have had to accept one simple fact over the years: Their analytical needs had outgrown Excel. They all met with fundamental issues that stemmed from one or more of Excel's three problem areas: scalability, transparency of analytical processes, and separation of data and presentation.

Scalability

Scalability is the ability for an application to develop flexibly to meet growth and complexity requirements. In the context of Excel, scalability refers to Excel's ability to handle ever-increasing volumes of data. Most Excel aficionados are quick to point out that as of Excel 2007, you can place 1,048,576 rows of data into a single Excel worksheet. This is an overwhelming increase from the limitation of 65,536 rows imposed by previous versions of Excel. However, this increase in capacity does not solve all of the scalability issues that inundate Excel.

Imagine that you're working in a small company and using Excel to analyze your daily transactions. As time goes on, you build a robust process complete with all the formulas, PivotTables, and macros you need to analyze the data that is stored in your neatly maintained worksheet.

As your data grows, you start to notice performance issues. Your spreadsheet becomes slow to load and then slow to calculate. Why does this happen? It has to do with the way Excel handles memory. When an Excel file is loaded, the entire file is loaded into RAM. Excel does this to allow for quick data processing and access. The drawback to this behavior is that each time something changes in your spreadsheet, Excel has to reload the entire spreadsheet into RAM. A large spreadsheet takes a great deal of RAM to process even the smallest change. Eventually, each action you take in your gigantic worksheet will result in an excruciating wait.

Your PivotTables will require bigger *pivot caches* (memory containers), almost doubling your Excel workbook's file size. Eventually, your workbook will become too big to distribute easily. You may even consider breaking down the workbook into smaller workbooks (possibly one for each region). This causes you to duplicate your work.

In time, you may eventually reach the 1,048,576-row limit of your worksheet. What happens then? Do you start a new worksheet? How do you analyze two datasets on two different worksheets as one entity? Are your formulas still good? Will you have to write new macros?

These are all issues that need to be dealt with.

You can find various clever ways to work around these limitations. In the end, though, they are just workarounds. Eventually you will begin to think less about the most effective way to perform and present analysis of your data and more about how to make something "fit" into Excel without breaking your formulas and functions. Excel is flexible enough that you can make most things "fit" into Excel just fine. However, when you think only in terms of Excel, you're limiting yourself, albeit in an incredibly functional way.

In addition, these capacity limitations often force you to have the data prepared for you. That is, someone else extracts large chunks of data from a large database, then aggregates and shapes the data for use in Excel. Should you always depend on someone else for your data needs? What if you have the tools to "access" vast quantities of data without relying on others to provide data? Could you be more valuable to the organization? Could you focus on the accuracy of the analysis and the quality of the presentation instead of routing Excel data maintenance?

A relational database system (like Access or SQL Server) is a logical next step. Most database system tables take very few performance hits with larger datasets and have no predetermined row limitations. This allows you to handle larger datasets without requiring the data to be summarized or prepared to fit into Excel. Also, if a process becomes more crucial to the organization and needs to be tracked in a more "enterprise-acceptable" environment, it's easier to upgrade and scale up if that process is already in a relational database system.

Transparency of analytical processes

One of Excel's most attractive features is its flexibility. Each individual cell can contain text, a number, a formula, or practically anything else you define. Indeed, this is one of the fundamental reasons Excel is such an effective tool for data analysis. You can use named ranges, formulas, and macros to create an intricate system of interlocking calculations, linked cells, and formatted summaries that work together to create a final analysis.

The problem with that is there is no transparency of analytical processes, meaning it is extremely difficult to determine what is actually going on in a spreadsheet. If you've ever had to work with a spreadsheet created by someone else you know all too well the frustration that comes with deciphering the various gyrations of calculations and links being used to perform an analysis. Small spreadsheets that perform a modest analysis are painful to decipher but are usually still workable, while large, elaborate, multi-worksheet workbooks are virtually impossible to decode, often leaving you to start from scratch.

Compared to Excel, database systems might seem rigid, strict, and unwavering in their rules. However, all this rigidity comes with a benefit.

Because only certain actions are allowable, you can more easily come to understand what is being done within structured database objects, such as queries or stored procedures. If a dataset is being edited, a number is being calculated, or any portion of the dataset is being affected as a part of an analytical process, you can readily see that action by reviewing the query syntax or reviewing the stored procedure code. Indeed, in a relational database system, you never encounter hidden formulas, hidden cells, or dead named ranges.

Separation of data and presentation

Data should be separate from presentation; you do not want the data to become too tied into any one particular way of presenting it. For example, when you receive an invoice from a company, you don't assume that the financial data on that invoice is the true source of your data. It is a presentation of your data. It can be presented to you in other manners and styles on charts or on Web sites, but such representations are never the actual source of the data.

What exactly does this concept have to do with Excel? People who perform data analysis with Excel tend to fuse the data, the analysis, and the presentation together. For example, you often see an Excel workbook that has 12 worksheets, each representing a month. On each worksheet, data for that month is listed along with formulas, PivotTables, and summaries. What happens when you're asked to provide a summary by quarter? Do you add more formulas and worksheets to consolidate the data on each of the month worksheets? The fundamental problem in this scenario is that the worksheets actually represent data values that are fused into the presentation of your analysis. The point here is that data should not be tied to a particular presentation, no matter how apparently logical or useful it may be. However, in Excel, it happens all the time.

In addition, because all manners and phases of analysis can be done directly within a spreadsheet, Excel cannot effectively provide adequate transparency to the analysis. Each cell has the potential of holding hidden formulas and containing links to other cells. In Excel, the line between analysis and data is blurred, which makes it difficult to determine exactly what is going on in a spreadsheet. Moreover, it takes a great deal of effort in the way of manual maintenance to ensure that edits and unforeseen changes don't affect previous analyses.

Relational database systems inherently separate analytical components into tables, queries, and reports. By separating these elements, databases make data less sensitive to changes and create a data analysis environment where you can easily respond to new requests for analysis without destroying previous analyses.

In these days of big data, there are more demands for complex data analysis, not fewer. You have to add some tools to your repertoire to get away from being simply "spreadsheet mechanics." Excel can be stretched to do just about anything, but maintaining such "creative" solutions can be a tedious manual task. You can be sure that the exciting part of data analysis is not in routine data management within Excel. Rather, it is in leveraging of BI tools to provide your clients with the best solution for any situation.

Database Terminology

The terms *database, table, record, field,* and *value* indicate a hierarchy from largest to smallest. These same terms are used with virtually all database systems, so you should learn them well.

Databases

Generally, the word *database* is a computer term for a collection of information concerning a certain topic or business application. Databases help you organize this related information in a logical fashion for easy access and retrieval. Some older database systems used the term *database* to describe individual tables. Current use of *database* applies to all elements of a database system.

Databases aren't only for computers. There are also manual databases; sometimes they're referred to as manual filing systems or manual database systems. These filing systems usually consist of people, folders, and filing cabinets — and paper, which is the key to a manual database system. In a real manual database system, you probably have in/out baskets and some type of formal filing method.

You access information manually by opening a file cabinet, taking out a file folder, and finding the correct piece of paper. Customers fill out paper forms for input, perhaps by using a keyboard to input information that is printed on forms. You find information by manually sorting the papers or by copying information from many papers to another piece of paper (or even into an Excel spreadsheet). You may use a spreadsheet or calculator to analyze the data or display it in new and interesting ways.

Tables

Databases store information in carefully defined structures called *tables*. A table is just a container for raw information (called *data*), similar to a folder in a manual filing system. Each table in a database contains information about a single entity, such as a person or product, and the data in the table is organized into rows and columns. A relational database system stores data in related tables. For example, a table containing employee data (names and addresses) may be related to a table containing payroll information (pay date, pay amount, and check number).

Note

In database-speak, a table is an object. As you design and work with databases, it's important to think of each table as a unique entity and consider how each table relates to the other objects in the database.

In most database systems, you can view the contents of a table in a spreadsheet-like form, called a *datasheet*, comprising rows and columns (known as *records* and *fields*, respectively — see the following section, "Records, fields, and values"). Although a datasheet and a spreadsheet are superficially similar, a datasheet is a very different type of object. You typically cannot make changes or add calculations directly within a table. Your interaction with tables primarily comes in the form of queries or views (see the later section, "Queries").

Records, fields, and values

A database table is divided into rows (called *records*) and columns (called *fields*), with the first row (the heading at the top of each column) containing the names of the fields in the database.

Each row is a single record containing fields that are related to that record. In a manual system, the rows are individual forms (sheets of paper), and the fields are equivalent to the blank areas on a printed form that you fill in.

Each column is a field that includes many properties that specify the type of data contained within the field, and how the database should handle the field's data. These properties include the name of the field (for example, CompanyName) and the type of data in the field (for example Text). A field may include other properties as well. For example, a field's Size property tells the database the maximum number of characters allowed for the address.

At the intersection of a record and a field is a *value* — the actual data element. For example, if you have a field called CompanyName, a company name entered into that field would represent one data value.

Note

When working with Access, the term *field* is used to refer to an attribute stored in a record. In many other database systems, including SQL Server, *column* is the expression you'll hear most often in place of field. Field and column mean the same thing. The exact terminology used relies somewhat on the context of the database system underlying the table containing the record.

Queries

Most relational database systems allow the creation of queries (sometimes called *views*). Queries extract information from the database tables. A query selects and defines a group of records that fulfill a certain condition. Most database outputs are based on queries that combine, filter, or sort data before it's displayed. Queries are often called from other database objects, such as stored procedures, macros, or code modules. In addition to extracting data from tables, queries can be used to change, add, or delete database records.

An example of a query is when a person at the sales office tells the database, "Show me all customers, in alphabetical order by name, who are located in Massachusetts and bought something over the past six months." Or "Show me all customers who bought Chevrolet car models within the past six months and sort them by customer name and then by sale date."

Instead of asking the question in words to query a database, you use a special syntax such as SQL (Structured Query Language).

How Databases Are Designed

The better a database is designed or structured, the better the reporting solutions are able to leverage the data within it. The design process of a database is not all that mysterious. The basic design steps described in this section provide a solid understanding of how best to think about and even design your own databases.

Step 1: The overall design — from concept to reality

All solution developers face similar problems, the first of which is determining how to meet the needs of the end client. It's important to understand the overall client's requirements before zeroing in on the details.

For example, a client may ask for a database that supports the following tasks:

➤ Entering and maintaining customer information (name, address, and financial history)

➤ Entering and maintaining sales information (sales date, payment method, total amount, customer identity, and other fields)

➤ Entering and maintaining sales line-item information (details of items purchased)

➤ Viewing information from all the tables (sales, customers, sales line items, and payments)

> ➤ Asking questions about the information in the database

> ➤ Producing a monthly invoice report

> ➤ Producing a customer sales history

> ➤ Producing mailing labels and mail-merge reports

When reviewing these eight tasks, database designers need to consider other peripheral tasks that weren't mentioned by the client. Before jumping into design, database designers typically prepare a series of questions that provide insight to the client's business and how the client uses data. For example, a database designer might ask these questions:

> ➤ What reports and forms are currently used?

> ➤ How are sales, customers, and other records currently stored?

> ➤ How are invoices processed?

As these types of questions get answered, database designers get a feel for the business process, how data should be structured, and what, if any, integration with other data systems need to be considered.

Step 2: Report design

Database designers often consider the types of reports needed when modeling a database. Although it may seem odd to start with output reports, in many cases, customers are more interested in the printed output from a database than they are in any other aspect of the application. Reports often include every bit of data managed by an application. Because they tend to be comprehensive, reports are often the best way to gather important information about a database's requirements.

Step 3: Data design

The next step in the design phase is to take an inventory of all the information needed by the reports. One of the best methods is to list the data items in each report. As database designers do so, they take careful note of items that are included in more than one report, making sure they keep the same name for a data item that is in more than one report because the data item is really the same item.

For example, note all the customer data needed for each report shown in in Table 1-1.

Table 1-1: Customer-Related Data Items Found in the Reports

Customer Report	Invoice Report
Customer Name	Customer Name
Street	Street
City	City
State	State

continued

Table 1-1: Customer-Related Data Items Found in the Reports *(continued)*

Customer Report	Invoice Report
Zip Code	Zip Code
Phone Number	Phone Number
E-Mail Address	
Web Site	
Discount Rate	
Customer Since	
Last Sales Date	
Sales Tax Rate	
Credit Information (four fields)	

As you can see by comparing the type of customer information needed for each report, there are several common fields. Most of the customer data fields are found in both reports. Table 1-1 shows only some of the fields that are used in each report — those related to customer information. Because the related row and the field names are the same, a database designer can make sure all the data items are included in a customer table in the database. Table 1-2 lists the fields in a needed Invoice Report that contains sales information.

Table 1-2: Sales Data Items Found in the Reports

Invoice Report	Line Item Data
Invoice Number	
Sales Date	
Invoice Date	
Payment Method	
Salesperson	
Discount (overall for sale)	
Tax Location	
Tax Rate	
Product Purchased (multiple lines)	Product Purchased
Quantity Purchased (multiple lines)	Quantity Purchased
Description of Item Purchased (multiple lines)	Description of Item Purchased
Price of Item (multiple lines)	Price of Item
Discount for Each Item (multiple lines)	Discount for Each Item
Payment Type (multiple lines)	
Payment Date (multiple lines)	
Payment Amount (multiple lines)	
Credit Card Number (multiple lines)	
Expiration Date (multiple lines)	

As you can see when you examine the type of sales information needed for the report, there are a few repeating items (fields) — for example, Product Purchased, Quantity Purchased, and Price of Item. Each invoice can have multiple items, and each of these items needs the same type of information — number ordered and price per item. Many sales have more than one purchased item. Also, each invoice may include partial payments, and it's possible that this payment information will have multiple lines of payment information, so these repeating items can be put into their own grouping.

This type of report leads you to create two tables: one table to hold the top-level invoice data such as invoice number, invoice data, and sales person; and another table to hold line item details such as the products purchased, quantity purchased, and purchase price.

Step 4: Table design

After determining the tables needed, you evaluate the fields and calculations that are needed to fulfill the reporting requirements. Initially, only the fields included in the reports are added to the tables. Other fields may be added later (for various reasons), although certain fields won't appear in any table.

It's important to understand that not every little bit of data must be added into the database's tables. For example, clients may want to add vacation and other out-of-office days to the database to determine which employees are available on a particular day. However, it's easy to burden a database's initial design by incorporating too many ideas during the initial development phases. In general, you can accommodate client requests after the database development project is underway.

After all the tables and fields are determined, database designers consolidate the data by purpose (for example, grouped into logical groups) and then compare the data across those functions. For example, customer information is combined into a single set of data items. The same action is taken for sales information and line-item information. Table 1-3 compares data items from these three groups of information.

Table 1-3: Comparing the Data Items

Customer Data	Invoice Data	Line Items
Customer Company Name	Invoice Number	Product Purchased
Street	Sales Date	Quantity Purchased
City	Invoice Date	Description of Item Purchased
State	Payment Method	Price of Item
Zip Code		Discount for Each Item
Phone Numbers (two fields)	Discount (overall for this sale)	Taxable?
E-Mail Address	Tax Rate	
Web Site	Payment Type (multiple lines) Payment Date (multiple lines)	
Discount Rate	Payment Amount (multiple lines)	
Customer Since	Credit Card Number (multiple lines)	

continued

Table 1-3: Comparing the Data Items *(continued)*

Customer Data	Invoice Data	Line Items
Last Sales Date	Expiration Date (multiple lines)	
Sales Tax Rate		
Credit Information (four fields)		

Consolidating and comparing data is a good way to start creating the individual table, but the customer data must be split into two groups. Some of these items are used only once for each customer, while other items have multiple entries. For example, in the Sales column, the payment information can have multiple lines of information.

For example, one customer can have multiple contacts with the company. Another customer may make multiple payments toward a single sale. Of course, for this example, the data goes into three categories: customers, invoices, and sales line items.

Keep in mind that one customer may have multiple invoices, and each invoice may have multiple line items on it. The invoice category contains information about individual sales and the line items category contains information about each invoice. Notice that these three columns are all related; for example, one customer can have multiple invoices and each invoice may require multiple detail lines (line items).

 # Why multiple tables?

The prospect of creating multiple tables almost always intimidates beginning database users. Most often, beginners want to create one huge table that contains all the information they need — for example, a customer table with all the sales placed by the customer and the customer's name, address, and other information. After all, if you've been using Excel to store data so far, it may seem quite reasonable to take the same approach when building tables in a database.

A single large table for all customer information quickly becomes difficult to maintain, however. You have to input the customer information for every sale a customer makes (repeating the name and address information in every row). The same is true for the items purchased for each sale when the customer has purchased multiple items as part of a single purchase. This makes the system more inefficient and prone to data-entry mistakes. The information in the table is inefficiently stored — certain fields may not be needed for each sales record — and the table ends up with a lot of empty fields.

You want to create tables that hold the minimum of information while still making the system easy to use and flexible enough to grow. To accomplish this, you need to consider making more than one table, with each table containing fields that are only related to the focus of that table. Then, after you create the tables, you link them so that you're able to glean useful information from them. Although this process sounds complex, the actual implementation is relatively easy.

The relationships between tables can be different. For example, each sales invoice has one and only one customer, while each customer may have multiple sales. A similar relationship exists between the sales invoice and the line items of the invoice.

Database table relationships require a unique field in both tables involved in a relationship. A unique identifier in each table helps the database engine to properly join and extract related data.

Only the sales table has a unique identifier (InvoiceNumber), which means at least one field must be added to each of the other tables to serve as the link to other tables; for example, adding a CustomerID field to tblCustomers, adding the same field to the invoice table, and establishing a relationship between the tables through CustomerID in each table. The database engine uses the relationship between customers and invoices to connect customers with their invoices. Relationships between tables is done through key fields. Chapter 3 shows you how to create relationships between key fields in tables.

When you understand the need for linking one group of fields to another group, you can add the required key fields to each group. Table 1-4 shows two new groups and link fields created for each group of fields. These linking fields, known as *primary* and *foreign* keys, are used to link these tables.

Table 1-4: Tables with Keys

Customer Data	Invoice Data	Line Items Data	Sales Payment Data
CustomerID	InvoiceID	InvoiceID	InvoiceID
Customer Name	CustomerID	Line Number	Payment Type
Street	Invoice Number	Product Purchased	Payment Date
City	Sales Date	Quantity Purchased	Payment Amount
State	Invoice Date	Description of Item Purchased	Credit Card Number
ZIP Code	Payment Method	Price of Item	Expiration Date
Phone Numbers (two fields)	Salesperson	Discount for Each Item	
E-Mail Address			
Web Site			
Discount Rate			
Customer Since			
Last Sales Date			
Sales Tax Rate	Tax Rate		

The field that uniquely identifies each row in a table is the primary key. The corresponding field in a related table is the foreign key. In this example, CustomerID in tblCustomers is a primary key, while CustomerID in tblInvoices is a foreign key.

Assume a certain record in tblCustomers has 12 in its CustomerID field. Any records in Invoices with 12 as its CustomerID is "owned" by customer 12.

With the key fields added to each table, you can now find a field in each table that links it to other tables in the database. For example, Table 1-4 shows CustomerID in both the Customer table (where it's the primary key) and the Invoice table (where it's a foreign key).

This way, you're not repeating information on every row, you're just providing a link back to the table containing the information that may be required to show up on the report or invoice. The database will handle retrieving all related information so you don't have to worry about it — the only thing you have to define is the link between the tables.

PivotTable Fundamentals

In This Chapter

- Creating PivotTables
- Customizing PivotTable fields, formats, and functions
- Using slicers to filter data
- Understanding the internal Data Model

As you gain an understanding of Microsoft's BI tools, it becomes clear that PivotTables are an integral part of delivering business intelligence. Whether you're working with Power Pivot (Chapters 3 and 4), Power View (Chapter 5), or even Power Map (Chapter 6), you eventually have to utilize some form of PivotTable structure to make those tools deliver the final solution to your audience.

If you're new to PivotTables, this chapter gives you the fundamental understanding you need to continue exploring Microsoft's BI tool set. If you're already familiar with PivotTables, we recommend you skim the "Understanding the Internal Data Model" section later in this chapter. The internal Data Model is a feature introduced in Excel 2013 that essentially allows Power Pivot to run natively in Excel.

On the Web

You can find the example file for this chapter on this book's companion Web site at `www.wiley.com/go/bitools` **in the workbook named** `Chapter 2 Samples.xlsx.`

Introducing the PivotTable

A *PivotTable* is a tool that allows you to create an interactive view of your source data (commonly referred to as a PivotTable report). A PivotTable can help transform endless rows and columns of numbers into a meaningful presentation of data. You can easily create groupings of summary items: For example, combine Northern Region totals with Western Region totals, filter that data using a variety of views, and insert special formulas that perform new calculations.

PivotTables get their name from your ability to interactively drag and drop fields within the Pivot Table to dynamically change (or pivot) the perspective, giving you an entirely new view using the same source data. You can then display subtotals and interactively drill down to any level of detail that you want. Note that the data itself doesn't change, and is not connected to the PivotTable. A PivotTable is well suited to a dashboard because you can quickly update the view of your PivotTable by changing the source data that it points to. This allows you to set up both your analysis and presentation layers at one time. You can then press a button to update your presentation.

Anatomy of a PivotTable

A PivotTable is comprised of four areas: Values, Rows, Columns, and Filters, as shown in Figure 2-1. The data you place in these areas defines both the use and presentation of the data in your PivotTable. In the following sections, we discuss the function of each area.

Filters

Region	(All) ▾			
Sales Amount	**Segment** ▾			
Market ▾	Accessories	Bikes	Clothing	Components
Australia	23,974	1,351,873	43,232	203,791
Canada	119,303	11,714,700	383,022	2,246,255
Central	46,551	6,782,978	155,874	947,448
France	48,942	3,597,879	129,508	871,125
Germany	35,681	1,602,487	75,593	337,787
Northeast	51,246	5,690,285	163,442	1,051,702
Northwest	53,308	10,484,495	201,052	1,784,207
Southeast	45,736	6,737,556	165,689	959,337
Southwest	110,080	15,430,281	364,099	2,693,568
United Kingdom	43,180	3,435,134	120,225	712,588

Columns ←

Rows   Values

Figure 2-1: The four areas of a PivotTable.

Values area

The Values area allows you to calculate and count the source data. It is the large rectangular area below and to the right of the column and row headings. In this example, the Values area contains a sum of the values in the Sales Amount field.

The data fields that you drag and drop here are typically those that you want to measure — fields, such as the sum of revenue, a count of the units, or an average of the prices.

Rows area

Dragging a data field into the Rows area displays the unique values from that field down the rows of the left side of the PivotTable. The Rows area typically has at least one field, although it's possible to have no fields.

The types of data fields that you would drop here include those that you want to group and categorize, such as products, names, and locations.

Columns area

The Columns area contains headings that stretch across the top of columns in the PivotTable. In this example, the Columns area contains the unique list of business segments.

Placing a data field into the Columns area displays the unique values from that field in a column-oriented perspective. The Columns area is ideal for creating a data matrix or showing trends over time.

Filters area

At the top of the PivotTable, the Filters area is an optional set of one or more drop-down controls. The Filters area contains the Region field, and the PivotTable is set to show all regions.

Placing data fields into the Filters area allows you to change the views for the entire PivotTable based on your selection. The types of data fields that you'd drop here include those that you want to isolate and focus on; for example, region, line of business, and employees. Data fields dropped into this area are commonly referred to as filter fields.

Creating the basic PivotTable

Now that you have a good understanding of its structure, follow these steps to create your first PivotTable:

1. Click any single cell inside your source data (the table you use to feed the PivotTable).

2. On the Insert tab, click the PivotTable button's drop-down list and choose PivotTable.

   The Create PivotTable dialog box opens, as shown in Figure 2-2.

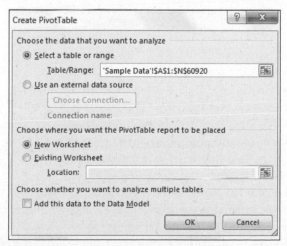

Figure 2-2: The Create PivotTable dialog box.

3. Specify the location of your source data.

4. Specify the worksheet where you want to put the PivotTable.

    The default location for the new PivotTable is New Worksheet. This means your PivotTable is placed in a new worksheet within the current workbook. If you want to add your PivotTable to an existing worksheet, select Existing Worksheet and specify the worksheet in which you want to place the PivotTable.

5. Click OK.

    At this point, you have an empty PivotTable report on a new worksheet, with the PivotTable Field pane next to it, as shown in Figure 2-3. You find out how to populate your PivotTable using this pane in the next section.

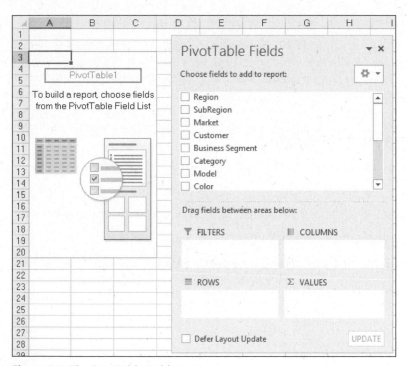

Figure 2-3: The PivotTable Fields List pane.

Laying out the PivotTable

You can add fields to the PivotTable by dragging and dropping the field names to one of the four areas found in the PivotTable Fields list — Filters, Columns, Rows, and Values.

Tip

If you don't see the PivotTable Fields List pane, right-click anywhere inside the PivotTable and select Show Field List. Alternatively, with your PivotTable selected, click the Field List icon in the Show group on the Options tab of the Ribbon.

Before you start dropping fields into the various areas, ask yourself two questions: "What am I measuring?" and "How do I want to see it?" The answers to these questions guide you in determining which fields go where.

Suppose you want to measure the dollar sales by market. You need to work with the Sales Amount and Market fields.

The best way to view that data is for the markets to go down the left side of the report and the sales amount to be calculated next to each market. You need to add the Market field to the Rows area, and the Sales Amount field to the Values area. Follow these steps to do so:

1. In the field list, select the Market field (see Figure 2-4).

    Now that you have regions in your PivotTable, it's time to add the dollar sales.

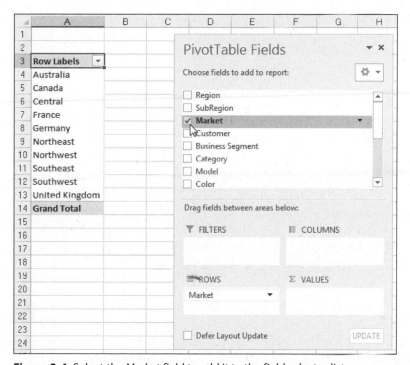

Figure 2-4: Select the Market field to add it to the field selector list.

Tip   Placing a check mark next to any field that is non-numeric (text or date) automatically places that field into the Rows area of the PivotTable. Placing a check mark next to any field that is numeric automatically places that field in the Values area of the PivotTable.

2. In the field list, select the Sales Amount field (see Figure 2-5).

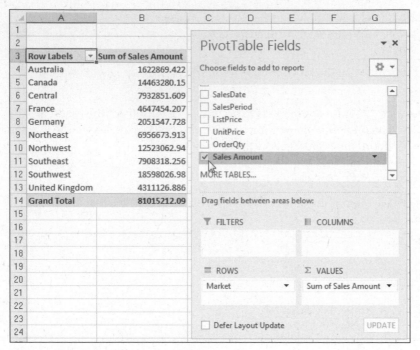

Figure 2-5: Add the Sales Amount field.

When you add new fields, you may find it difficult to see all the fields in the box for each area. You can expand the PivotTable Fields List pane by clicking and dragging the borders of the pane.

As you can see, you have just analyzed the sales for each market in just a few steps! That's an amazing feat considering you start with over 60,000 rows of data. With a little formatting, this modest PivotTable can become the starting point for a dashboard or report.

Modifying the PivotTable

Here's the wonderful thing about PivotTables: For your data model, you can add as many analysis layers as you like by changing or rearranging the fields in your source data table. Say you want to show the dollar sales each market earned by business segment. Because your PivotTable already contains the Market and Sales Amount fields, all you have to add is the Business Segment field.

Click anywhere in your PivotTable to open the PivotTable Fields List pane and then select the Business Segment field to add it to the Rows area. Figure 2-6 shows what your PivotTable now looks like.

What if this layout doesn't work for you? Maybe you want to see business segments listed at the top of the PivotTable results. No problem. Simply drag the Business Segment field from the Rows area to the Columns area. As shown in Figure 2-7, this instantly restructures the PivotTable to your specifications.

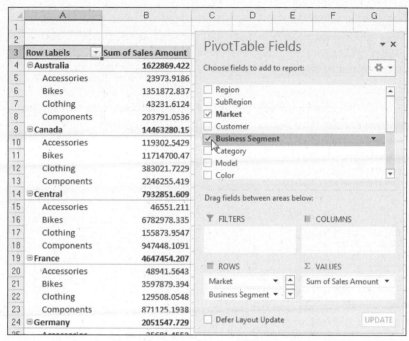

Figure 2-6: Adding a new analysis layer to your data model is as easy as selecting another field.

Row Labels	Sum of Sales Amount
⊟ Australia	1622869.422
Accessories	23973.9186
Bikes	1351872.837
Clothing	43231.6124
Components	203791.0536
⊟ Canada	14463280.15
Accessories	119302.5429
Bikes	11714700.47
Clothing	383021.7229
Components	2246255.419
⊟ Central	7932851.609
Accessories	46551.211
Bikes	6782978.335
Clothing	155873.9547
Components	947448.1091
⊟ France	4647454.207
Accessories	48941.5643
Bikes	3597879.394
Clothing	129508.0548
Components	871125.1938
⊟ Germany	2051547.729

Figure 2-7: Your business segments are now column oriented.

Sum of Sales Amount	Column Labels		
Row Labels	Accessories	Bikes	Clothing
Australia	23973.9186	1351872.837	43231.6
Canada	119302.5429	11714700.47	383021.7
Central	46551.211	6782978.335	155873.9
France	48941.5643	3597879.394	129508.0
Germany	35681.4552	1602487.163	75592.5
Northeast	51245.8881	5690284.732	163441.7
Northwest	53308.4547	10484495.02	201052.0
Southeast	45736.1077	6737555.913	165689.0
Southwest	110079.5882	15430280.58	364098.8
United Kingdom	43180.2218	3435134.262	120224.8
Grand Total	578000.9525	66827668.7	1801734

Changing the PivotTable view

You may frequently be asked to produce reports for one particular region, market, product, and so on. Instead of spending hours building separate PivotTables for every possible scenario, you can leverage PivotTables to help create multiple views of the same data. For example, you can create a region filter in your PivotTable.

Click anywhere in your PivotTable to open the PivotTable Fields List pane and then drag the Region field to the Filters area. A drop-down control is added to your PivotTable, as shown in Figure 2-8. You can then use this control to view one particular region at a time.

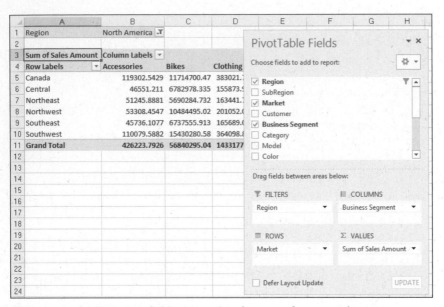

Figure 2-8: Add the Region field to view data for a specific geographic area.

Updating your PivotTable

Your data may change and grow with newly added rows and columns. To update the PivotTable, right-click inside your PivotTable and select Refresh.

Sometimes, the source data that feeds your PivotTable changes in structure. For example, you may want to add or delete rows or columns from your data table. These types of changes affect the range of your data source, not just a few data items in the table.

In this case, a simple update of your PivotTable data won't do. You have to update the range that is captured by the PivotTable. Here's how:

1. Click anywhere inside your PivotTable.

   Whenever your PivotTable is selected, the Ribbon activates the PivotTable Tools tabs for you to work with your PivotTable.

2. On the Analyze tab, click the Change Data Source button.

   The Change PivotTable Data Source dialog box opens, as shown in Figure 2-9.

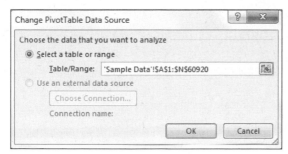

Figure 2-9: Select the new range that feeds your PivotTable.

3. Change the range selection to include any new rows or columns.

4. Click OK.

Customizing Your PivotTable

PivotTables often need to be tweaked to achieve the look and feel you want. In this section, we cover some of the ways that you can customize your PivotTables to suit your dashboard's needs.

Changing the PivotTable layout

Excel 2013 gives you a choice in the layout of your data in a PivotTable. The three layouts, shown side by side in Figure 2-10, are Compact Form, Outline Form, and Tabular Form. Although no layout stands out as being better than another, most people prefer the Tabular Form layout because it's easiest to read and most people who have seen PivotTables are used to it.

The layout you choose not only affects the look and feel of your reporting mechanisms, but it may also affect the way you build and interact with any dashboard models based on your PivotTables.

Changing the layout of a PivotTable is easy. Follow these steps:

1. Click anywhere inside your PivotTable.

2. On the Design tab of the Ribbon, click the Report Layout icon's drop-down menu and choose the layout you like.

Renaming the fields

Every field in your PivotTable has a name. The fields in the rows, columns, and filter areas inherit their names from the data labels in your source data. For example, the fields in the Values area are given a name, such as Sum of Sales Amount.

Compact		Outline			Tabular		

Compact

Row Labels ⟋	Sales
⊟Australia	1622869.422
Accessories	23973.9186
Bikes	1351872.837
Clothing	43231.6124
Components	203791.0536
⊟Canada	14463280.15
Accessories	119302.5429
Bikes	11714700.47
Clothing	383021.7229
Components	2246255.419
⊟Central	7932851.609
Accessories	46551.211
Bikes	6782978.335
Clothing	155873.9547
Components	947448.1091
⊟France	4647454.207
Accessories	48941.5643
Bikes	3597879.394
Clothing	129508.0548
Components	871125.1938
⊟Germany	2051547.729
Accessories	35681.4552
Bikes	1602487.163
Clothing	75592.5945
Components	337786.516

Outline

Market ⟋	Segment ▾	Sales
⊟Australia		1622869.422
	Accessories	23973.9186
	Bikes	1351872.837
	Clothing	43231.6124
	Components	203791.0536
⊟Canada		14463280.15
	Accessories	119302.5429
	Bikes	11714700.47
	Clothing	383021.7229
	Components	2246255.419
⊟Central		7932851.609
	Accessories	46551.211
	Bikes	6782978.335
	Clothing	155873.9547
	Components	947448.1091
⊟France		4647454.207
	Accessories	48941.5643
	Bikes	3597879.394
	Clothing	129508.0548
	Components	871125.1938
⊟Germany		2051547.729
	Accessories	35681.4552
	Bikes	1602487.163
	Clothing	75592.5945
	Components	337786.516

Tabular

Market ⟋	Segment ▾	Sales
⊟Australia	Accessories	23973.9186
	Bikes	1351872.837
	Clothing	43231.6124
	Components	203791.0536
Australia Total		**1622869.422**
⊟Canada	Accessories	119302.5429
	Bikes	11714700.47
	Clothing	383021.7229
	Components	2246255.419
Canada Total		**14463280.15**
⊟Central	Accessories	46551.211
	Bikes	6782978.335
	Clothing	155873.9547
	Components	947448.1091
Central Total		**7932851.609**
⊟France	Accessories	48941.5643
	Bikes	3597879.394
	Clothing	129508.0548
	Components	871125.1938
France Total		**4647454.207**
⊟Germany	Accessories	35681.4552
	Bikes	1602487.163
	Clothing	75592.5945
	Components	337786.516
Germany Total		**2051547.729**

Figure 2-10: The three layouts for a PivotTable report.

You might prefer the name Total Sales instead of a default name like Sum of Sales Amount. If so, you can change a field name using the following steps:

1. Right-click any value within the target field and select Value Field Settings.

    For example, if you want to change the name of the field Sum of Sales Amount, right-click any value under that field.

    The Value Field Settings dialog box opens, as shown in Figure 2-11.

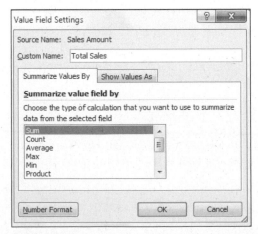

Figure 2-11: Use the Custom Name box to change the name.

2. Type the new name in the Custom Name box.

3. Click OK.

Tip

If you use the same name of the data label that you specified in your source data, you receive an error. In our example, if you try to rename the Sum of Sales Amount field to Sales Amount, you get an error message. To avoid this, you can add a space to the end of any field name. Excel considers Sales Amount (followed by a space) to be different from Sales Amount. This way you can use the name you want, and no one will notice any difference.

Formatting numbers

You can format numbers in a PivotTable to fit your needs (such as currency, percent, or number). You control the numeric formatting of a field using the Value Field Settings dialog box. Here's how:

1. Right-click any value within the target field and choose one of the following:

   - *To format a value field:* Select Value Field Settings, which opens the Value Field Setting dialog box.

   - *To format a number field:* Select Number Format, which opens the Format Cells dialog box.

2. Indicate the number format you want, just as you normally would on your worksheet.

3. Click OK.

After you set a new format for a field, the applied formatting remains even if you refresh or rearrange your PivotTable.

Changing summary calculations

When you create your PivotTable, Excel, by default, summarizes your data by either counting or summing the items. You can also choose other functions, such as Average, Min, and Max. In all, 11 options are available:

- ➤ **Sum:** Adds all numeric data.

- ➤ **Count:** Counts all data items within a given field, including numeric-, text-, and date-formatted cells.

- ➤ **Average:** Calculates an average for the target data items.

- ➤ **Max:** Displays the largest value in the target data items.

- ➤ **Min:** Displays the smallest value in the target data items.

- ➤ **Product:** Multiplies all target data items.

- ➤ **Count Nums:** Counts only the numeric cells in the target data items.

- ➤ **StdDevP and StdDev:** Calculates the standard deviation for the target data items. Use StdDevP if your data source contains the complete population. Use StdDev if your data source contains a sample of the population.

➤ **VarP and Var:** Calculates the statistical variance for the target data items. Use VarP if your data contains a complete population. If your data contains only a sampling of the complete population, use Var to estimate the variance.

To change the summary calculation for any given field, follow these steps:

1. Right-click any value within the target field and select Value Field Settings.

   The Value Field Settings dialog box opens. Refer to Figure 2-11.

2. Select the type of calculation you want to use from the list of calculations.

3. Click OK.

Note

A single blank cell causes Excel to count instead of sum. If all the cells in a column contain numeric data, Excel chooses Sum. If just one cell is either blank or contains text, Excel chooses Count. Be sure to pay attention to the fields that you place into the Values area of the PivotTable. If the field name starts with Count Of, Excel counts the items in the field instead of summing them.

Suppressing subtotals

Each time you add a field to your PivotTable, Excel adds a subtotal for that field. However, there may be times when subtotals don't make sense or hinders your PivotTable report. For example, Figure 2-12 shows a PivotTable where the subtotals hide the data.

	A	B	C	D	E
1	Region	SubRegion	Market	Business Segment	Sum of Sales Amount
2	North America	United States	Central	Accessories	46,551
3				Bikes	6,782,978
4				Clothing	155,874
5				Components	947,448
6			Central Total		7,932,852
7			Northeast	Accessories	51,246
8				Bikes	5,690,285
9				Clothing	163,442
10				Components	1,051,702
11			Northeast Total		6,956,674
12			Northwest	Accessories	53,308
13				Bikes	10,484,495
14				Clothing	201,052
15				Components	1,784,207
16			Northwest Total		12,523,063
17			Southeast	Accessories	45,736
18				Bikes	6,737,556
19				Clothing	165,689
20				Components	959,337
21			Southeast Total		7,908,318
22			Southwest	Accessories	110,080
23				Bikes	15,430,281
24				Clothing	364,099
25				Components	2,693,568
26			Southwest Total		18,598,027
27		United States Total			53,918,934
28	North America Total				53,918,934

Figure 2-12: Subtotals sometimes muddle the data you're trying to show.

Here's how to remove subtotals:

➤ **Remove all subtotals at one time:** Click anywhere inside your PivotTable. On the Design tab, click the Subtotals drop-down list and select Do Not Show Subtotals. Figure 2-13 shows a report without any subtotals.

	A	B	C	D	E
1	Region ▼	SubRegion ▼	Market ▼	Business Segment ▼	Sum of Sales Amount
2	⊟North America	⊟United States	⊟Central	Accessories	46,551
3				Bikes	6,782,978
4				Clothing	155,874
5				Components	947,448
6			⊟Northeast	Accessories	51,246
7				Bikes	5,690,285
8				Clothing	163,442
9				Components	1,051,702
10			⊟Northwest	Accessories	53,308
11				Bikes	10,484,495
12				Clothing	201,052
13				Components	1,784,207
14			⊟Southeast	Accessories	45,736
15				Bikes	6,737,556
16				Clothing	165,689
17				Components	959,337
18			⊟Southwest	Accessories	110,080
19				Bikes	15,430,281
20				Clothing	364,099
21				Components	2,693,568
22	Grand Total				53,918,934

Figure 2-13: A report without subtotals.

➤ **Remove the subtotals for only one field:** Right-click any value within the target field and choose Field Settings. Select None under the Subtotals area and click OK.

➤ **Remove grand totals:** Right-click anywhere in your PivotTable and select PivotTable Options. On the Totals & Filters tab, deselect the Show Grand Totals for Rows and Show Grand Totals for Columns options. Click OK.

Hiding and showing data items

A PivotTable summarizes and displays all the information in your source data. However, you may want to inhibit certain data items from being included in your PivotTable summary. In these situations, you can choose to hide a data item.

Note

In terms of PivotTables, hiding doesn't mean preventing the data item from displaying on the dashboard; hiding a data item also prevents it from being factored into the summary calculations.

The PivotTable shown in Figure 2-14 shows sales amounts for all Business Segments by Market. Suppose you want to show totals without taking sales from the Bikes segment into consideration.

	A	B	C
1	Market	Business Segment	Sum of Sales Amount
2	⊟Australia	Accessories	$23,974
3		Bikes	$1,351,873
4		Clothing	$43,232
5		Components	$203,791
6	Australia Total		$1,622,869
7	⊟Canada	Accessories	$119,303
8		Bikes	$11,714,700
9		Clothing	$383,022
10		Components	$2,246,255
11	Canada Total		$14,463,280
12	⊟Central	Accessories	$46,551
13		Bikes	$6,782,978
14		Clothing	$155,874
15		Components	$947,448
16	Central Total		$7,932,852
17	⊟France	Accessories	$48,942

Figure 2-14: We want to remove Bikes from this analysis.

You need to hide the Bikes segment. Deselect Bikes from the Business Segment drop-down list (see Figure 2-15).

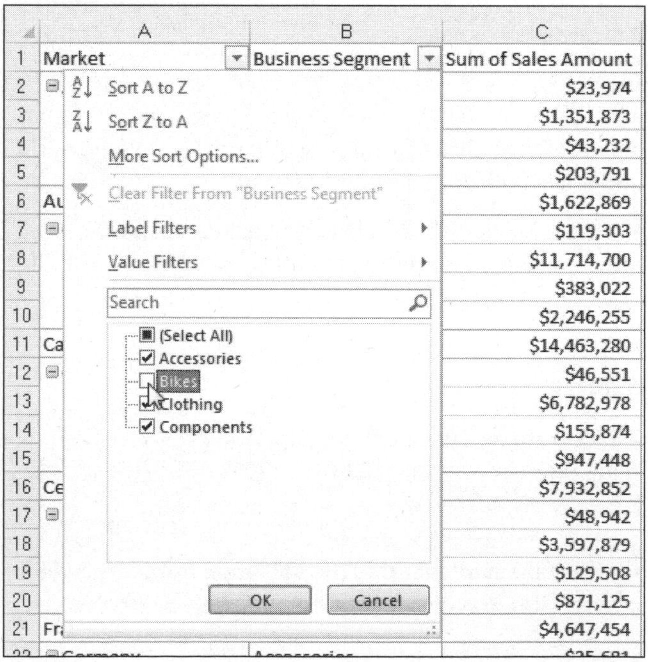

	A	B	C
1	Market	Business Segment	Sum of Sales Amount
2	⊟ A↓ Sort A to Z		$23,974
3	Z↓ Sort Z to A		$1,351,873
4	More Sort Options...		$43,232
5			$203,791
6	Au ⊽ₓ Clear Filter From "Business Segment"		$1,622,869
7	⊟ Label Filters ▸		$119,303
8	Value Filters ▸		$11,714,700
9			$383,022
10	Search 🔍		$2,246,255
11	Ca ▣ (Select All)		$14,463,280
12	⊟ ☑ Accessories		$46,551
13	☐ Bikes		$6,782,978
14	☑ Clothing		$155,874
15	☑ Components		$947,448
16	Ce		$7,932,852
17	⊟		$48,942
18			$3,597,879
19			$129,508
20	OK Cancel		$871,125
21	Fr		$4,647,454
22	⊟Germany	Accessories	$35,681

Figure 2-15: Removing the check mark from the Bike items hides the Bikes segment.

Click OK, and the PivotTable instantly recalculates, leaving out the Bikes segment. As shown in Figure 2-16, the Market total sales now reflect the sales without Bikes.

⊿	A	B	C
1	Market ▾	Business Segment ▼	Sum of Sales Amount
2	⊟Australia	Accessories	$23,974
3		Clothing	$43,232
4		Components	$203,791
5	Australia Total		$270,997
6	⊟Canada	Accessories	$119,303
7		Clothing	$383,022
8		Components	$2,246,255
9	Canada Total		$2,748,580
10	⊟Central	Accessories	$46,551
11		Clothing	$155,874
12		Components	$947,448
13	Central Total		$1,149,873
14	⊟France	Accessories	$48,942

Figure 2-16: Segment analysis without the Bikes segment.

You can just as quickly reinstate all hidden data items for the field. Choose Select All from the Business Segment drop-down list. (Refer to Figure 2-15.) All the segments are now showing again.

Hiding or showing items without data

By default, your PivotTable shows only items that have data. This may cause unintended problems for your data.

Look at Figure 2-17, which shows a PivotTable with the SalesPeriod field in the Rows area and the Region field in the Filters area. Note that the Region field is set to (All), and every sales period appears in the report.

⊿	A	B
1	Region	(All) ▾
2		
3	SalesPeriod ▾	Sum of Sales Amount
4	01/01/08	$713,230
5	02/01/08	$1,900,797
6	03/01/08	$1,455,282
7	04/01/08	$883,011
8	05/01/08	$2,269,722
9	06/01/08	$1,137,250
10	07/01/08	$2,411,569
11	08/01/08	$3,615,926
12	09/01/08	$2,894,658
13	10/01/08	$1,804,184
14	11/01/08	$3,055,007

Figure 2-17: All sales periods are showing.

If you display only Europe in the filter area, a portion of all the sales periods now show (see Figure 2-18).

	A	B
1	Region	Europe ▾ᴛ
2		
3	SalesPeriod ▾	Sum of Sales Amount
4	07/01/08	$180,241
5	08/01/08	$448,373
6	09/01/08	$373,122
7	10/01/08	$119,384
8	11/01/08	$330,026
9	12/01/08	$254,011
10	01/01/09	$71,313
11	02/01/09	$264,487
12	03/01/09	$177,006
13	04/01/09	$105,153
14	05/01/09	$300,602

Figure 2-18: Filtering for the Europe region hides some of the sales periods.

But displaying only those items with data could cause trouble if you plan on using this PivotTable as the source for your charts or other dashboard components. With that in mind, it isn't ideal if half the year disappears each time a customer selects Europe.

Here's how you can prevent Excel from hiding pivot items without data:

1. Right-click any value within the target field and choose Field Settings.

   In this example, the target field is the SalesPeriod field.

2. On the Layout & Print tab, select Show Items with No Data.

3. Click OK.

All the sales periods appear whether the selected region had sales that period or not, as shown in Figure 2-19.

	A	B
1	Region	Europe ▾ᴛ
2		
3	SalesPeriod ▾	Sum of Sales Amount
4	01/01/08	
5	02/01/08	
6	03/01/08	
7	04/01/08	
8	05/01/08	
9	06/01/08	
10	07/01/08	$180,241
11	08/01/08	$448,373
12	09/01/08	$373,122
13	10/01/08	$119,384
14	11/01/08	$330,026

Figure 2-19: All sales periods display even if there is no data.

Now that you're confident that the structure of the PivotTable is locked, you can use it as the source for all charts and other components in your dashboard.

Sorting your PivotTable

By default, items in each pivot field are sorted in ascending order based on the item name. Excel enables you to change the sort order of the items in your PivotTable.

Like many actions you can perform in Excel, there are several different ways you can sort data within a PivotTable. The easiest way, and the way that's used most often, is to apply the sort directly in the PivotTable. Right-click any value within the target field (the field you need to sort), choose Sort, and then select the sort direction. The changes take effect immediately and remain while you work with your PivotTable.

Understanding Slicers

Slicers allow you to filter your PivotTable, similar to the way Filter fields filter a PivotTable. As dis cussed in the "Anatomy of a PivotTable" section earlier in this chapter, Filter fields are those placed in the Filters area, allowing your users to interactively filter for specific data items. As useful as Filter fields are, they have a couple of drawbacks.

➤ **Filter fields are not cascading filters.** Filters don't work together to limit selections when needed. Look at the left side of Figure 2-20, for example. You can see that the Region filter is set to North. However, the Market filter still allows you to select markets that are clearly not in the North region (California, for example). Because the Market filter is not in any way limited based on the Region Filter field, you could select a market that yields no data because it is not in the North region.

   Slicers respond to one another. Shown on the right side of Figure 2-20, the Market slicer visibly highlights the relevant markets when the North region is selected. The rest of the markets are muted, signaling they are not part of the North region.

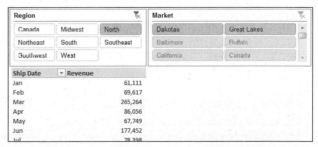

Figure 2-20: Default PivotTable Filter fields do not work together (left); slicers work together to show relevant data items (right).

➤ **Filter fields don't provide an easy way to tell what exactly is being filtered when you select multiple items.** The left side of Figure 2-21 shows an example of this. The Region filter has been limited to three regions: Midwest, North, and Northeast. However, the Region filter shows (Multiple Items). By default, Filter fields show (Multiple Items) when you select more than one item. The only way to tell what has been selected is to click the drop-down list. You can imagine the confusion on a printed version of this report, where there is no way to click to see which data items make up the numbers on the page.

When selecting multiple items in a slicer, you can easily see what's been chosen. On the right side of Figure 2-21, you can see that the PivotTable is being filtered by the Midwest, North, and Northeast regions — no more (Multiple Items).

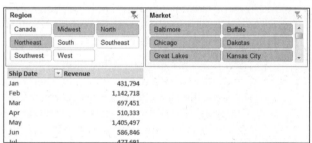

Figure 2-21: Filter fields show the words "(Multiple Items)" when multiple selections are made (left); slicers do a better job at displaying multiple items (right).

Creating a standard slicer

To create a slicer, follow these steps:

1. Place your cursor anywhere inside your PivotTable.

2. On the Analyze tab, click the Insert Slicer button.

   The Insert Slicers dialog box opens.

3. Select the dimensions you want to filter.

4. Click OK.

After the slicers are created, click the filter values to filter your PivotTable. As shown in Figure 2-22, clicking Midwest in the Region slicer not only filters your PivotTable, but the Market slicer responds by highlighting the markets that belong to the Midwest region.

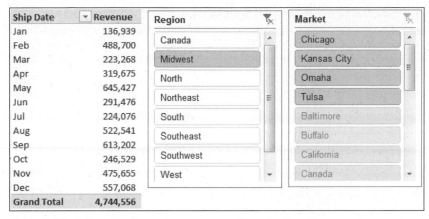

Figure 2-22: Select the dimensions you want filtered using slicers.

Tip

To select multiple values, press the Ctrl key while selecting the filters.

To clear the filtering on a slicer, simply click the Clear Filter icon on the target slicer (see Figure 2-23).

Clear your filter.

Figure 2-23: Clearing the filters on a slicer.

Formatting slicers

If you're using slicers in a dashboard, you'll want to do some formatting to make sure your slicers match the theme and layout of your dashboard. Here are a few common formatting adjustments you can make to your slicers.

Size and placement

A slicer behaves like a standard Excel shape object in that you can move it around and adjust its size by clicking it and dragging its position points. Or right-click the slicer and select Size and Properties.

You can then adjust the size of the slicer in the Format Slicer pane shown in Figure 2-24. You can specify how the slicer should behave when cells are shifted and specify whether the slicer should be shown when printed.

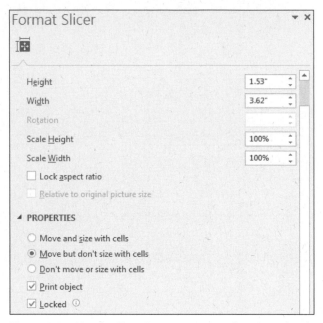

Figure 2-24: Use the Slicer Format pane to adjust how the slicer behaves in relation to the worksheet it's on.

Data item columns

By default, all slicers are created with one column of data items. You can change this by right-clicking the slicer and selecting Size and Properties. In the Position and Layout section of the Format Slicer pane, you can specify the number of columns in the slicer. Adjust the number to 2 (as shown in Figure 2-25) and the data is displayed in two columns, adjust the number to 3 and the data is displayed in three columns, and so on.

Slicer color and style

To change the color and style of your slicer, click it, and then select a style from the Slicer Style gallery on the Slicer Tools Options tab. The default styles available suit a majority of dashboards, but if you want more control over the color and style of your slicer, you can click the New Slicer Style button on the lower left-hand corner. You can then specify the detailed formatting of each part of the slicer.

Other slicer settings

Right-click your slicer and select Slicer Settings to open the Slicer Settings dialog box. With this dialog box, you can control the look of your slicer's header, how your slicer is sorted, and how filtered items are handled.

With minimal effort, your slicers can be integrated nicely into your dashboard layout. Figure 2-26 shows how two slicers and a chart work together as a cohesive dashboard component.

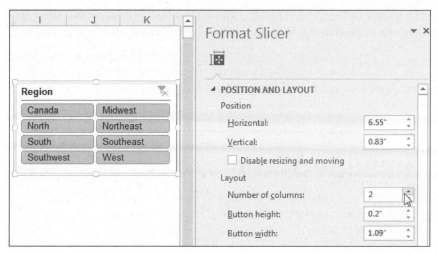

Figure 2-25: Adjust the Number of Columns property to display the slicer data items in more than one column.

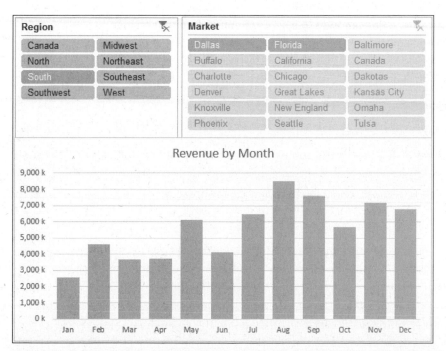

Figure 2-26: With a little formatting, slicers can be made to adopt the look and feel of your overall dashboard.

Controlling multiple PivotTables with one slicer

Another advantage you gain with slicers is that each slicer can be tied to more than one PivotTable. That is, any filter you apply to your slicer can be applied to multiple PivotTables.

To connect your slicer to more than one PivotTable, right-click the slicer and select Report Connections. In the Report Connections dialog box, place a check mark next to any PivotTable that you want to filter using the current slicer. Click OK when you're done.

At this point, any filter you apply to your slicer is applied to all the connected PivotTables. Controlling the filter state of multiple PivotTables is a powerful feature; especially in dashboards that run on multiple PivotTables.

Creating a Timeline Slicer

The Timeline slicer works in the same way a standard slicer does in that it lets you filter a PivotTable using a visual selection mechanism instead of the old Filter fields. The difference is the Timeline slicer is designed to work exclusively with date fields, providing an excellent visual method to filter and group the dates in your PivotTable.

Note

To create a Timeline slicer, your PivotTable must contain a field where all the data is formatted as a date. It's not enough to have a column of data that contains a few dates. All the values in your date field must be a valid date, and formatted as such.

To create a Timeline slicer, follow these steps:

1. Place your cursor anywhere inside your PivotTable.

2. On the Analyze tab, click the Insert Timeline icon.

   The Insert Timelines dialog box opens, showing you all the available date fields in the chosen PivotTable.

3. Select the date fields for which you want to create the timeline.

4. Click OK.

After you create your Timeline slicer, you can filter the data in your PivotTable using this dynamic data selection mechanism. Figure 2-27 shows how selecting Mar, Apr, and May in the Timeline slicer automatically filters the pivot chart.

Figure 2-27 also illustrates how you can expand the slicer range with the mouse to include a wider range of dates in your filtered numbers by clicking and dragging the pull handles at the edges of the selected months.

Want to quickly filter your PivotTable by quarters? Well that's easy with a Timeline slicer. Click the time period drop-down list and select Quarters. As shown in Figure 2-28, you also have the option of switching to Years, Months, or Days, if needed.

Caution

Timeline slicers are not backward-compatible, meaning they are only usable in Excel 2013. If you open a workbook with Timeline slicers in Excel 2010 or previous versions, the Timeline slicers are disabled.

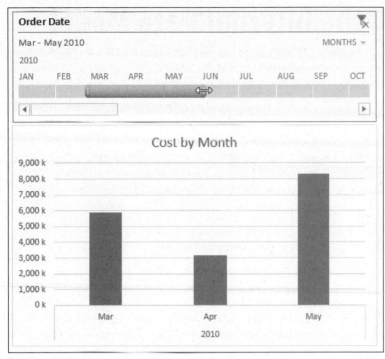

Figure 2-27: Click a date selection to filter your PivotTable.

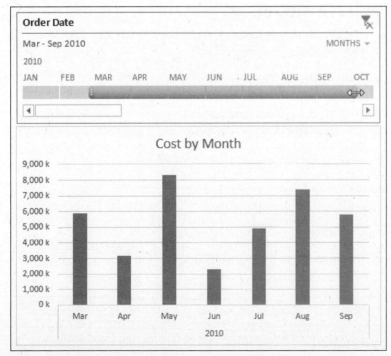

Figure 2-28: Quickly switch between Years, Quarters, Months, or Days.

Understanding the Internal Data Model

Excel 2013 introduces several new BI features that we discuss in this book, such as Power Pivot, Power Map, and Power View. These features run on the internal Data Model found in Excel 2013. The internal Data Model is an in-memory analytics engine that allows you to store disparate data sources in a kind of OLAP cube within Excel. OLAP is a category of data warehousing that allows you to mine and analyze vast amounts of data with ease and efficiency. Every workbook has one internal Data Model that allows you to analyze disparate data sources like never before.

The idea behind the Data Model is simple. Say you have two tables — an Orders table and a Customers table. The Orders table has basic information about invoices (Customer Number, Invoice Date, and Revenue). The Customers table has basic information like Customer Number, Customer Name, and State.

If you wanted to analyze revenue by state, you would have to join the two tables and aggregate the Revenue field in the Orders table by the State field in the Customers table.

In the past, to do this you would have to go through a series of gyrations involving VLookups, SumIfs, or other formulas. With the Excel 2013 data model, however, you can simply tell Excel how the two tables are related (they both have a customer number) and then pull them into the internal Data Model. The Excel Data Model then builds an analytical cube based on that customer number relationship and exposes the data through a PivotTable. With the PivotTable, you can create the aggregation by state with a few clicks of the mouse.

Building out your first Data Model

Imagine you have the Transactions table. On another worksheet, you have a Generators table that contains location information about each generator. See Figure 2-29.

Convert your data ranges to tables

The first step in building your data model is to convert your separate data ranges to named Excel tables. Converting a range to a table ensures that the internal Data Model recognizes it as an actual data source.

1. Click anywhere inside the Transactions data table and press Ctrl+T.

   The Create Table dialog box opens.

2. Ensure that the range for the table is correct and click OK.

3. On the Table Tools Design tab, type a name in the Table Name field.

   Choose a name that you can recognize as belonging to the table when adding it to the internal Data Model.

4. Repeat Steps 1 through 3 for each of the data ranges you want to import into the internal Data Model.

   In this scenario, you want to also convert the Generators table to a named Excel table.

Figure 2-29: Two tables: transactions by generator number (top) and location information on each generator (bottom).

Add your tables to the internal Data Model

Each 2013 workbook has an internal Data Model that (by default) is exposed as a connection called `ThisWorkbookDataModel` when you add data sources to it. You can add your newly created tables to the internal Data Model using the Workbook Connections dialog box.

1. Click the Data tab on the Ribbon and click the Connections button.

2. In the Workbook Connections dialog box, click the drop-down arrow next to the Add button and select Add to the Data Model.

   Excel opens the Existing Connections dialog box shown in Figure 2-30.

	A	B	C	D	E
1	GENERATOR _ID	WASTE_CODE	GENERATOR_SIZE	ON_SITE_MANAGEMENT	GENERATED_QTY
2	RID001201508	W205	MEDIUM	N	2,392
3	RID001201508	W205	MEDIUM	N	2,392
4	RID001201508	W219	MEDIUM	N	1,020
5	RID001201508	W206	MEDIUM	N	1,587
6	RID001201508	W200	MEDIUM	N	4,795
7	RID980914550	W219	MEDIUM	N	6,800
8	RIR000508416	W203	MEDIUM	N	1,845
9	SC0000029843	W211	LARGE	N	3,895

	A	B	C	D	E
1	GENERATOR_ID	GENERATOR_NAME	GEN_CITY	GEN_STATE	GEN_ZIP
2	AK1210022157	USARMY FT RICH	ANCHORAGE	AK	99505
3	AK1570028646	USAF EIELSON A	EIELSON AFB	AK	99702
4	AK3210022155	US ARMY FT GRE	DELTA JUNCTIOI	AK	99737
5	AK4170024323	FORMER U. S. N/	ADAK	AK	99546
6	AK6210022426	US ARMY FT WA	FT WAINWRIGH	AK	99703
7	AK8570028649	USAF ELMENDOI	ANCHORAGE	AK	99506
8	AK8690360492	USDHS CG BSU K	KETCHIKAN	AK	99901
9	AK9570028705	USAF EARECKSO	SHEMYA ISLAND	AK	98736
10	AK9690330742	USDHS CG BASE	KODIAK	AK	99619

Figure 2-30: Select a table to add and click Open.

3. Click the Tables tab, select your first table, and then click Open.

4. Repeat Steps 2 and 3 for each table you want added to the internal Data Model.

After adding all your tables, the Workbook Connections dialog box shows a connection called `ThisWorkbookDataModel`, listing all the data sources associated with it.

Note Any changes made to the tables (such as adding or deleting records or columns) are automatically captured in the internal Data Model. There's no need to perform any sort of refresh action.

Build relationships for the tables in the internal Data Model

Although your data now exists in the internal Data Model, Excel does not inherently know how your tables relate to one another. For example, both tables have a column called Generator_ID (see Figure 2-29). This column is the key that connects the two tables, allowing you to match transactions with customer location. You have to explicitly define this relationship before Excel recognizes how to handle the data in the Data Model.

1. Click the Data tab on the Ribbon and click the Relationships button.

   The Manage Relationships dialog box opens.

2. Click the New button.

   The Create Relationship dialog box opens, as shown in Figure 2-32.

3. Select the tables and fields that define the relationship.

   In Figure 2-31, the Transactions table has a Generator_ID field. It is related to the Generators table via the Generator_ID field.

4. Click OK.

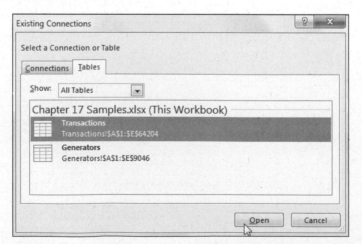

Figure 2-31: Create the relationships between your tables, defining each table and the associated fields.

You return to the Manage Relationships dialog box where you can add, delete, and edit relationships.

Note

In Figure 2-31, notice that the lower right-hand drop-down list is called Related Column (Primary). The term *Primary* means that the internal Data Model uses this field from the associated table as the primary key. Every relationship must have a field you designate as the primary key. Primary key fields are necessary in the Data Model to prevent aggregation errors and duplications. In that light, the Excel Data model must impose some strict rules around the primary key. You cannot have any duplicates or null values in a field being used as the primary key. So the Generators table (in the scenario in Figure 2-31) must have all unique values in its Generator_ID field; with no blanks or null values. This is the only way Excel can ensure data integrity when joining multiple tables.

Using your Data Model in a PivotTable

After you have filled your internal Data Model, you can start using it. Later, of course, you learn how to leverage it with Power View (Chapter 5).

Follow these steps to leverage the Data Model in PivotTables to analyze the data within:

1. Click the Insert tab and click the PivotTable icon.

2. In the Create PivotTable dialog box, select the Use an External Data Source option and click the Choose Connection button.

   The Existing Connections dialog box opens.

3. Click the Tables tab and select Tables in Workbook Data Model. Click Open.

4. Click OK in the Create PivotTable dialog box.

After the PivotTable is created, the PivotTable Fields list shows each individual Table in the internal Data Model (see Figure 2-32).

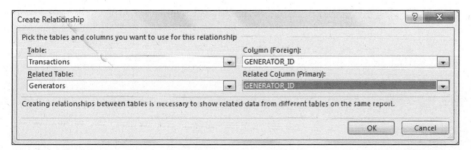

Figure 2-32: PivotTables that use the internal Data Model as the source show all the tables within the Data Model.

With a Data Model–driven PivotTable, you have the ability to merge disparate data sources into one analytical engine. Figure 2-33 demonstrates how you can build a view using data fields from the different tables in the Data Model.

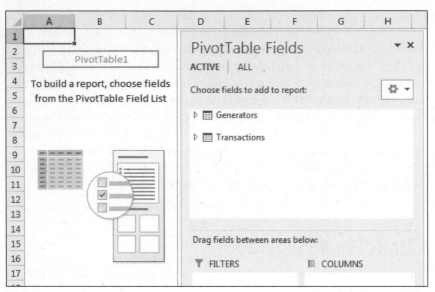

Figure 2-33: With a Data Model–driven PivotTable, you can analyze data using the fields for each table in the Data Model.

Introduction to Power Pivot

3

In This Chapter

- Getting started with Power Pivot
- Linking to Excel data
- Managing relationships
- Creating a Power Pivot–driven PivotTable
- Creating your own calculated columns
- Utilizing DAX to create calculated columns
- Using calculated fields

Over the last decade or so, corporate managers, eager to turn impossible amounts of data into useful information, drove the BI industry to innovate new ways of consolidating data into meaningful insights.

The key product of Excel's business intelligence endeavor is Power Pivot (introduced in Excel 2010 as an add-in). With Power Pivot, you can set up relationships between large disparate data sources. For the first time, you can add a relational view to your reporting without using problematic functions such as `vlookup`. The ability to merge data sources with hundreds of thousands of rows into one analytical engine within Excel was groundbreaking.

With the release of Excel 2013, Microsoft incorporated Power Pivot directly into Excel — making its powerful capabilities available to you right out of the box!

On the Web

You can find the example file for this chapter on this book's companion Web site at `www.wiley.com/go/bitools` **in the workbook named** `Chapter 3 Samples.xlsx.`

In this chapter, you get an overview of those capabilities, exploring the key features, benefits, and capabilities of Power Pivot.

Understanding the Power Pivot Internal Data Model

At its core, Power Pivot is essentially an SQL Server Analysis Services engine made available through an in-memory process that runs directly within Excel. The technical name for this engine is the xVelocity analytics engine. However, in Excel, it's referred to as the internal Data Model. You can leverage the internal Data Model in Excel 2013 to create PivotTables that analyze data from multiple data sources (which you can find out about in Chapter 2).

The internal Data Model can contain unlimited rows and columns of data. The only real limitation is the 2GB maximum file size for a workbook and available memory. But you probably won't reach that limit, because Power Pivot's compression algorithm is typically able to shrink imported data to about one-tenth of its original size. This means a 100MB text file would only take up approximately 10MB in the internal Data Model.

Every Excel 2013 workbook contains an internal Data Model; a single instance of the Power Pivot in-memory engine. In Chapter 2, you interacted with the internal Data Model in a limited capacity through the Data tab on the Ribbon. However, the most effective way to interact with the internal Data Model is to use the Power Pivot Ribbon interface, which becomes available once you activate the Power Pivot Add-In.

The Power Pivot Add-In doesn't install with every edition of Office 2013. If you have the Office Home Edition, you won't able to activate the Power Pivot Add-In, thus you will not have access to the Power Pivot Ribbon interface.

As of this writing, the Power Pivot Add-In is only available if you have one of the following editions of Office or Excel:

> **Office 2013 Professional Plus:** Available through volume licensing only
>
> **Office 365 ProPlus:** Available with an ongoing subscription to Office365.com
>
> **Excel 2013 Stand-alone Edition:** Available for purchase through any retailer

If you see the Power Pivot Add-In tab on the Ribbon (see the upcoming Figure 3-1), you don't have to do anything! The Power Pivot Add-In is already activated.

If you still need to activate the Power Pivot Add-In, follow these steps:

1. Choose File ➜ Options.

2. Choose the Add-Ins option on the left.

3. Select COM Add-Ins from the Manage drop-down list and then click Go.

4. Select the Microsoft Office Power Pivot for Excel 2013 in the list of available COM Add-Ins. Click OK.

If the Power Pivot tab does not appear on the Ribbon, close and restart Excel 2013.

After installing the add-in, the Power Pivot tab appears on the Ribbon, as shown in Figure 3-1.

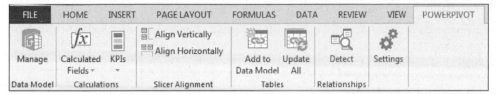

Figure 3-1: After you activate the add-in, you see the Power Pivot tab on the Ribbon.

The Power Pivot Ribbon interface exposes the full set of functionality you don't get with the standard Data tab. Here are a few examples of functionality available with the Power Pivot interface:

➤ Browse, edit, filter, and custom sort data import.

➤ Create custom calculated columns that apply to all rows in your data import.

➤ Define a default number format to use when the field appears in a PivotTable.

➤ Configure relationships via a handy graphical diagram view.

➤ Prevent certain fields from appearing in the PivotTable Field List.

➤ Configure specific fields to be read as Geography or Image fields.

➤ Access Key Performance Indicators (KPI).

Linking Excel Tables to Power Pivot

The first step in using Power Pivot is to fill it with data. You can either import data from external data sources or link to Excel tables in your current workbook. See Chapter 4 for more about importing data from external data sources. For now, you can link three Excel tables to Power Pivot.

In this scenario, you have three datasets in three different worksheets (see Figure 3-2):

➤ The **Customers** dataset contains basic information like CustomerID, CustomerName, and Address.

➤ The **InvoiceHeader** dataset contains data that points specific invoices to specific customers.

➤ The **InvoiceDetails** dataset contains the specifics of each invoice.

If you want to analyze revenue by customer and month, you need to join these three tables. In the past, you'd have to go through a series of gyrations involving `vlookup` or other clever formulas. But with Power Pivot, you can build these relationships in just a few clicks.

	A	B	C	D	E	F	G
1	CustomerID	CustomerName	Address	Country	City	State	Zip
2	DOLLISCO0001	Dollis Cove Resort	765 Kingway	Canada	Charlottetown	PEI	C1A 1W3
3	GETAWAYI0001	Getaway Inn	234 E Cannon Ave.	USA	Saginaw	MI	48605

◄ ►   **Customers**   InvoiceHeader   InvoiceDetails   ⊕

	A	B	C	D
1	InvoiceDate	InvoiceNumber	CustomerID	
2	5/8/2005	ORDST1025	BAKERSEM0001	
3	4/12/2007	STDINV2251	BAKERSEM0001	

◄ ►   Customers   **InvoiceHeader**   InvoiceDetails

	A	B	C	D	E
1	InvoiceNumber	Quantity	UnitCost	UnitPrice	
2	ORDST1022	1	59.29	119.95	
3	ORDST1015	1	3290.55	6589.95	

◄ ►   Customers   InvoiceHeader   **InvoiceDetails**

Figure 3-2: Use Power Pivot to analyze the data in the Customers, InvoiceHeader, and InvoiceDetails worksheets.

Preparing your Excel tables

When linking Excel data to Power Pivot, it's best to first convert your data to explicitly named tables. Although it's not technically necessary, giving your tables easy-to-remember names helps track and manage your data in the Power Pivot Data Model. If you don't convert your data to tables first, Excel does it for you and gives your tables useless names like Table1 and Table2.

Follow these steps to convert each dataset into an Excel table:

1. On the Customers tab, click anywhere inside the data range.

2. Press Ctrl+T.

3. In the Create Table dialog box, check that the range for the table is correct and that the My Table Has Headers option is selected. Click the OK button.

   The Table Tools Design tab appears on the Ribbon.

4. On the Table Tools Design tab, click in the Table Name input and give your table an easy to remember name (see Figure 3-3).

   This ensures that you will be able to recognize the table when adding it to the internal Data Model.

5. Repeat Steps 1–4 for the InvoiceHeader and InvoiceDetails datasets.

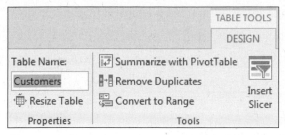

Figure 3-3: Give your newly created Excel table a friendly name.

Adding your Excel tables to the Data Model

After you've converted your data to Excel tables, you're ready to add the tables to the Power Pivot Data Model. Follow these steps to add your new created Excel tables to the Data Model using the Power Pivot tab:

1. Place your cursor anywhere inside your Customers table.

2. On the Power Pivot tab, click the Add to Data Model button.

    Power Pivot creates a copy of your table and opens the Power Pivot window (shown in Figure 3-4).

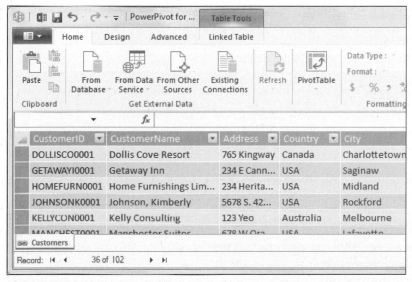

Figure 3-4: The Power Pivot window shows all the data that currently exists in your data model.

3. Repeat Steps 1 and 2 for your other Excel tables: InvoiceHeader and InvoiceDetails.

   After you have imported all your Excel tables into the Data Model, your Power Pivot window shows each dataset on its own tab, as shown in Figure 3-5.

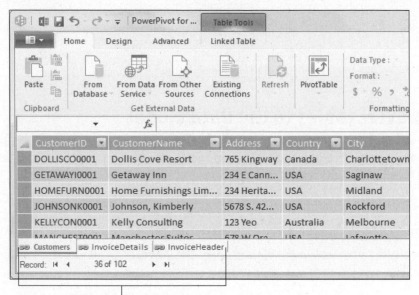

Each table has a tab.

Figure 3-5: Each table you add to the Data Model is placed on its own tab in Power Pivot.

When working with Power Pivot, note the following:

➤ Although the Power Pivot window looks like Excel, it's actually a separate program.

➤ The grid for your table does not have any row or column references.

➤ You can't edit the data within the table. This data is simply a snapshot of the actual Excel table you imported.

➤ You can switch between Excel and the Power Pivot window by clicking each respective program in the taskbar.

Note

The tabs in the Power Pivot window shown in Figure 3-6 have a hyperlink icon next to the tab names. This icon indicates that the data contained in the tab is a linked Excel table. This means that even though the data is a snapshot of the data at the time you added it, the data automatically updates when you edit the source table in Excel.

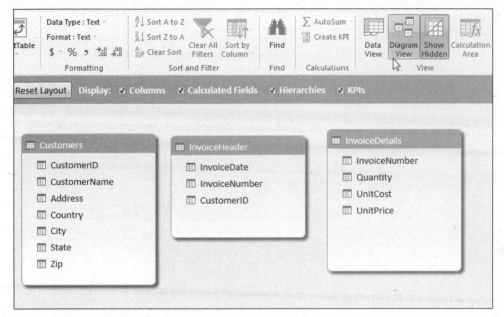

Figure 3-6: The Diagram View allows you to see all the tables in your Data Model.

Creating Relationships Among Your Power Pivot Tables

You can think of a relationship like a `vlookup`, in which you relate the data in one range to the data in another range using an index or unique identifier. In Power Pivot, you use relationships to do the same thing, but without the hassle of writing a formula.

At this point, Power Pivot knows you have three tables in the Data Model, but it has no idea how these three tables relate to one another. You need to connect these tables by defining relationships among the Customers, InvoiceDetails, and InvoiceHeader tables. You can do so within the Power Pivot window. Follow these steps:

1. Open the Power Pivot window and click the Diagram View button on the Home tab.

Tip

If you inadvertently closed the Power Pivot window, you can open it by clicking the Manage button on the Power Pivot tab.

Power Pivot displays a screen that shows a visual representation of all the tables in the Data Model (see Figure 3-6).

Tip   **You can move the tables in the Diagram View around by clicking and dragging them.**

The idea is to identify the primary index keys in each table and connect them. In this scenario, the Customers and InvoiceHeader tables can be connected using the CustomerID field. The InvoiceHeader and InvoiceDetails tables can be connected using the InvoiceNumber field.

2. Click and drag a line from the CustomerID field in the Customers table to the CustomerID field in the InvoiceHeader table (as shown in Figure 3-7).

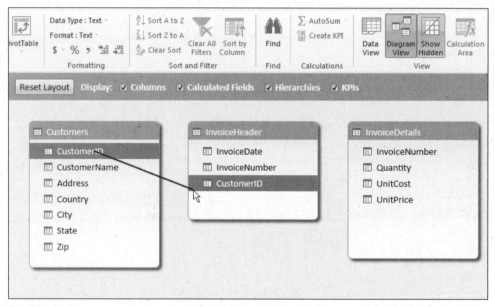

Figure 3-7: To create a relationship, simply click and drag a line between the fields in your tables.

3. Click and drag a line from the InvoiceNumber field in the InvoiceHeader table to the InvoiceNumber field in the InvoiceDetails table.

At this point, your diagram looks similar to Figure 3-8. Notice Power Pivot shows a line between the tables you just connected. In database-speak, these are referred to as *joins.*

The joins in Power Pivot are always *one to many* joins. This means that when a table is joined to another, one of the tables has unique records with unique index numbers, while the other can have many records where index numbers are duplicated.

A common example, shown in Figure 3-8, is the relationship between the Customers table and the InvoiceHeader table. In the Customers table, you have a unique list of customers, each with its own identifier. No CustomerID in that table is duplicated. The InvoiceHeader table has many rows for each CustomerID; each customer can have many invoices.

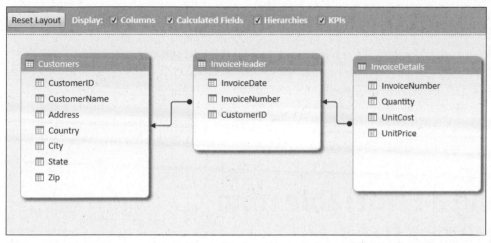

Figure 3-8: When you create relationships, the Power Pivot diagram shows join lines between your tables.

Notice that the join lines have arrows pointing from one table to another. The arrow in these join lines always points to the table that has the non-duplicated unique index.

Tip

To close the diagram and get back to seeing the data tables, click the Data View button in the Power Pivot window.

If you need to edit or delete a relationship between two tables in your Data Model, you can do so by following these steps:

1. Open the Power Pivot window. On the Design tab, click the Manage Relationships button.

2. In the Manage Relationships dialog box, click the relationship you want to work with and then click Edit or Delete.

    Clicking Edit opens the Edit Relationship dialog box shown in Figure 3-9.

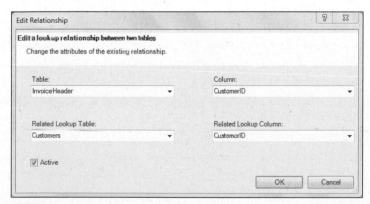

Figure 3-9: Define the relationship by selecting the appropriate table and field names from the drop-down lists.

3. Select the appropriate table and field names from the drop-down lists to redefine the relationship.

4. Click OK when you're done. Click the Close button in the Manage Relationships dialog box to get back to the Power Pivot model.

Note In Figure 3-9, you see that the lower-left field is called Related Lookup Table. In this drop-down list, you must select the table that contains unique non-duplicated rows. The column you select in the Related Lookup Column must contain unique items.

Creating a PivotTable from Power Pivot Data

After you define the relationships in your Power Pivot Data Model, it's essentially ready for action. In terms of Power Pivot, "action" means analysis with a PivotTable. Creating a PivotTable from a Power Pivot Data Model is relatively straightforward:

1. Open the Power Pivot window. On the Home tab, click the PivotTable button.

2. Specify whether you want the PivotTable placed on a new worksheet or an existing sheet.

Limitations of Power Pivot–driven PivotTables

It's important to note that Power Pivot–driven PivotTables come with some limitations that you don't encounter with standard PivotTables:

- The Group feature is disabled for Power Pivot–driven PivotTables. You can't roll dates into months, quarters, years, and so on. You can work around this using your own calculated columns described later in this chapter.

- In a standard PivotTable, you can double-click a cell to drill down to the rows that make up the figure in that cell. In Power Pivot–driven PivotTables, however, you only get the first 1,000 rows.

- Power Pivot–driven PivotTables won't allow you to create the traditional Calculated Fields and Calculated Items found in standard Excel PivotTables.

- Workbooks that use the Power Pivot Data Model cannot be refreshed or configured if opened in a version of Excel earlier than Excel 2013.

- You cannot use custom lists to automatically sort the data in your Power Pivot–driven PivotTables.

- The Product and Count Numbers summary calculations are not available with Power Pivot–driven PivotTables.

3. Build your needed analysis just as you would any other standard PivotTable, using the Pivot Field List.

Turn to Chapter 2 if you need to configure a PivotTable with the Pivot Field List.

The PivotTable shown in Figure 3-10 contains all the tables in the Power Pivot Data Model. With this configuration, you have a powerful cross-table analytical engine in the form of a familiar PivotTable. From here, you can calculate the average Unit Price by customer.

Row Labels	Average of UnitPrice
Aaron Fitz Electrical	$271.62
Adam Park Resort	$639.95
Advanced Paper Co.	$191.75
Advanced Tech Satellite System	$63.48
American Science Museum	$156.62
Associated Insurance Company	$324.95
Astor Suites	$1,583.28
Atmore Retirement Center	$39.95
Baker's Emporium Inc.	$601.06
Blue Yonder Airlines	$856.10
Boyle's Country Inn's	$609.95
Breakthrough Telemarketing	$864.24
Castle Inn Resort	$119.95
Central Communications LTD	$768.52
Central Distributing	$124.95
Central Illinois Hospital	$1,704.98
Communication Connections	$126.62
Computerized Phone Systems	$119.95
Contoso, Ltd.	$8,912.45

Figure 3-10: You now have a Power Pivot–driven PivotTable that aggregates across multiple tables.

In the days before Power Pivot, this analysis would have been difficult to get to. You needed to build `vlookup` formulas to get from Customer to Invoice Numbers, then another set of `vlookup` formulas to get from Invoice Numbers to Invoice Details. And after all that formula building, you still wouldn't have a way to aggregate the data to average Unit Price per customer.

With Power Pivot, you get to your analysis in just a few clicks!

Enhancing Power Pivot Data with Calculated Columns

When analyzing data with Power Pivot, you may need to expand your analysis to include data based on calculations that are not in your original dataset. Power Pivot provides a way to add your own calculations with calculated columns. *Calculated columns* are columns you create to enhance a Power Pivot table with your own formulas. Calculated columns are entered directly in the Power Pivot window, becoming part of the source data you use to feed your PivotTable. Calculated columns work at the row level; that is, the formulas you create in a calculated column perform their operations based on the data in each individual row. For example, imagine you have a Revenue column and a Cost column in your Power Pivot table. You could create a new column that calculates revenue minus cost. This calculation is simple and valid for each row in the dataset.

Creating a calculated column

Creating a calculated column works very much like building formulas in an Excel table. Follow these steps to create a calculated column:

1. Open the Power Pivot window and click the Invoice Details tab.

   Tip

   If you inadvertently closed the Power Pivot window, you can open it by clicking the Manage button on the Power Pivot Ribbon.

2. Click in the first blank cell in the Add Column column.

3. Enter the following formula on the formula bar:

   ```
   =[UnitPrice]*[Quantity]
   ```

4. Press Enter to see your formula populate the entire column.

   Power Pivot automatically renames the column to CalculatedColumn1.

5. Double-click the column label and rename the column Total Revenue.

   Your table now has a calculated column similar to that shown in Figure 3-11.

This is a calculated column.

[Total Revenue] ▼	fx =[UnitPrice]*[Quantity]			
InvoiceNu... ▼	Quantity ▼	UnitCost ▼	UnitPrice ▼	Total Revenue ▼
ORDST1022	1	59.29	119.95	119.95
ORDST1015	1	3290.55	6589.95	6589.95
ORDST1016	10	35	34.95	349.5
ORDST1017	50	91.59	189.95	9497.5
ORDST1018	1	59.29	119.95	119.95
INV1010	1	674.5	1349.95	1349.95
INV1011	1	91.25	189.95	189.95
INV1012	1	303.85	609.95	609.95
ORDST1020	1	59.29	119.95	119.95

Figure 3-11: Your formula automatically populates all rows in your new calculated column.

6. Create another calculated column called Total Cost.

   The formula is =[UnitCost]*[Quantity].

In Figure 3-11, notice how calculated columns are slightly darker than the standard imported columns. This allows you to easily see the calculated columns.

Note

You can rename any column in the Power Pivot window by double-clicking the column name and entering a new name. Alternatively, you can right-click any column and select Rename.

Tip

You can build your calculated columns by clicking instead of typing. For example, instead of manually entering = [UnitPrice] * [Quantity], you can enter the equal sign (=), click the UnitPrice column, enter the asterisk (*), and then click the Quantity column. Note that you can also enter your own static data. For example, you can enter a formula to calculate a 10-percent tax rate by entering = [UnitPrice] *1.10.

After you have your two calculated columns, go back to the PivotTable you created earlier in this chapter (see "Creating a PivotTable from Power Pivot Data"). Take a look at the field list. If you accidentally closed your field list, right-click anywhere in the PivotTable and select Show Field List.

Your newly created calculated columns are now available in the field list, as shown in Figure 3-12. Notice that you didn't have to take any action to get your calculated columns into the PivotTable. Each calculated column you create is automatically available in any PivotTable connected to the Power Pivot Data Model. You can use these calculated columns just as you would any other field in your PivotTable.

Sum of Total Revenue	Sum of Total Cost
45668.4	23199.07
6238.5	3615.26
131930.45	130385.18
2278.7	1300.75
6357.8	3053.48
1299.8	646.8
174604.55	87902.76
39.95	18.65
18418	9842.36
26138.3	12584.68
1829.85	911.55
91437	49504.57
239.9	118.58
36816.2	19671.22
9637.8	9558.2
10229.9	10180.49
928.85	439.57
239.9	118.58
224137.6	112241.81
95294.55	92402.09
119.95	59.29
6745.95	3070.13

PivotTable Fields

ACTIVE | ALL

Choose fields to add to report:

▲ 🗔 **InvoiceDetails**
- ☐ InvoiceNumber
- ☐ Quantity
- ☐ UnitCost
- ☐ UnitPrice
- ☑ **Total Revenue**
- ☑ **Total Cost**

Drag fields between areas below:

▼ FILTERS

▥ COLUMNS

Σ Values

▤ ROWS

CustomerName ▼

Σ VALUES

Sum of Total Revenue

Sum of Total Cost

Figure 3-12: Calculated columns automatically show up in the PivotTable Field List.

Note

If you need to edit the formula in a calculated column, find the calculated column in the Power Pivot window, click the column, and then make your changes directly in the formula bar.

Formatting your calculated columns

You often need to change the formatting of your Power Pivot columns to appropriately match the data within them; for example, to show numbers as currency, remove decimal places, or display dates in a certain way.

You are by no means limited to formatting just calculated columns. You can format any column; just click in the column you want to format and use the tools in the Formatting group on the Home tab of the Ribbon.

Tip

Veterans of Excel PivotTables know that changing PivotTable number formats one data field at a time is a pain. One fantastic feature of Power Pivot formatting is that any format you apply to your columns in the Power Pivot window is automatically applied to all PivotTables connected to the Data Model.

Referencing calculated columns in other calculations

Like all calculations in Excel, Power Pivot allows you to reference a calculated column as a variable in another calculated column. Figure 3-13 shows a calculated column called Gross Margin. The formula bar shows the calculation is using the previously created `[Total Revenue]` and `[Total Cost]` calculated columns.

`=([Total Revenue]-[Total Cost])/[Total Revenue]`

Total Revenue	Total Cost	Gross Margin
$69,109.95	$34,550.00	50 %
$899.50	$419.80	53 %
$1,349.95	$674.50	50 %
$189.95	$91.25	52 %
$609.95	$303.85	50 %
$949.75	$467.75	51 %
$29.85	$9.87	67 %
$359.95	$179.85	50 %
$9.95	$3.29	67 %
$5,999.95	$2,998.15	50 %

Figure 3-13: The Gross Margin calculation is using the previously created [Total Revenue] and [Total Cost] calculated columns.

Hiding calculated columns from end users

Because calculated columns can reference each other, you can imagine creating columns simply as helper columns for other calculations. You may not want your end users to see these columns in your client tools. In this context, the term "client tools" refers to PivotTables, Power View dashboards, and Power Map.

Similar to hiding columns on an Excel worksheet, Power Pivot allows you to hide any column (it doesn't have to be a calculated column). To hide columns, select the columns you want hidden, right-click the selection, and then select Hide from Client Tools.

Your selected columns become subdued and grayed out, as shown in Figure 3-14; you can easily identify which columns are hidden.

These columns are hidden.

UnitPrice	Total Revenue	Total Cost	Gross Margin
69109.95	$69,109.95	$34,550.00	50 %
89.95	$899.50	$419.80	53 %
1349.95	$1,349.95	$674.50	50 %
189.95	$189.95	$91.25	52 %
609.95	$609.95	$303.85	50 %
189.95	$949.75	$467.75	51 %
9.95	$29.85	$9.87	67 %
359.95	$359.95	$179.85	50 %
9.95	$9.95	$3.29	67 %
5999.95	$5,999.95	$2,998.15	50 %

Figure 3-14: The [Total Revenue] and [Total Cost] columns are hidden.

When a column is hidden, it doesn't appear as an available selection in your PivotTable Field List. However, if the column you're hiding is already part of the pivot report, meaning you already dragged it onto the PivotTable, hiding the column doesn't automatically remove it from the report. Hiding it merely affects the ability to see the column in the PivotTable Field List.

Note To unhide columns, select the hidden columns in the Power Pivot window, right-click the selection, and then select Unhide from Client Tools.

Utilizing DAX to Create Calculated Columns

DAX (Data Analysis Expression) is the formula language Power Pivot uses to perform calculations within its own construct of tables and columns. The DAX formula language comes with its own set of functions. Some of these functions can be used in calculated columns for row level calculations, while others are designed to be used in calculated fields for aggregate operations.

In this section, we touch on some of the DAX functions that can be leveraged in calculated columns.

Identifying DAX functions that are safe for calculated columns

In the previous section, we showed you how to use the formula bar within the Power Pivot window to enter calculations. Next to that formula bar, you may have noticed the Insert Function button (labeled with an fx). This is similar to the Insert Function button found in Excel. You can browse, search for, and insert the available DAX functions.

Click the fx button and the Insert Function dialog box opens, as shown in Figure 3-15.

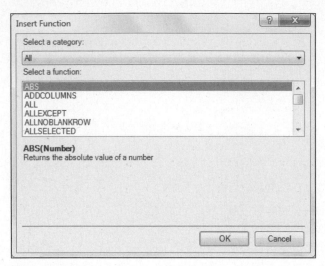

Figure 3-15: The Insert Function dialog box shows you all available DAX functions.

Note

As you look through the list of DAX functions, notice many of them look like the Excel functions you're already familiar with. But make no mistake; these aren't Excel functions. Where Excel functions work with cells and ranges, these DAX functions are designed to work at the table and column levels.

To see how these DAX functions work, add a calculated column on the Invoice Details tab. Enter the SUM function SUM([UnitCost]) in the formula bar. The result you get is shown in Figure 3-16.

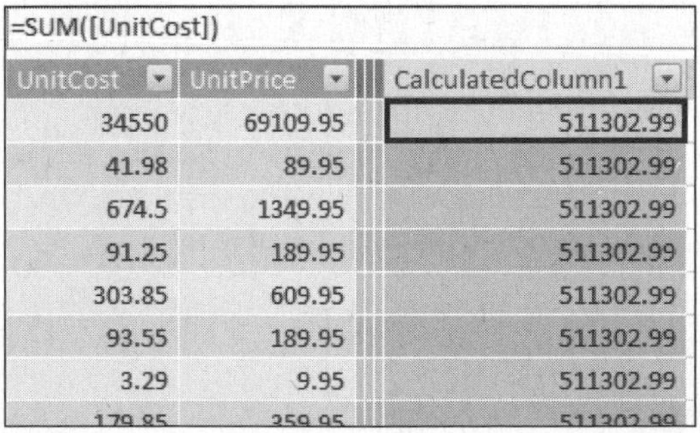

=SUM([UnitCost])		
UnitCost	**UnitPrice**	**CalculatedColumn1**
34550	69109.95	511302.99
41.98	89.95	511302.99
674.5	1349.95	511302.99
91.25	189.95	511302.99
303.85	609.95	511302.99
93.55	189.95	511302.99
3.29	9.95	511302.99
179.85	359.95	511302.99

Figure 3-16: The DAX SUM function can only sum the column as a whole.

As you can see, the SUM function sums the entire column. This is because Power Pivot and DAX are designed to work with tables and columns. Power Pivot has no construct for cells and ranges. It doesn't even have column letters and row numbers on its grid. So where you would normally reference a range (such as in an Excel SUM function), DAX basically takes the entire column.

The bottom line is that you can't use all DAX functions with calculated columns. Because a calculated column evaluates at the row level, only DAX functions that evaluate single data points can be used in a calculated column.

A good rule is that if the function requires an array or a range of cells as an argument, then it's not viable in a calculated column. So functions such as SUM, MIN, MAX, AVERAGE, and COUNT don't work in calculated columns. Functions such as YEAR, MONTH, MID, LEFT, RIGHT, IF, and IFERROR that require only single data point arguments are better suited for use in calculated columns.

Building DAX-driven calculated columns

To use a DAX function to enhance calculated columns, click the Invoice Header tab in the Ribbon.

Figure 3-17 contains an InvoiceDate column. Although this column is valuable in the raw table, the individual dates aren't convenient when analyzing the data with a PivotTable. It would be beneficial to have a column for Month and a column for Year. This way, you could aggregate and analyze data by month and year.

InvoiceDate	InvoiceNumber	CustomerID	Add Column
5/8/2005 12:00:00 AM	ORDST1025	BAKERSEM0001	
4/12/2007 12:00:00 AM	STDINV2251	BAKERSEM0001	
5/8/2005 12:00:00 AM	ORDST1026	AARONFIT0001	
4/12/2007 12:00:00 AM	STDINV2252	AARONFIT0001	
5/7/2004 12:00:00 AM	ORD1002	METROPOL0001	
2/10/2004 12:00:00 AM	INV1024	AARONFIT0001	
2/15/2004 12:00:00 AM	INV1025	AARONFIT0001	
5/10/2004 12:00:00 AM	ORDPH1005	LECLERC0001	
5/8/2004 12:00:00 AM	ORD1000	MAGNIFIC0001	

Figure 3-17: Although this table has an InvoiceDate field, adding Year and Month columns would allow for better time-based analysis.

For this endeavor, you use the `year()`, `month()`, and `format()` DAX functions to add time dimensions to your data model. Follow these steps:

1. In the InvoiceHeader table, click in the first blank cell in the Add Column column on the far right.

2. In the formula bar, type **=YEAR([InvoiceDate])** and press Enter.

   Power Pivot automatically names the column CalculatedColumn1.

3. Double-click the CalculatedColumn1 column label and rename the column **Year**.

4. Repeat Steps 1–3 to add two additional columns:

- *Month:* Enter **=MONTH([InvoiceDate])** in the formula bar and rename the column **Month**.

- *Month Name:* Enter **=FORMAT([InvoiceDate],"mmm")** in the formula bar and rename the column **Month Name**.

You now have three new calculated columns similar to those shown in Figure 3-18.

[Month Name] ▼	f_x =FORMAT([InvoiceDate],"mmm")		
InvoiceDate	Year	Month	Month Name
5/8/2005 12:00:00 AM	2005	5	May
4/12/2007 12:00:00 AM	2007	4	Apr
5/8/2005 12:00:00 AM	2005	5	May
4/12/2007 12:00:00 AM	2007	4	Apr
5/7/2004 12:00:00 AM	2004	5	May
2/10/2004 12:00:00 AM	2004	2	Feb
2/15/2004 12:00:00 AM	2004	2	Feb
5/10/2004 12:00:00 AM	2004	5	May
5/8/2004 12:00:00 AM	2004	5	May
5/10/2004 12:00:00 AM	2004	5	May

Figure 3-18: Using DAX functions to supplement a table with Year, Month, and Month Name columns.

As mentioned previously, creating calculated columns automatically makes them available through your PivotTable Field Lists (see Figure 3-19).

PivotTable Fields

ACTIVE | ALL

Choose fields to add to report:

▲ ▦ **InvoiceHeader**
 ☐ InvoiceDate
 ☐ InvoiceNumber
 ☐ CustomerID
 ☑ **Year**
 ☑ **Month**
 ☑ **Month Name**

Drag fields between areas below:

▼ FILTERS   ▥ COLUMNS
                    Σ Values

▤ ROWS   Σ VALUES

Figure 3-19: DAX calculations are immediately available in any connected PivotTable.

Month sorting in Power Pivot–driven PivotTables

One of the more annoying things about Power Pivot is that it doesn't inherently know how to sort months. Unlike standard Excel, Power Pivot doesn't use the built-in custom lists that define the order of month names. So when you create a calculated column like [Month Name] and place it into your PivotTable, Power Pivot puts those months in alphabetical order.

The fix for this is fairly easy. Open the Power Pivot window and click the Sort by Column button.

In the Sort by Column dialog box, select the column you want sorted, and then select the column you want to sort by.

Click OK, and you might think you did something wrong because nothing happens. This is because the sort order you defined is not for the Power Pivot window. The sort order is applied to your PivotTable. Switch to Excel to see the result in the PivotTable.

Row Labels ▼	Sum of Total Revenue
Jan	$239,739.00
Feb	$179,334.20
Mar	$824,469.20
Apr	$473,330.10
May	$378,596.45
Jul	$1,469.00
Sep	$2,519.85
(blank)	$21,404.45
Grand Total	**$2,120,862.25**

Understanding Calculated Fields

You can enhance the functionality of your Power Pivot reports with another kind of calculation called a *calculated field*. Calculated fields are used to perform more complex calculations that work on an aggregation of data. These calculations are not applied to the Power Pivot window like calculated columns. Instead, they're applied directly to your PivotTable, creating a sort of virtual column that can't be seen in the Power Pivot window. You use calculated fields when you need to calculate based on an aggregated grouping of rows.

Imagine you wanted to show the dollar variance between the years 2007 and 2006 for each of your customers. Think about what technically has to be done to achieve this calculation. You'd have to figure out the sum of revenue for 2007, then you'd have to get the sum of revenue for 2006, then you'd have to subtract the sum of 2007 from the sum of 2006. This is a calculation that simply can't be done using calculated columns. Using calculated fields is the only way to get the dollar variance between 2007 and 2006.

Follow these steps to create a calculated field:

1. Start with a PivotTable created from a Power Pivot model.

2. Click the Power Pivot tab on the Ribbon and choose Calculated Fields ➜ New Calculated Field.

   The Calculated Field dialog box opens, as shown in Figure 3-20.

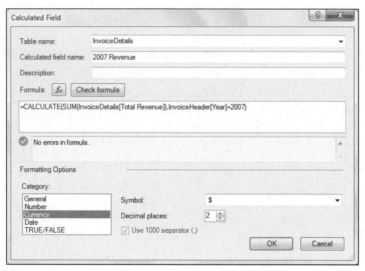

Figure 3-20: Creating a new calculated field.

3. Set the following inputs:

   - *Table Name:* Choose the table that will contain the calculated field when looking at the PivotTable Fields list.

   - *Calculated Field Name:* Give your calculated field a descriptive name.

   - *Formula:* Enter the DAX formula that will calculate the results of your new field.

   - *Formatting Options:* Specify the formatting for the calculated field results.

   In this example, we use the following DAX formula:

   ```
   =CALCULATE(SUM(InvoiceDetails[Total Revenue]),
       InvoiceHeader[Year]=2007)
   ```

   This formula uses the `Calculate` function to sum the Total Revenue column from the InvoiceDetails table, where the Year column in the InvoiceHeader is equal to 2007. This is just one of a limitless number of formulas you can use to define a calculated field.

4. Click the Check Formula button to ensure there are no syntax errors.

   If your formula is well formed, you see the message `No errors in formula`. If there are errors, you see a full description of the errors.

5. Click OK to confirm your changes and close the Calculated Field dialog box.

 You immediately see your newly created calculated field in the PivotTable.

6. Repeat Steps 2–5 for any other calculated field you need to create.

In this example, we created two additional calculated fields:

```
=CALCULATE(SUM(InvoiceDetails[Total Revenue]),InvoiceHeader[Year]=2006)
=[2007 Revenue]-[2006 Revenue]
```

Figure 3-21 shows the newly created calculated fields. The calculated fields are applied to each customer, showing the variance between their 2007 and 2006 revenues. Note that once you create calculated fields, they're available for selection in the PivotTable Fields list.

CustomerName	2007 Revenue	2006 Revenue	2007 vs 2006
Aaron Fitz Electrical	$15,500.80	$24,448.20	(8,947.40)
Adam Park Resort	$2,519.75	$3,598.95	(1,079.20)
Advanced Paper Co.	$479.60	$959.60	(480.00)
American Science Museum	$3,178.90	$2,279.40	899.50
Associated Insurance Company	$649.90		649.90
Astor Suites	$84,577.60	$89,937.40	(5,359.80)
Baker's Emporium Inc.	$8,859.50		8,859.50
Blue Yonder Airlines	$6,919.30	$16,519.10	(9,599.80)
Breakthrough Telemarketing	$45,638.90	$45,718.50	(79.60)
Central Communications LTD	$11,819.20	$24,937.30	(13,118.10)
Communication Connections	$69.65		69.65
Computerized Phone Systems	$119.95		119.95
Contoso, Ltd.	$75,829.25	$9,758.60	66,070.65

PivotTable Fields

ACTIVE   ALL

Choose fields to add to report:

- ☐ Total Revenue
- ☐ Total Cost
- ☐ Gross Margin
- ☑ 2007 Revenue
- ☑ 2006 Revenue
- ☑ 2007 vs 2006

Drag fields between areas below:

Figure 3-21: Calculated fields can be seen in the PivotTable Fields list.

Note

There are over 140 different DAX functions. You can click the fx button in the Calculated Field dialog box to see all the available DAX functions that can be used to implement a new calculated field. A full overview of DAX is out of the scope of this book. If after reading this section, you have a desire to learn more about DAX, consider picking up *Microsoft Excel 2013: Building Data Models with PowerPivot,* **by Alberto Ferrari and Marco Russo (Microsoft Press).**

You may find that you need to either edit or delete a calculated field. You can do so by following these steps:

1. Click anywhere inside your PivotTable, then click the Power Pivot tab on the Ribbon and choose Calculated Fields ➜ Manage Calculated Fields.

 The Manage Calculated Field dialog box opens, as shown in Figure 3-22.

2. Select the target calculated field and click either the Edit or Delete button.

 Clicking the Edit button opens the Calculated Field dialog box, where you can make changes to the calculation setting. Clicking the Delete button opens a message box asking you to confirm that you want to remove the calculated field.

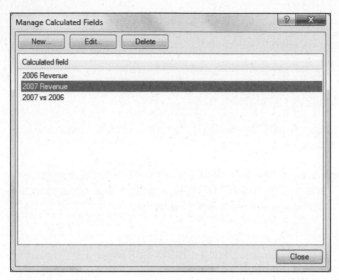

Figure 3-22: The Manage Calculated Fields dialog box lets you edit or delete your calculated fields.

Loading External Data into Power Pivot

In This Chapter

- Importing from relational databases

- Importing from flat files

- Loading data from other data sources

- Refreshing and managing external data connections

In Chapter 3, you loaded the data already contained within the workbook in which you're working. But as you discover in this chapter, you're not limited to using only the data that already exists in your Excel workbook.

Power Pivot has the ability to reach outside the workbook and import data found in external data sources. Indeed, what makes Power Pivot so powerful is its ability to consolidate data from disparate data sources and build relationships among them. This means you can theoretically create a Power Pivot Data Model that contains some data from an SQL Server table, some data from a Microsoft Access database, and even data from a one-off text file.

In this chapter, we show you how to import external data into your Power Pivot Data Models.

Loading Data from Relational Databases

Relational databases are one of the more common data sources used by Excel analysts. It's not difficult to find an analyst who frequently uses data from Microsoft Access, SQL Server, or Oracle databases. In this section, we walk through the steps for loading data from external database systems.

Loading data from SQL Server

SQL Server databases are some of the most commonly used for the storing of enterprise-level data. Most SQL Server databases are managed and maintained by the IT department. To connect to an SQL Server database, you have to work with your IT department to obtain read access to the database you're trying to pull from.

After you have access to the database, follow these steps to load the data:

1. Open the Power Pivot window and click the From Other Sources button on the Home tab.

2. In the Table Import Wizard, shown in Figure 4-1, select the Microsoft SQL Server option and then click Next.

Figure 4-1: Select Microsoft SQL Server to start loading data.

The Table Import Wizard asks for the information it needs to connect to your database (see Figure 4-2).

3. Fill in the following fields. When you're done, click Next.

- *Friendly Connection Name:* This field allows you to specify your own name for the external source. Enter a name that is descriptive and easy to read.

- *Server Name:* This is the name of the server that contains the database you're trying to connect to. You get this from your IT department when you're given access.

Figure 4-2: Provide the basic information needed to connect to the target database.

- *Log on to the Server:* These are your login credentials. Depending on how your IT department gives you access, you select either Use Windows Authentication or Use SQL Server Authentication. Windows Authentication essentially means that the server recognizes you by your windows login. SQL Server Authentication means that the IT department created a distinct username and password for you. If you're using SQL Server Authentication, you need to provide a username and password.

- *Save My Password:* Select the Save My Password check box if you want your username and password to be stored in the workbook. This allows your connections to remain refreshable when being used by other people. There are obviously security issues with this option, because anyone can view the connection properties and see your username and password. You should only use this option if your IT department set you up with an application account — that is, an account created specifically to be used by multiple people.

- *Database Name:* Every SQL Server can contain multiple databases. Enter the name of the database you are connecting to. You get this from your IT department when you are given access.

4. In the Choose How to Import the Data screen, shown in Figure 4-3, choose whether to select from a list of tables and views, or write your own custom query using SQL syntax. Click Next when done.

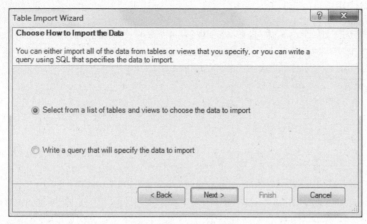

Figure 4-3: Choose to select from a list of tables and views.

The latter requires an advanced technique that we cover in Chapter 11. In most cases, you choose the option to select from a list of tables.

The Table Import Wizard reads the database and shows you a list of all available tables and views (see Figure 4-4). The tables have an icon that looks like a grid, while views have an icon that looks like a box on top of another box.

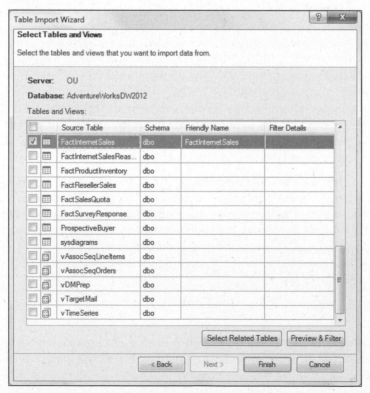

Figure 4-4: The Table Import Wizard offers a list of tables and views.

Importing tables versus importing views

Views are query objects that are built to extract subsets of data from database tables based on certain predefined conditions. Views are typically created by someone familiar with the database as a kind of canned reporting mechanism that outputs a ready-to-use dataset.

There are pros and cons to importing tables versus views.

Tables come with the benefit of defined relationships. When you import tables, Power Pivot can recognize the relationships among the tables and automatically duplicate those relationships in the Data Model. Tables are also more transparent, allowing you to see all the raw unfiltered data. However, when you import tables, you have to have some level of understanding of the database schema and how the values within the tables are utilized in the context of your organization's business rules. In addition, importing a table imports all the columns and records, whether you need them or not. In order to keep the size of your Power Pivot Data Model manageable, this often forces you to take the extra step of explicitly filtering out the columns you don't need.

Views are often cleaner datasets because they are already optimized to include only the columns and data that are necessary. In addition, you don't need to have an intimate knowledge of the database schema. Someone with that knowledge has already done the work for you; joined the correct tables, applied the appropriate business rules, optimized output, and so on. What you lose with views, however, is the ability for Power Pivot to automatically recognize and build relationships within the Data Model. Also, if you don't have the rights to open the views in design mode, you lose transparency because you won't be able to see exactly what the view is doing to come up with its final output.

It's generally considered a best practice to use views rather than tables whenever possible. They not only provide you with cleaner, more user-friendly data, but they can help streamline your Power Pivot Data Model by limiting the amount of data you import. That said, using tables is by no means frowned upon, and is often the only option due to the lack of database rights or availability of predefined views. You may even find yourself importing both tables and views from the same database.

5. Select the tables and views you want to import by checking the box.

   In Figure 4-4, the FactInternetSales table is selected. The Friendly Name column allows you to enter a new name that is used to reference the table in Power Pivot.

6. Click the Select Related Tables button.

   Power Pivot scans for and automatically selects any other tables that have a relationship with the table(s) you've already selected. This is a handy feature to have when sourcing large databases with dozens of tables.

Note

Remember that importing a table imports all the columns and records for that table. This can impact the size and performance of your Power Pivot Data Model. You may find you need only a handful of the columns from the tables you import. In those cases, you can use the Preview & Filter button.

7. Click the table name to highlight it and then click the Preview & Filter button.

The Table Import Wizard displays the preview screen shown in Figure 4-5, where you see all the columns available in the table, with a sampling of rows.

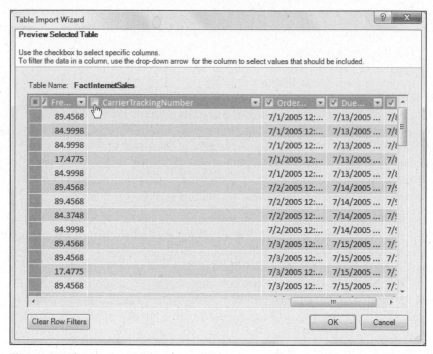

Figure 4-5: The Preview & Filter screen allows you to filter out columns you don't need.

8. Choose the columns that you want to import in the table.

Each column header has a check box next to it, indicating that the column will be imported with the table. Deselecting the check box tells Power Pivot to not include that column in the Data Model.

You can also filter certain records. Click the drop-down arrow for any of the columns and choose the criteria to filter unwanted records, as shown in Figure 4-6. This works just like the standard filtering in Excel. You can select and deselect the data items in the filtered list, or if there are too many choices, you can apply broader criteria by choosing Date Filters (if you're filtering a textual column, this is Text Filters).

9. After you're done selecting your data and applying any needed filters, click the Finish button in the Table Import Wizard.

The import log shown in Figure 4-7 shows the progress of the import and summarizes the import actions taken after completion.

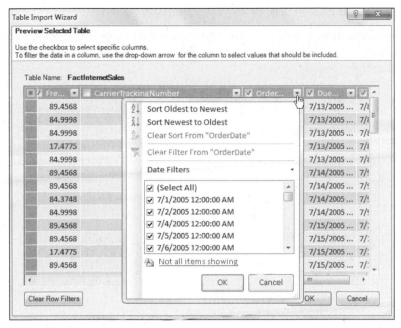

Figure 4-6: Use the drop-down arrows in each column to filter out unneeded records.

Figure 4-7: The last screen of the Table Import Wizard shows you the progress of your import actions.

10. Open the Power Pivot window and click the Diagram View button on the Home tab.

The final step in loading data from SQL Server is to review and create any needed relationships. Power Pivot displays the diagram screen (see Figure 4-8), where you can view and edit relationships as needed. Chapter 3 covers relationships.

Tip

Don't panic if you feel like you've botched the column and record filtering on your imported Power Pivot table. Select the worrisome table in the Power Pivot window and open the Edit Table Properties dialog box (choose Design ➜ Table Properties). Notice this dialog box is basically the same Preview & Filter screen in the Import Table Wizard (refer to Figure 4-5). From here, you can select columns you originally filtered, edit record filters, clear filters, or even use a different table or view.

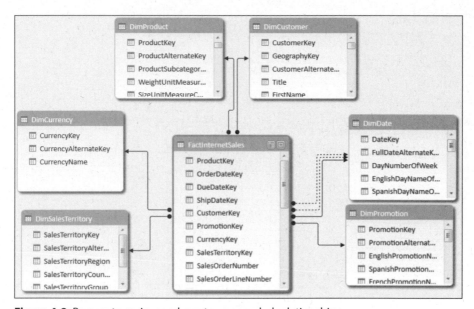

Figure 4-8: Be sure to review and create any needed relationships.

Loading data from Microsoft Access databases

Because Microsoft Access has traditionally been available with the Microsoft Office suite of applications, Access databases have long been used by organizations to store and manage mission-critical departmental data. Walk into any organization, and you will likely find several Access databases that contain useful data.

Unlike SQL Server databases, Microsoft Access databases are typically found on local desktops and directories. This means you can typically import data from Access without the help of your IT department. Follow these steps to do so:

1. Open the Power Pivot window and click the From Other Sources button on the Home tab.

2. In the Table Import Wizard, shown in Figure 4-9, select the Microsoft Access option and click the Next button.

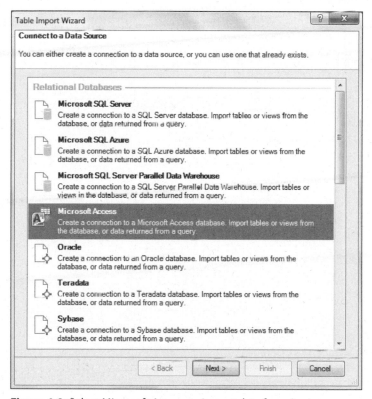

Figure 4-9: Select Microsoft Access to import data from Access.

3. Fill in the information the wizard needs to connect to your database (see Figure 4-10).

   In this screen, you need to provide

   - *Friendly Connection Name:* This field allows you to specify your own name for the external source. Enter a name that is descriptive and easy to read.

   - *Database Name:* Enter the full path of your target Access database. You can click the Browse button to search for and select the database you want to pull from.

- *Log on to the Database:* Most Access databases aren't password-protected. But if you're connecting to one that does require a username and password, enter your login credentials.

- *Save My Password:* Select the Save My Password check box if you want your username and password to be stored in the workbook. This allows your connections to remain refreshable when being used by other people. Keep in mind that anyone can view the connection properties and see your username and password.

Caution

Because Access databases are essentially desktop files (`.mdb` or `.accdb`), they are susceptible to being moved, renamed, or deleted. Be aware that the connections in your workbook are hard-coded, so if you do move, rename, or delete your Access database, you will no longer be able to connect to it.

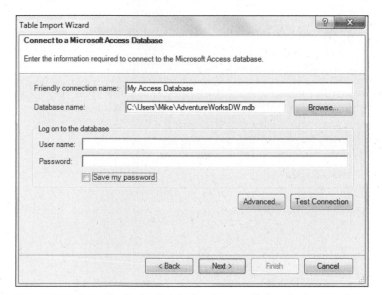

Figure 4-10: Provide the basic information needed to connect to the target database.

4. Click the Next button to continue with the Table Import Wizard.

   From this point, the process is virtually identical to importing SQL Server data (refer to the previous section).

Loading data from other relational database systems

Whether your data lives in Oracle, Dbase, or MySQL, you can load data from virtually any relational database system. As long as you have the appropriate database drivers installed, you have a way to connect Power Pivot to your data.

Open the Power Pivot window and click the From Other Sources button on the Home tab to open the Table Import Wizard dialog box shown in Figure 4-11. Then select the appropriate relational database system that you're using. For example, if you need to import data from Oracle, select Oracle. If you need to import data from Sybase, select Sybase.

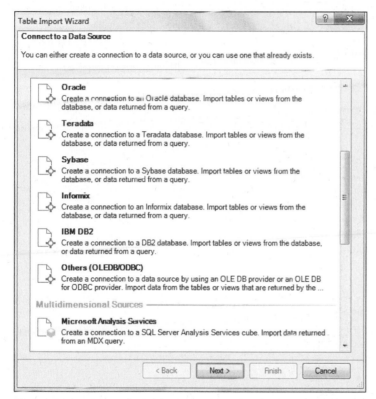

Figure 4-11: Activate the Table Import Wizard and select your target relational database system.

Connecting to any of these relational systems takes you through roughly the same steps you take when importing SQL Server data. You may see some alternate dialog boxes based on the needs of the database system you select.

Understandably, Microsoft cannot possibly create a named connection option for every database system out there, so you may not find your database system listed. In that case, select the Others (OLEDB/ODBC) option. Selecting this option opens the Table Import Wizard, starting with a screen asking you to enter or paste the connection string for your database system (see Figure 4-12). Ask your IT department for this connection string if you don't have it.

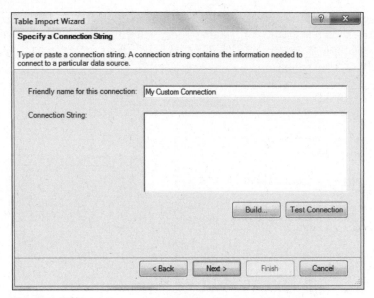

Figure 4-12: Enter the connection string for your database system.

If you're having trouble finding the correct syntax for your connection string, follow these steps to create the string:

1. Click Build to open the Data Link Properties dialog box shown in Figure 4-13.

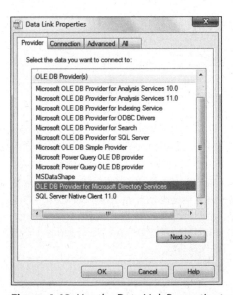

Figure 4-13: Use the Data Link Properties to configure a custom connection string to your relational database system.

2. On the Provider tab, select the appropriate driver for your database system.

3. Enter all the information needed on the Connection, Advanced, and All tabs.

4. When you're done, click OK to get back to the Table Import Wizard, where you see the connection string input box populated with the connection string needed to connect to your database system (see Figure 4-14).

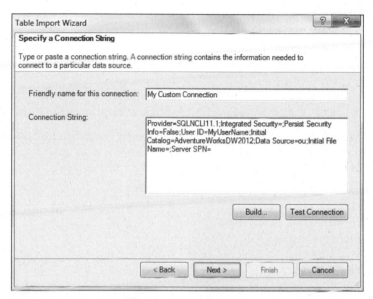

Figure 4-14: Use the options on the Data Link Properties dialog box to automatically build the syntax for your connection string.

From this point, the process is virtually identical to importing SQL Server data.

Note

To connect to any database system, you must have that system's drivers installed on your PC. SQL Server and Access are Microsoft, whose drivers are virtually guaranteed to be installed on most machines you'll encounter. The drivers for other database systems, however, need to be installed. This is typically done by the IT department, either at the time the machine is loaded with corporate software or upon demand. If you don't see the needed drivers for your database system, contact your IT department.

Loading Data from Flat Files

The term *flat file* refers to a file that contains some form of tabular data without any sort of structural hierarchy or relationship between records. The most common types of flat files are Excel files and text files. A ton of important data is maintained in flat files. In this section, you discover how to import these flat file data sources into the Power Pivot Data Model.

Loading data from external Excel files

If your source data is contained within the same workbook as your data model, you can create a linked table (see Chapter 3). Linked tables have a distinct advantage over other types of imported data in that they immediately respond to changes in the source data within the workbook. If you change the data in one of the tables in the workbook, the linked table automatically changes within the Power Pivot Data Model. The real-time interactivity you get with linked tables is nice to have.

The drawback to linked tables is that the source data must be kept in the same workbook as the Power Pivot Data Model. This isn't always possible. You'll encounter plenty of scenarios where you need to incorporate Excel data into your analysis, but that data lives in another workbook. In those cases, you can use Power Pivot's Table Import Wizard to connect to external Excel files. Follow these steps:

1. Open the Power Pivot window and click the From Other Sources button on the Home tab.

2. In the Table Import Wizard dialog box shown in Figure 4-15, select the Excel File option and click the Next button.

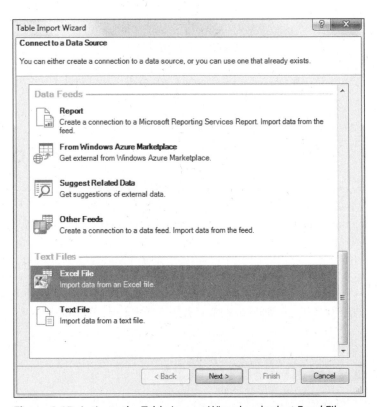

Figure 4-15: Activate the Table Import Wizard and select Excel File.

3. Fill in the information the wizard needs to connect to your target workbook. Click Next when you're done.

In this screen (see Figure 4-16), you need to provide

- *Friendly Connection Name:* This field allows you to specify your own name for the external source. Enter a name that is descriptive and easy to read.

- *Excel File Path:* Enter the full path of your target Excel workbook. You can click the Browse button to search for and select the workbook you want to pull from.

- *Use First Row as Column Headers:* In most cases, your Excel data will have column headers. Select the Use First Row as Column Headers check box to make sure your column headers are recognized as headers when imported.

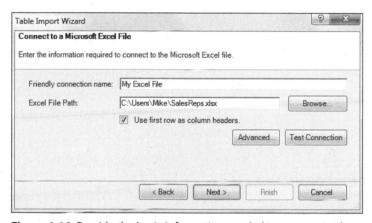

Figure 4-16: Provide the basic information needed to connect to the target workbook.

4. In the Select Tables and Views screen (see Figure 4-17), select the worksheets you want to import.

The Friendly Name column allows you to enter a new name that will be used to reference the table in Power Pivot.

Note

When reading from external Excel files, Power Pivot cannot identify individual table objects. As a result, you can only select entire worksheets in the Table Import Wizard (shown in Figure 4-17). Keeping this in mind, make sure you import worksheets that contain one single range of data.

5. (Optional) Click the Preview & Filter button if you need to filter unwanted columns and records.

6. Click Finish to complete the import process.

As always, be sure to review and create relationships to any other tables you've loaded into the Power Pivot Data Model.

Figure 4-17: Select the worksheets you want to import.

Note

Be aware that loading external Excel data does not give you the same interactivity you get with linked tables. Just as with importing database tables, the data you bring from an external Excel file is simply a snapshot. You need to refresh the data connection to see any new data that may have been added to the external Excel file (see the section "Refreshing and Managing External Data Connections" later in this chapter).

Loading data from text files

Text files are another type of flat file used to distribute data. These files are commonly outputs from legacy systems and Web sites. Excel has always been able to consume text files. With Power Pivot, you can go further and integrate them with other data sources. Follow these steps to do so:

1. Open the Power Pivot window and click the From Other Sources button on the Home tab.

2. In the Table Import Wizard dialog box shown in Figure 4-18, select the Text File option and click the Next button.

   The Table Import Wizard asks for the information it needs to connect to the target text file (see Figure 4-19).

Figure 4-18: Activate the Table Import Wizard and select Text File.

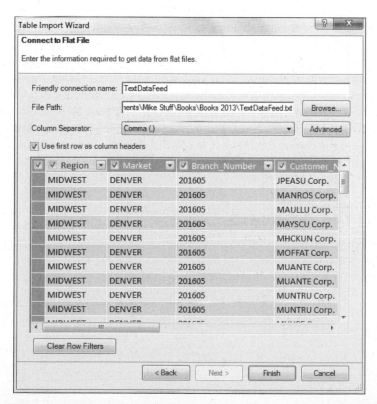

Figure 4-19: Provide the basic information needed to connect to the target text file.

3. Fill in the following information and when you're finished, click Next.

   - *Friendly Connection Name:* This field allows you to specify your own name for the external source. Enter a name that is descriptive and easy to read.

   - *File Path:* Enter the full path of your target text file. You can click the Browse button to search for and select the file you want to pull from.

   - *Column Separator:* Select the character used to separate the columns in the text file. Before you can do this, you need to know how the columns in your text file are delimited. For example, a comma-delimited file has commas separating the columns. A tab-delimited file has tabs separating the columns. Click the drop-down arrow next to the Comma Separator field to see choices for the more common delimiters: Tab, Comma, Semicolon, Space, Colon, and Vertical bar.

   - *Use First Row as Column Headers:* If your text file contains header rows, be sure to select the Use First Row as Column Headers check box to make sure the column headers are recognized as headers when imported.

   After you click Next, you get an immediate preview of the data in the text file.

4. Filter any unwanted columns by removing the check next to the column names. You can also click the drop-down arrows next to each column to apply any record filters.

5. Click the Finish button to start the import process.

   Upon completion, the data from your text file will be part of the Power Pivot Data Model. As always, be sure to review and create relationships to any other tables you've loaded into Power Pivot.

Note

Anyone who's worked with text files in Excel knows they are notorious for importing numbers that look like numbers, but are really coded as text. In standard Excel, Text to Columns fixes these kinds of issues. This can be a problem in Power Pivot, too. When importing text files, you'll want to take the extra step of verifying that all columns have been imported with the correct data formatting. You can use the formatting tools found on the Power Pivot window's Home tab to format any column in the Data Model.

Loading data from the clipboard

Power Pivot includes an interesting option for loading data straight from the clipboard — that is, pasting data you've copied from some other place. This option is meant to be used as a one-off technique to quickly get useful information into the Power Pivot Data Model.

Caution

As you consider this option, keep in mind that there is no real data source. It's just you manually copying and pasting. There is no way to refresh the data or to trace back where you actually copied the data from.

Imagine you received a Word document (similar to the one shown in Figure 4-20). You like the nifty table of holidays within the document. Here's how to import the data:

Day	Date	Holiday
Wednesday	1/1/2013	New Year's Day
Monday	1/20/2013	Martin Luther King's Birthday
Monday	2/17/2013	Presidents Day
Sunday	4/20/2013	Easter
Monday	5/26/2013	Memorial Day
Friday	7/4/2013	Independence Day
Monday	9/1/2013	Labor Day
Monday	10/13/2013	Columbus Day
Tuesday	11/11/2013	Veterans Day
Thursday	11/27/2013	Thanksgiving Day
Friday	11/28/2013	Friday after Thanksgiving
Wednesday	12/25/2013	Christmas Day

Figure 4-20: You can copy data straight out of Microsoft Word.

1. Copy the table; then go to the Power Pivot window and click the Paste button on the Home tab.

   The Paste Preview dialog box opens as shown in Figure 4-21, where you can review what exactly will be pasted.

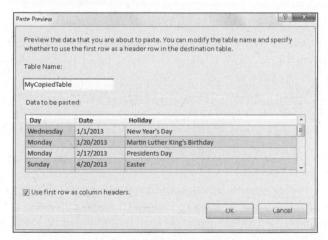

Figure 4-21: The Paste Preview dialog box gives you a chance to see what you're pasting.

2. Specify the name that is used to reference the table in Power Pivot and specify if the first row is a header.

3. Click OK to import the pasted data into Power Pivot.

At this point, you can adjust the data formatting and create the needed relationships.

Loading Data from Other Data Sources

We've covered the data sources that are most important to a majority of Excel analysts. Still, there are a few more data sources that Power Pivot is able to connect to and load data from. We touch on some of these data sources later in this book, but others are outside the scope of this book.

Although you're probably not likely to use the following data sources, it's worth knowing they exist and are available if you need them:

➤ **Microsoft SQL Azure:** SQL Azure is a cloud-based relational database service some companies use as an inexpensive way to get the benefits of SQL Server without taking on the full cost of hardware, software, and IT staff. Power Pivot can load data from SQL Azure in much the same way as the other relational databases we discuss in this chapter.

➤ **Microsoft SQL Parallel Data Warehouse:** SQL Parallel Data Warehouse (SQL PDW) is an appliance that partitions very large data tables into separate servers and manages query processing among them. SQL PDW is used to provide scalability and performance for big data analytics. From a Power Pivot perspective, it's no different from connecting to any other relational database.

➤ **Microsoft Analysis Services:** This selection refers to Microsoft's Analysis Services Online Analytical Processing product. We take a closer look at Analysis Services and using Analysis Services in Power Pivot in Chapter 13.

➤ **Report:** The curiously named report data source refers to SQL Server Reporting Services reports. In a basic sense, Reporting Services is a BI tool used to create stylized PDF-style reports from SQL Server data. In Chapter 12, you get a feel for Reporting Services as it relates to Microsoft's suite of BI tools. In the context of Power Pivot, a Reporting Services report can be used as a Data Feed Service, providing a refreshable connection to the underlying SQL Server data.

➤ **From Windows Azure Marketplace:** Windows Azure Marketplace is an OData (Open Data Protocol) service that provides both free and paid data sources. If you register for a free Azure Marketplace account, you get instant access to governmental data, industrial market data, consumer data, and much more. You can enhance your Power Pivot analyses by loading the data from the Azure Marketplace using this connection type.

➤ **Suggested Related Data:** This data source reviews the content of your Power Pivot Data Model and, based on its findings, suggests Azure Marketplace data you may be interested in.

➤ **Other Feeds:** The Other Feeds data source allows you to import data from OData Web services into Power Pivot. OData connections are facilitated by XML Atom files. Point the OData connection to the URL of the `.atomsvcs` file, and you essentially have a connection to the published Web service.

Refreshing and Managing External Data Connections

When you load data from an external data source into Power Pivot, you essentially create a static snapshot of that data source at the time of creation. Power Pivot uses that static snapshot in its internal Data Model.

The external data source may change and grow as new records are added. However, Power Pivot is still using its snapshot so it can't incorporate any of the changes in your date source until you take another snapshot.

The action of updating the Power Pivot Data Model by taking another snapshot of your data source is called *refreshing* your data. You can refresh manually, or you can set up an automatic refresh.

Manually refreshing your Power Pivot data

On the Home tab of the Power Pivot window, click the drop-down arrow on the Refresh button and choose one of these options:

➤ **Refresh:** Use the Refresh option to refresh the Power Pivot table that's currently active. For example, if you are on the Dim_Products tab in Power Pivot, clicking Refresh reaches out to the external SQL Server and requests an update for just the Dim_Products table. This works nicely when you need to strategically refresh only certain data sources.

➤ **Refresh All:** Use the Refresh All option to refresh all the tables in the Power Pivot Data Model.

Setting up automatic refreshing

You can configure your data sources to automatically pull the latest data and refresh Power Pivot. Here's how:

1. Click the Data tab on the Ribbon and click the Connections button.

    The Workbook Connections dialog box opens.

2. Select the data connection you want to work with and then click the Properties button.

3. With the Connection Properties dialog box open, click the Usage tab.

    You'll find an option to refresh the chosen data connection every X minutes and an option to refresh the data connection when the Excel work is opened (see Figure 4-22).

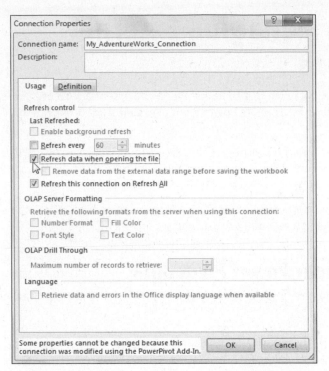

Figure 4-22: The Connection Properties dialog box lets you configure the chosen data connection to refresh automatically.

4. Choose a refresh rate:

- *Refresh Every X Minutes:* Refresh the chosen data connection every specified number of minutes. This refreshes all tables associated with that connection.

- *Refresh Data When Opening the File:* Automatically refresh the chosen data connection when the workbook is opened. This refreshes all tables associated with that connection as soon as the workbook is opened.

5. Click OK when you're done.

Preventing Refresh All

In addition to the Refresh All command on the Ribbon, there are actually two more places you can refresh your data in Excel 2013: the Ribbon's Data tab and the PivotTable's Analyze tab.

Clicking any Refresh All button anywhere in Excel essentially completely reloads Power Pivot, refreshes all PivotTables, and updates all workbook data connections. If your Power Pivot Data Model imports millions of lines of data from an external data source, you may want to avoid the processing hit taken when clicking Refresh All.

In the Connection Properties dialog box (refer to Figure 4-22), deselect the Refresh This Connection on Refresh All check box.

Editing your data connection

There may be times when you need to edit your source data connection after you've already created it. Unlike refreshing, where you simply take another snapshot of the same data source, editing the source data connection allows you to go back and reconfigure the connection itself. Here are a few reasons you may need to edit your data connection:

➤ The location or server or data source file has changed.

➤ The name of the server or data source file has changed.

➤ You need to edit your login credentials or authentication mode.

➤ You need to add tables you left out during initial import.

In the Power Pivot window, click the Home tab and click the Existing Connections button. The Existing Connections dialog box shown in Figure 4-23 opens. Your Power Pivot connections are under the Power Pivot Data Connections subheading. Select the data connection that you need to edit.

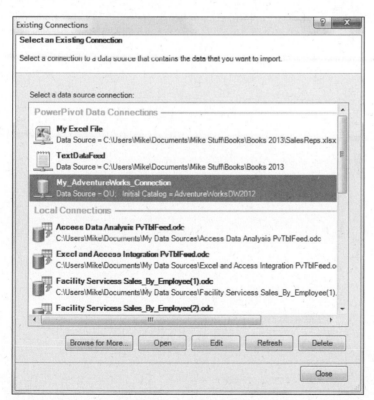

Figure 4-23: Use the Existing Connections dialog box to reconfigure your Power Pivot source data connections.

After you select your target data connection, click either the Edit or Open button, depending on what you need to change:

➤ **Edit:** Lets you reconfigure the server address, file path, and authentication settings.

➤ **Open:** Lets you import a new table from the existing connection. This is handy if you inadvertently missed a table during the initial loading of data.

Creating Dashboards with Power View

In This Chapter

- Starting a Power View dashboard
- Creating and working with Power View charts
- Visualizing data on a Power View map

Excel 2013 introduces a feature called Power View. Power View is an interactive canvas that allows you to display charts, tables, maps, and slicers in one dashboard window. The components in the Power View window are inherently linked so that they all work together and respond to any filtering or slicing you apply while using the dashboard. Select a region in one chart, and the other components in the Power View dashboard automatically respond to show you data for only that region.

This powerful feature runs on the internal Data Model in Excel 2013. This chapter shows you how to combine the internal Data Model and Power View to create powerful interactive dashboards.

Activating the Power View Add-In

Similar to the Power Pivot functionality covered in Chapter 3, the Power View functionality is only available when you activate the Power View Add-In. It's important to note that the Power View Add-In does not install with every edition of Office 2013. For example, if you have the Office Home Edition, you will not be able to see or activate the Power View Add-In.

As of this writing, the Power View Add-In is only available to you if you have one of the following editions of Office or Excel:

Office 2013 Professional Plus: Available through volume licensing only

Office 365 Pro Plus: Available with an ongoing subscription to Office365.com

Excel 2013 Stand-alone Edition: Available for purchase through any retailer

To check whether you have the Power View Add-In, look for the Power View icon on the Insert tab of the Ribbon. If you see it, then the Power View Add-In is already activated. But if you're not so lucky, you can activate the Power View Add-In by following these steps:

1. Choose File ➜ Options.

2. Select the Add-Ins option on the left, select COM Add-Ins from the Manage drop-down menu, and click Go.

3. Select Power View in the list of available COM Add-Ins, and click OK.

   The Power View command now appears on the Insert tab. If you don't see it, restart Excel 2013.

Note

You must have Silver Light installed on your machine in order to use Power View. Search for Silver Light using your favorite search engine to get the free download from Microsoft.

Creating a Power View Dashboard

In Chapters 2 and 3, you discovered how you can leverage the internal Data Model in Excel 2013 to create powerful PivotTable analyses. After you've loaded your data into the internal Data Model, you can create a Power View dashboard from that Data Model. Click the Power View button on the Insert tab. Excel takes a moment to create a new worksheet called Power ViewX, where X represents a number that makes the sheet name unique (for example, Power View1).

This new worksheet has the three main sections shown in Figure 5-1:

➤ **Canvas:** Contains the charts, tables, and maps you add to your dashboard.

➤ **Filter pane:** Contains the data filters you define.

➤ **Field list:** Add and configure the data for your dashboard.

You build up your Power View dashboard by dragging the fields from the field list to the respective sections. For example, dragging the Generator_Size field to the filter pane creates a list of filterable items (see Figure 5-2) with check boxes that can be selected or deselected. The filter pane has a few icons that help you work with the filters. These icons enable you to expand or collapse the entire filter pane, clear applied filters, call up advanced filter options, or delete the filter.

To add data to the canvas, use the field list to drag the needed data fields to the FIELDS drop zone. Figure 5-3 show the Waste_Code and Generated_Qty fields moved to the FIELDS drop zone. This results in a new table of data on the canvas.

Canvas   Filter pane   Field list

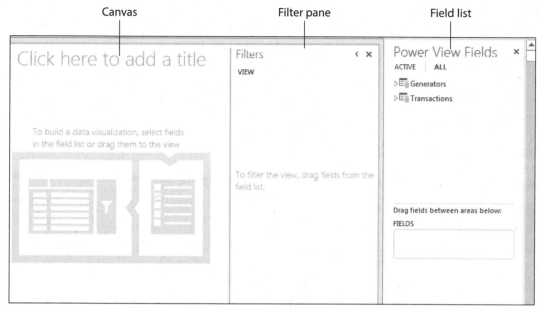

Figure 5-1: The three main sections of a Power View worksheet.

Open advanced folder options.

Expand or collapse Filter pane.

Clear applied filters.

Remove filter.

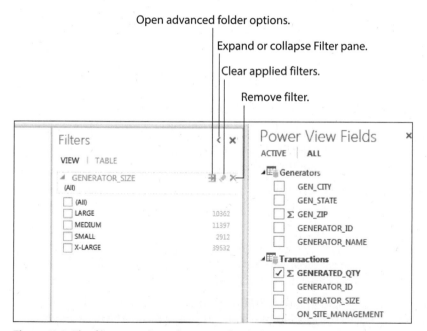

Figure 5-2: The filter pane has a few icons that help you work with the filters.

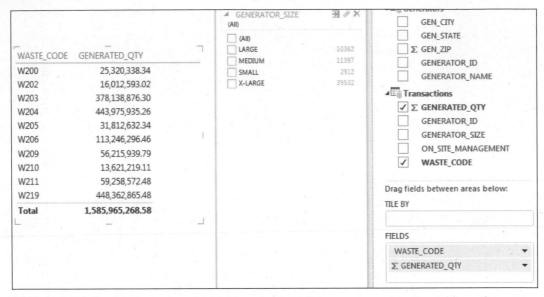

Figure 5-3: Use the field list to drag data fields to the FIELDS drop zone, resulting in a table on the canvas.

Creating and working with Power View charts

All data in Power View starts off as a table, as shown in Figure 5-3. Again, dragging fields to the FIELDS drop zone creates these tables. After you have a data table on the canvas, you can work with it in several ways.

Transform data into a chart. Click the data table and select a chart type from the Ribbon's Design tab. Your choices are Stacked Bar, 100% Stacked Bar, and Clustered Bar.

Figure 5-4 shows the data converted to a Clustered Bar chart, with new drop zones appearing in the field list. You use the new drop zones to configure the look and utility of the chart.

Sort, filter, or expand the chart to full screen. When you click a Power View chart, a context menu appears above the chart. With this menu, you can sort the chart series, filter the chart, and expand or collapse the chart to full screen (see Figure 5-5).

Apply custom filters. When you select a chart in the Power View canvas, the filter pane provides a CHART option. You can click that link to see and apply custom filters to the selected chart. Figure 5-6 shows a chart filtered by the Generated_Qty field using a nifty slider.

Slice your chart series. Drag a new data field into the LEGEND drop zone. In Figure 5-7, the On_Site_Management field is placed in the LEGEND drop zone; as a result, the original chart is sliced by the data items in the newly placed field.

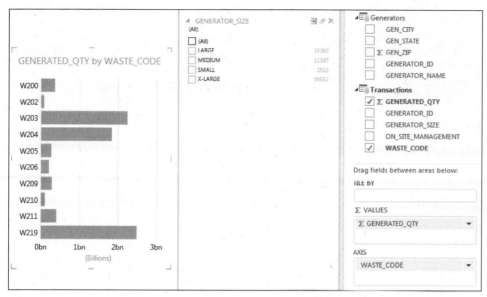

Figure 5-4: When your table is transformed into a chart, new drop zones appear in the field list.

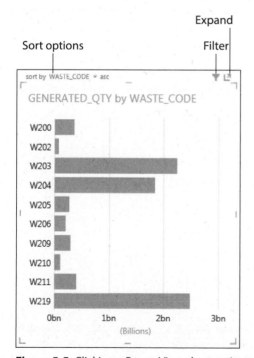

Figure 5-5: Clicking a Power View chart activates a context menu for that chart.

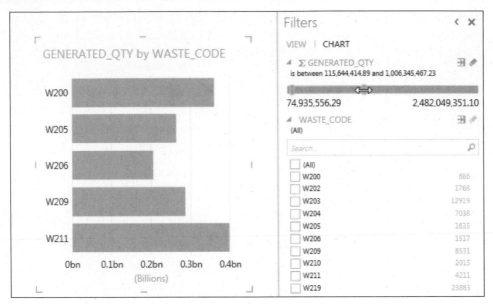

Figure 5-6: Use the filter pane to apply chart-specific custom filters.

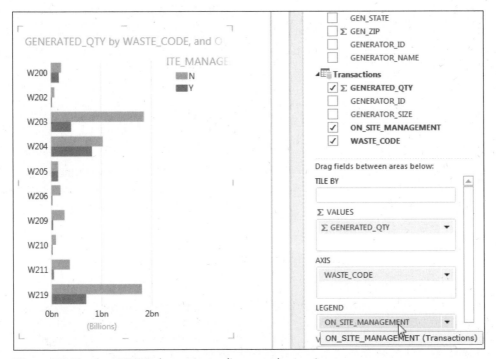

Figure 5-7: Use the LEGEND drop zone to slice your chart series.

Convert your chart into a panel of charts. You can use the VERTICAL MULTIPLES or the HORIZONTAL MULTIPLES drop zone to turn the original chart into a panel of charts (simply drag the data field into any one of the drop zones). Figure 5-8 shows how the original chart has been replicated to show a separate chart for each data item in the On_Site_Management field.

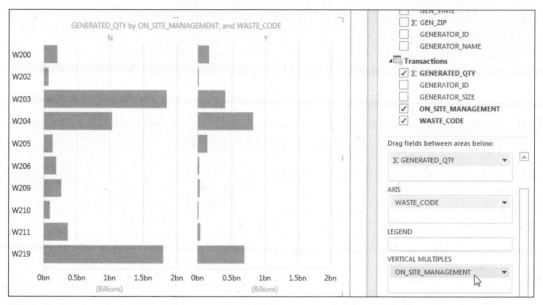

Figure 5-8: Dragging the On_Site_Management field to the VERTICAL MULTIPLES drop zone creates a panel of charts.

Add drill-down capabilities. Drag a new data field to the AXIS drop zone. Figure 5-9 shows the Gen_State field dragged to the AXIS drop zone. Initially, it seems as though nothing has happened. But in the background, Power View has layered in the newly selected field as a new category axis.

After you add your new field to the AXIS drop zone, double-click any data point in the chart. The chart automatically drills into the next level. In Figure 5-10, Gen_State (generator state) was added to the AXIS drop zone, so the chart drills down to show the breakdown by state for the selected data point.

Tip   **Click the arrow icon to drill back up.**

You can add as many charts as you want to your Power View canvas. All components in the Power View window are automatically linked so that they respond to one another. For example, Figure 5-11 shows two charts on the same Power View canvas. Clicking the pie slice for Arkansas (AR) dynamically recolors the bar chart so that it highlights the portion of the bar with the Arkansas data — all without any extra work from you!

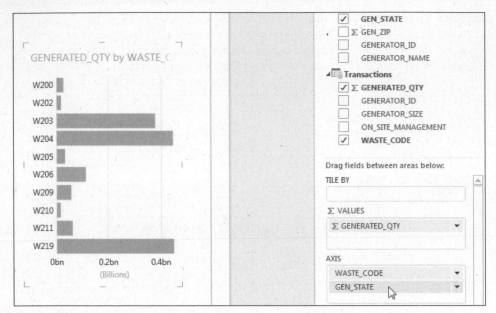

Figure 5-9: Dragging a new field to the AXIS drop zone creates a drill-down effect.

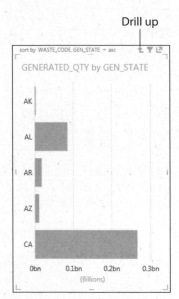

Figure 5-10: With multiple data fields in the AXIS drop zone, you can drill into the next layer of data and then drill back up clicking the arrow icon.

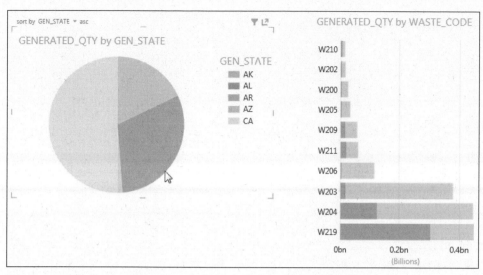

Figure 5-11: Charts in a Power View dashboard automatically respond to one another.

Visualizing data in a Power View map

The latest buzz in the dashboarding world is location intelligence: visualizing data on a map to quickly compare performance by location. Since Excel 2003, you haven't had a good way of building map-based visualizations without convoluted work-arounds. Excel 2013 changes all that with the introduction of Power View maps.

To add a map to your Power View dashboard, select your location data in the Power View canvas. Location data can be zip codes, which is what Figure 5-12 shows. Click the Map button on the Design tab (you can find it in the Switch Visualization group). Excel gives you a Bing map, as shown in Figure 5-13.

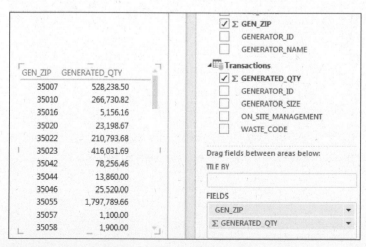

Figure 5-12: Add location data to your Power View canvas.

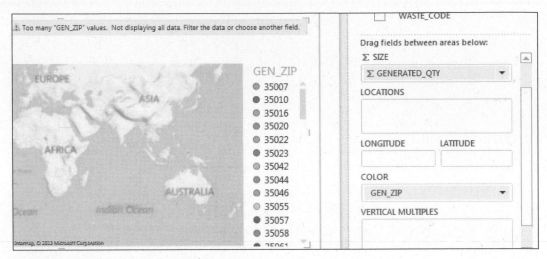

Figure 5-13: Excel generates an initial Bing map.

The initial map is often fairly useless. How Excel decides to initially handle your data varies from dataset to dataset. As you can see in Figure 5-13, Excel gives you a warning there are too many zip codes to plot on the map. In this case, we'll need to make some adjustments to get the view you need.

Move your location field to different drop zones in the field list. Figure 5-14 shows how moving the Gen_Zip field to the LOCATIONS drop zone fixes the map and creates a nice view of the data by zip code.

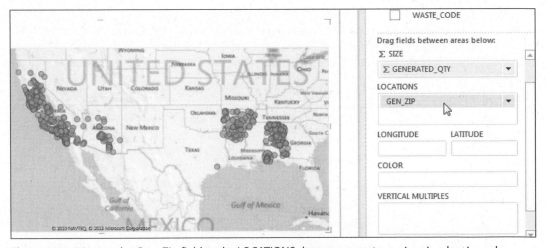

Figure 5-14: Moving the Gen_Zip field to the LOCATIONS drop zone creates a nice view by zip code.

Customize the map title, legend, data labels, and background. You have limited control over how your map looks. With your map selected, click the Layout tab and customize the map title, legend, data labels, and map background (see Figure 5-15).

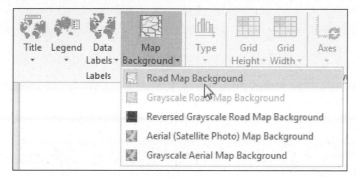

Figure 5-15: The Layout tab provides a limited set of options for customizing your Power View map.

Zoom in and out and move around. The map is fully interactive. Use the buttons at the top-right corner of the map to get the view you want, as shown in Figure 5-16.

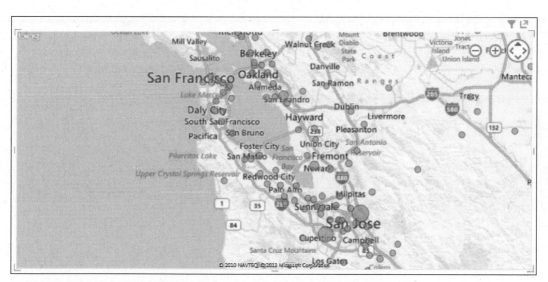

Figure 5-16: You can interactively zoom in and out and move around on the map.

Add an extra layer of analysis. Use the COLOR drop zone to add an extra layer of analysis to your map. Figure 5-17 shows how adding the Waste_Code field to the COLOR drop zone differentiates each plotted location based on waste code.

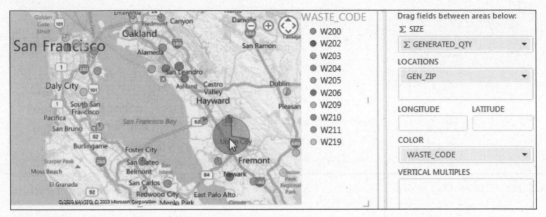

Figure 5-17: Add data fields to the COLOR drop zone to add an extra layer of analysis to your map.

Changing the look of your Power View dashboard

You have limited control over how your Power View dashboard looks. From the Themes group on the Power View tab (see Figure 5-18), you can set the overall font, text size, and background.

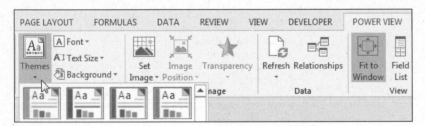

Figure 5-18: Changing the theme of your Power View dashboard.

The theme you choose changes the colors for your charts, backgrounds, filters, tables, and plotted map points, but the Bing map doesn't change to match your theme. Figure 5-19 illustrates a full Power View dashboard with an applied theme.

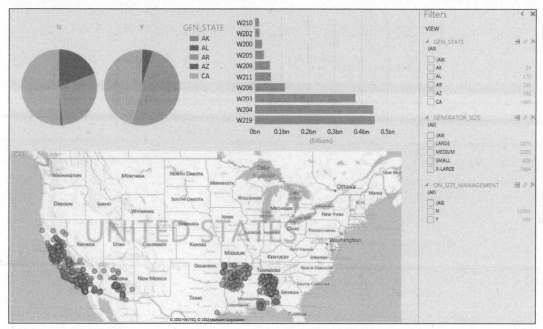

Figure 5-19: A completed Power View dashboard with an applied theme.

Adding Location Intelligence with Power Map

In This Chapter

- Installing Power Map
- Loading data into Power Map
- Adding and managing map visualizations
- Customizing map components
- Sharing your Power Map tours

Location intelligence is an area of business intelligence where data is represented in terms of geospatial plots on a map. With it, you can show your audience a visual representation of how certain data points relate to others in terms of location.

The Power Map Add-In is a tool that facilitates location intelligence by leveraging Microsoft Bing maps to plot geographic and temporal data. With Power Map, your audience can analyze data in an interactive map, offer new geographical perspectives and understandings, and create cinematic video tours that engage audiences like never before.

In this chapter, you explore the Power Map Add-In and discover how you can leverage it to add location intelligence to your cache of BI solution offerings.

Installing and Activating the Power Map Add-In

The Power Map Add-In does not come with Excel out of the box. If you find a Power Map button on the Insert tab (see Figure 6-1), then the Power Map Add-In is already activated.

Figure 6-1: The Power Map Add-In is on the Insert tab.

If you don't see a Power Map button, then you have to download and install it.

As of this writing, the Power Map Add-In is only available if you have one of the following editions of Office or Excel:

➤ **Office 2013 Professional Plus:** Available through volume licensing only

➤ **Office 365 Pro Plus:** Available with an ongoing subscription to Office365.com

➤ **Excel 2013 Stand-alone Edition:** Available for purchase through any retailer

If you have any of these editions, you can install and activate the Power Map Add-In. Type the term "Excel Power Map Add-In" into your favorite search engine to find the free installation package.

After it is installed, activate the Add-In by following these steps:

1. Choose File ➜ Options.

2. Select the Add-Ins option on the left, select COM Add-Ins from the Manage drop-down menu, and click Go.

3. Look for Power Map for Excel in the list of available COM Add-Ins. Select the box next to each one of these options and then click OK.

4. Close and restart Excel 2013.

You now find the Power Map button on the Insert tab.

Loading Data into Power Map

To start loading data into Power Map, all you need is a named Excel table that contains geographical data. Note that when you load a table into Power Map, it automatically gets added to the Excel's internal Data Model.

Tip

> You can convert your data range to named Excel tables by clicking anywhere inside your data range and pressing Ctrl+T. In the Create Table dialog box, ensure that the range for the table is correct and click OK.

The data you utilize needs at least one geographical data point per row, as shown in Figure 6-2. You don't necessarily need a full address along with the latitude and longitude. Power Map accepts any combination (but at least) of one of these geographic points:

➤ Latitude/Longitude pair

➤ City name

➤ Country name

➤ Zip code/postal code

➤ State/province name

➤ Address

	Store #	Address	City	State	Zip	Lat	Long
2	1	3601 N.W. 27th Avenue	Miami	FL	33142	25.8092	-80.24
3	2	8995 N. W. 7th Avenue	Miami	FL	33150	25.8587	-80.209
4	3	30390 South Dixie Highway	Homestead	FL	33030	25.4849	-80.461
5	4	7975 N. W. 27th Avenue	Miami	FL	33147	25.8471	-80.242
6	5	9201 South Dixie Highway	Miami	FL	33156	25.6849	-80.313
7	6	3051 Coral Way	Miami	FL	33145	25.7502	-80.243
8	7	18240 South Dixie Highway	Perrine	FL	33157	25.6003	-80.354
9	8	775 East 9th Street	Hialeah	FL	33010	25.8306	-80.266
10	9	1910 N. E. 163rd Street	Miami	FL	33162	25.926	-80.162
11	10	18750 N. W. 2nd Avenue	North Miami Bea	FL	33169	25.9466	-80.206
12	11	9675 Bird Road	Miami	FL	33165	25.7328	-80.351
13	12	1445 West Sunrise Boulevard	Fort Lauderdale	FL	33311	26.1368	-80.162

Figure 6-2: Start with a named Excel table that contains at least one valid geographic data column.

Tip

> Whenever you can, use Latitude and Longitude as your geographic points. Latitude/Longitude processes much faster than standard address elements. You also get better plotting accuracy.

When your data is ready to go, click the Map button on the Insert tab. Excel immediately opens the Power Map window and starts processing the geographic points in the table. It passes the points to Microsoft Bing, receives the geospatial data back, and then draws a plot point on the map.

After all points have been plotted, you see the window shown in Figure 6-3. There are three main sections: the Tour task pane, an interactive Bing map, and the Layer Manager task pane.

Tour task pane   Bing map   Layer Manager task pane

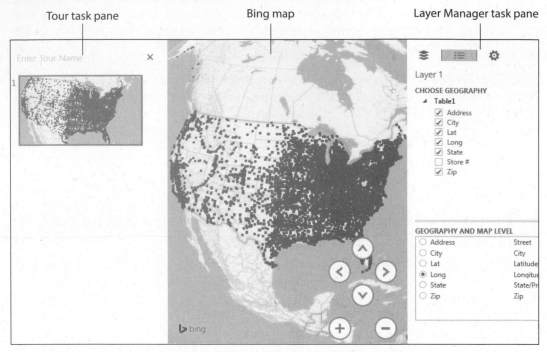

Figure 6-3: The Power Map window provides a Tour task pane, the Bing map, and a Layer Manager task pane.

Note

Because your data is geocoded with Microsoft Bing, you need access to the Internet to use the Power Map Add-In. As the data points are processed, the status bar displays the progress of plotting all the required data points.

Choosing geography and map level

It's important to note that Power Map initially plots the points on your map based on what it thinks you're trying to do regarding your geographical data. If you have multiple geographical data points, you need to tell Power Map which geospatial level you want to plot.

When you add data to Power Map, it creates a map "layer" that can be configured and customized to show a particular geospatial visualization. The first layer is, by default, called Layer 1.

Select the geography level you want to see in the Layer Manager task pane, which determines the data points plotted. For example, selecting Address gives you the map shown at the top of Figure 6-4. Selecting State gives you the map shown at the bottom of Figure 6-4. Click Next when you've selected your geography.

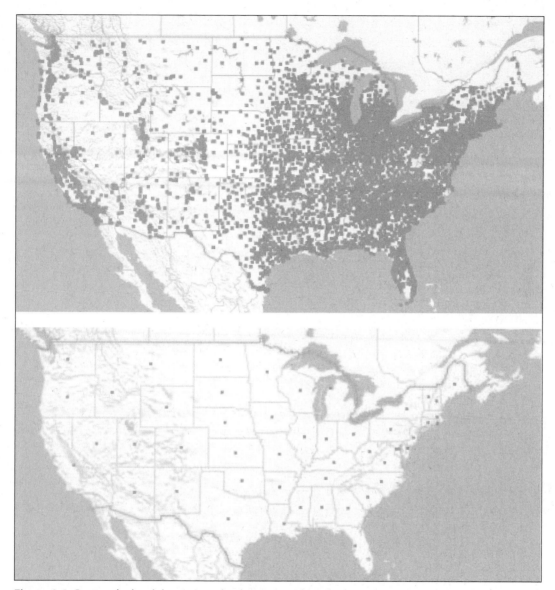

Figure 6-4: Geography level determines the data points plotted on your map.

Handling geocoding alerts

Bing Maps can't always plot all your geographical points. If it doesn't, you can find its success rate at the top of the pane, as shown in Figure 6-5. Only 87 percent of data points were plotted with a high confidence.

You need to investigate which data points Bing couldn't plot so you can fix them. Click the percentage shown to open the Geocoding Alerts dialog box shown in Figure 6-6. You see each problematic geographical data point and how Bing handled it. Some data is tagged as "No resolution for this address." In these cases, the data is simply excluded from the final map.

Find your success rate.

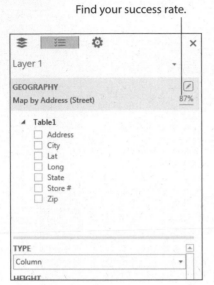

Figure 6-5: The Geography header alerts you if Bing Maps had trouble plotting any of the geographical data points.

Geocoding Alerts

We plotted 87% of locations on Layer 1 with high confidence.
Below is the list of locations we weren't sure about.

State	City	Zipcode	Street	Result
AL	Thomasvill	36784	#12 Highw	❌ No resolution for this address
MO	Charleston	63834	#2 Charles	❌ No resolution for this address
VA	Wise	24293	#4 Ridgevi	⚠ 4 Ridgeview Dr, Big Stone Gap, VA 24219
OR	Eugene	97401-218	016 Valley	❌ No resolution for this address
LA	Delhi	71232	1 Broadwa	❌ No resolution for this address
NY	Geneseo	14454	1 College (	❌ No resolution for this address
OH	Cincinnati	45219	1 Corry St	⚠ 1 Corry St W, Cincinnati, OH 45219
NC	Fort Bragg	28307-500	1 Fort Brag	❌ No resolution for this address

Figure 6-6: The Geocoding Alerts dialog box shows you each problematic geographical data point and how Bing handled it.

If you encounter geocoding alerts, it's best to step back and try resolving the errors by correcting your source data table. Consider taking any of these actions:

➤ If possible, use latitude and longitude as your geographic points. You'll get much better plotting accuracy.

➤ Try to include the full address, city, state, and zip or postal code for your data. Each should be in its own column. Remember that the more geographic data you can include, the better.

➤ Check to make sure your address field is not truncated.

➤ Ensure that your city and state names are spelled correctly.

After you've made all the changes to your source Excel table, you need to refresh your data. To do so, click the Refresh Data button on the Power Map Ribbon.

Navigating the map

The map initially starts out looking like a globe. You can flatten the map by clicking the Flat Map button on the Ribbon (see Figure 6-7).

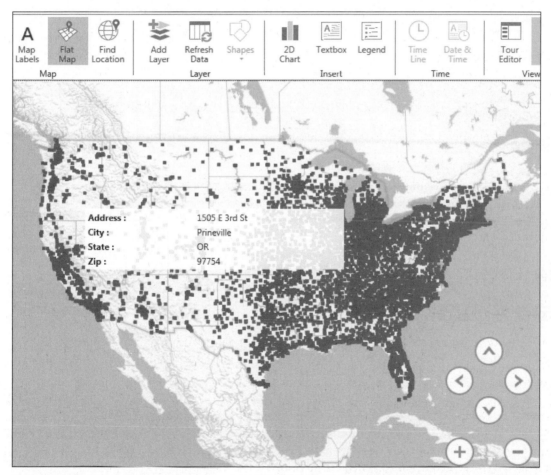

Figure 6-7: The interactive map enables you to navigate intuitively and see details by hovering over any data point.

The navigation buttons in the lower right-hand corner of the map allow you to zoom, pan, and change pitch. You can also navigate the map by taking any of the following actions using your mouse or keyboard:

➤ **To zoom**

- Double-click in any portion of the map to zoom in.

- Use the scroll wheel on your mouse to zoom in and zoom out.

- Press the plus (+) to zoom in or minus (–) key on your keyboard to zoom out.

➤ **To pan**

- Click and drag the map in any direction to pan left, right, up, or down.

- Press the arrow keys on your keyboard to pan up, down, left, or right.

➤ **To change the pitch**

- Hold the Alt key, and then click and drag.

- Press and hold the Alt key while pressing the arrow keys on your keyboard.

Hovering over any point on the map opens a pop-up window that shows you the details of that data point.

Tip

To snap the map back to the center of your screen, click the Reset View icon at the bottom-right corner of the Power Map status bar.

Managing and Modifying Map Visualizations

After the geography is plotted, you can start visualizing your data by using the Layer Manager task pane shown in Figure 6-8. You can select a visualization type and a quantitative value to aggregate.

Figure 6-8 shows Column as the visualization type and the Orders field as the quantitative value.

Note

The quantitative input box is named differently based on the visualization type you select. In Figure 6-8, this box is called Height when the Column visualization type is selected. When you select the Bubble visualization type, this box is called Size. When you select Heat Map or Region, this box is called Value.

Figure 6-9 shows the resulting map. Note that the sum of orders is represented by the height of each plotted column. This gives the user a comparative view between each county.

Figure 6-8: Use the Layer Manager task pane to build your visualization.

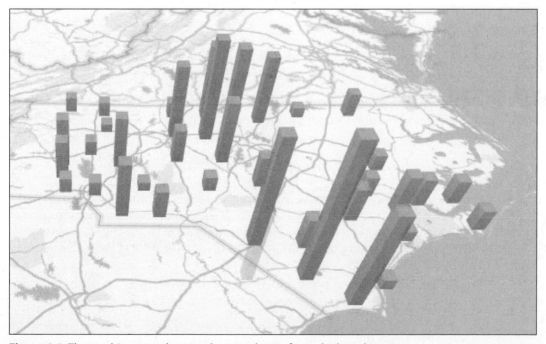

Figure 6-9: The resulting map shows orders as columns for each plotted county.

Click the drop-down arrow next to your quantitative field (see Figure 6-10) to select a different aggregation type. Power Map defaults to Sum in most cases, but you can select Average, Count, Maximum, Minimum, or No Aggregation. You can also select Remove to remove the field.

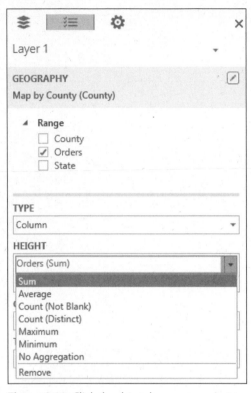

Figure 6-10: Click the drop-down arrow next to your quantitative field to select a different aggregation type.

Visualization types

In terms of visualization types, you can choose Column, Bubble, Heat Map, or Region. Simply click the drop-down arrow in the Type field to select the one you want.

Column

The Column visualization type lets you present your quantitative values as columns with varying heights. This is the default type. You can format the columns by clicking the Scene Options icon (it looks like a gear) in the Layer Manager task pane. As shown in Figure 6-11, the Layer Options allow you to adjust the overall height and thickness of the columns; change the color of the columns; and specify whether to show zeroes, negative values, or nulls.

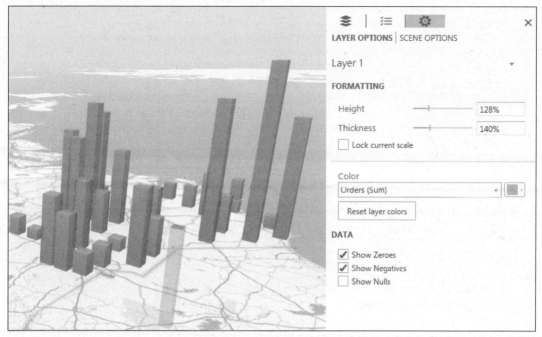

Figure 6-11: The Column visualization type.

Bubble

The Bubble visualization type lets you present your quantitative values as bubbles with varying sizes. You can format the bubbles by clicking the Scene Options icon (it looks like a gear) in the Layer Manager task pane. As shown in Figure 6-12, the Layer Options allow you to adjust the size and thickness of the bubbles; change the color of the bubbles; and specify whether to show zeroes, negative values, or nulls.

Heat Map

The Heat Map visualization type lets you present your quantitative values as color scales where the intensity of the colors is based on the data. You can format the heat map by clicking the Scene Options icon (it looks like a gear) in the Layer Manager task pane. As shown in Figure 6-13, the Layer Options allow you to adjust the color scale; adjust the radius of influence; and specify whether to show zeroes, negative values, or nulls.

Region

The Region visualization type lets you present your quantitative values as color scales plotted within county, state, or other regional boundaries. The intensity of the colors is based on the data values as they compare to one another. You can format the region by clicking the Scene Options icon (it looks like a gear) in the Layer Manager task pane. As shown in Figure 6-14, the Layer Options allow you to define the colors and specify whether to show zeroes, negative values, or nulls.

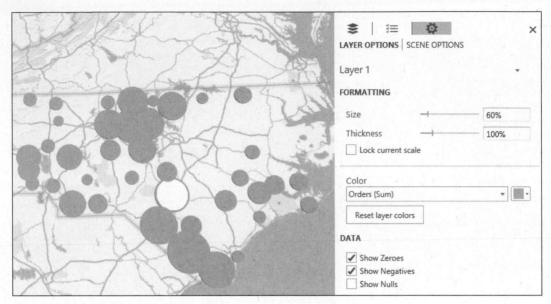

Figure 6-12: The Bubble visualization type.

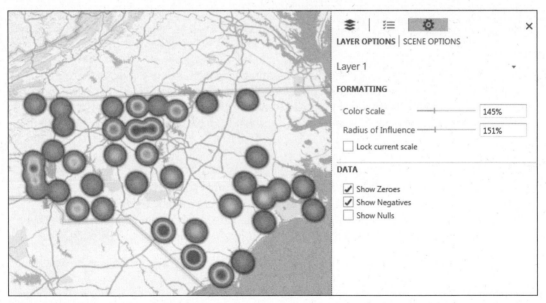

Figure 6-13: The Heat Map visualization type.

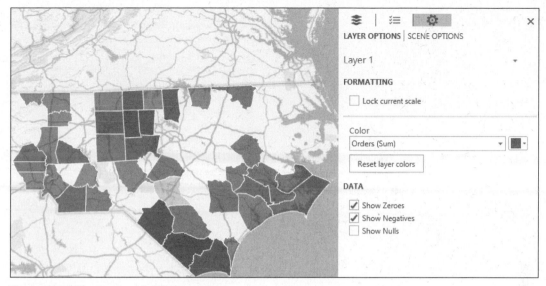

Figure 6-14: The Region visualization type.

Adding categories

You can add analyses to your maps by selecting different dimension fields from the Category menu. You can turn your ordinary column plots into multicolored clustered or stacked columns.

Figure 6-15 shows the path of Hurricane Katrina in the Column visualization type and the Wind Speed measure in the Height field. So the varying column sizes are based on wind speed.

To enhance the map, we've added the Hurricane Category field to the Category field. This adds a legend to the map and gives each column a different color based on the Hurricane Category status defined at each plot point.

Use the two chart icons next to the Category box to switch between seeing the data as clustered columns or stacked columns.

Note

If you add a dimension field to the Category box and you leave the Height box blank, Power Map automatically adds that same field to Height and draws a visual that represents the count of each category.

Visualizing data over time

Power Map can create time-based animations, allowing you to visualize how your data points change over time.

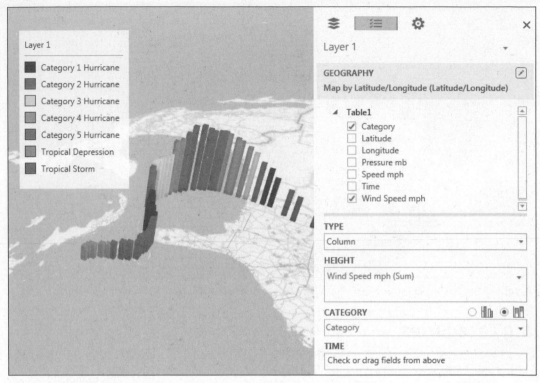

Figure 6-15: Dimensions enhance your map visualizations.

Figure 6-16 shows the Time dimension in the Time input box found in the Layer Manager task pane. You can then choose the appropriate behavior from the Time drop-down menu. The behavior option you choose dictates how your time animation will play:

➤ **Data accumulates over time:** Plot data points over time.

➤ **Data shows for an instant:** Plot each data point for its respective location at each particular time.

➤ **Data stays until it is replaced:** Show the last plotted data point for each location as time progresses until that point is replaced by a new one. This setting ignores a null or 0 value.

When a time dimension is added to the Time input box, a new player shows up on your map. Clicking the Play button starts the animation, showing a label that displays the time increments as the animation plays.

Note

Click the Settings icon (it looks like a gear) in the player at the bottom of the map to open the Time task pane, where you can adjust the properties of the player. You can slow down or speed up playback as well as specify a start and end time.

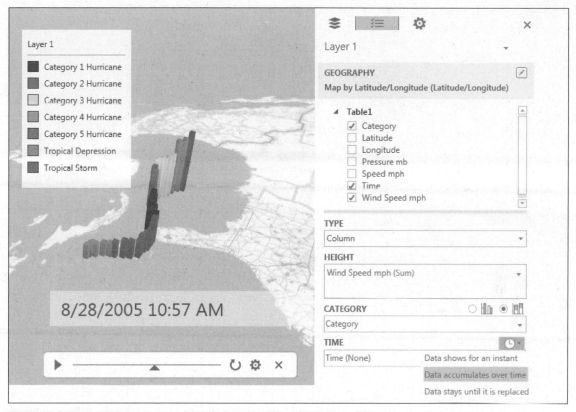

Figure 6-16: You can create a time-based animation by placing a Time field into the Time input box.

Adding layers

After building the visualizations for one layer of your map, you may want to add another perspective on your data. Power Map supports the use of multiple layers so you can stack and present geospatial visualizations on the same map at the same time.

To add a layer, click the Add Layer button on the Power Map Ribbon. The Layer Manager task pane opens with the configuration settings for your new layer; see Figure 6-17. At this point, you can build the visualization needed just as you did for the first layer.

The new layer (Layer 2) enhances the map with a Heat Map visualization representing the air pressure at each point in Hurricane Katrina's path. This new layer is presented on the same map as the first layer, which shows wind speed and category.

You can manage the layers in your Power Map model by clicking the Layers icon (see Figure 6-18) in the Layers Manager task pane. The Layers pane shows all of the existing layers, allowing you to hide, delete, or edit each layer.

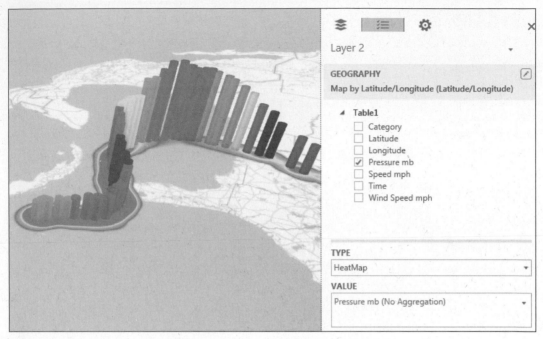

Figure 6-17: You can add multiple layers to enhance your Power Map analysis.

Manage your layers.

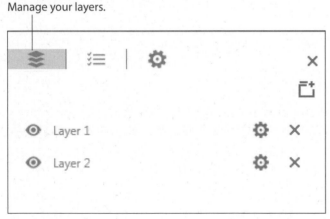

Figure 6-18: Click the Layers icon to activate a panel of all existing layers, which you can use to manage the layers in your Power Map model.

Adding Custom Components

To help support the geospatial visualizations you build, Power Map offers a few additional components. These custom components give you a way to add supplemental analyses, useful annotations, and clarifying comments.

Adding a top/bottom chart

The Power Map Add-In lets you add rudimentary charts to your maps. Although these charts don't come with the full functionality of Power View or standard Excel charts, they do offer a relatively easy way to expose the highest or lowest data points on your map.

To add a chart, click the 2D Chart button on the Power Map Ribbon. If your Power Map model has more than one layer, you see a dialog box asking you to choose the layer for which you want to show the chart. Otherwise, the chart is automatically created.

Power Map charts always show either the top or bottom locations based on the data used to geocode and aggregate the data. For example, in Figure 6-19, the chart shows the top 100 locations based on the Orders (Sum) by County.

After the chart is created, you can take the following actions:

➤ **Resize the chart:** Click it and use the resize handles.

➤ **Switch between top and bottom:** Click the word Top above the chart to toggle to the bottom view.

➤ **Change the number of columns displayed on the chart:** Drag each end of the chart's slider bar (or scroll bar). The smaller you make the slider bar, the fewer columns show in the chart at one time.

➤ **Change the chart type:** Click the chart type drop-down menu next to the chart title.

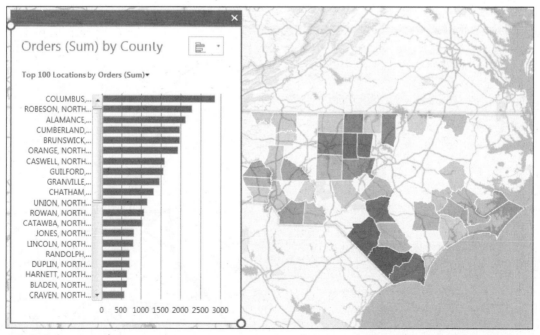

Figure 6-19: Power Map charts offer a way to expose the highest and lowest locations based on the data used to geocode and aggregate the data.

Note

Clicking any column in the chart highlights both that column and the associated data point on the map. The other data points and columns are grayed out, allowing you to see where the selected value is located. The map also pans so that the selected data point is centered in the map viewing area.

Adding annotations and text boxes

You can highlight noteworthy data points by using annotations. Figure 6-20 shows an annotation on the data point with the highest wind speed.

To add an annotation, right-click the target data point and select Add Annotation. In the dialog box that appears, enter your desired title and text for the annotation.

After the annotation is associated with a data point, Power Map automatically places the annotation so that it's always visible.

Note

Annotations are not available for Heat Map visualizations.

Text boxes work similar to annotations, but they aren't tied to a specific data. Text boxes retain their position within the Power Map window. Because of this, they are handy mechanisms for adding titles and other textual commentary.

To add a text box, click the Text Box button on the Power Map Ribbon. Then enter your desired title and text in the dialog box.

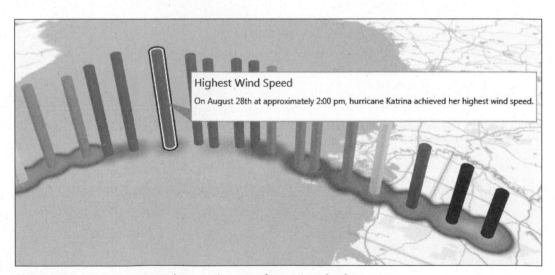

Figure 6-20: Annotations provide textual context for noteworthy data points.

Adding legends

As we mentioned earlier in this chapter, legends are automatically added when a field is added to the Category box. If you accidentally remove a legend, you can add it back by clicking the Legend button on the Power Map Ribbon. Legends can be resized, but not edited or formatted.

Customizing map themes and labels

Power Map comes with a predefined gallery of themes that can be accessed via the Themes drop-down menu on the Power Map Ribbon; see Figure 6-21. The themes range from standard monochromatic maps to satellite imagery. Clicking Map Labels button on the Ribbon toggles map labels on and off.

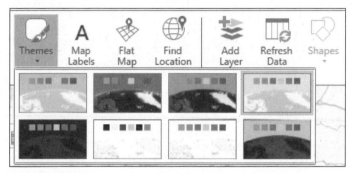

Figure 6-21: Power Map offers a handful of predefined map themes.

Customizing and Managing Power Map Tours

A tour Is essentially a saved Power Map model. You can think of a tour as a document that saves all your data and visualization settings. When you load data into Power Map, a tour is automatically created. From there, Power Map continuously saves any changes you make to that tour. Tours automatically save in the last state they were in when they were closed.

After you saved tours in Power Map, you can open it again by opening the Power Map window. You can open an existing Power Map tour or create a new tour; see Figure 6-22. You can create as many tours as you wish in a workbook.

Note

You can also duplicate or delete tours. Right-click the desired tour and select either Duplicate or Delete. Be absolutely certain you want to delete a tour — once you do, you can't get it back.

Figure 6-22: You can either open an existing Power Map tour or create a new tour.

Understanding scenes

When you open a tour, you see a Tour task panel on the left side of the Power Map window. This panel contains scenes. Each tour contains at least one scene. The default scene always represents the state of your map the last time it was closed. You can think of scenes as storyboards that, when viewed together, create a narrative around the data in your map.

You can add as many new scenes as you'd like by following these steps:

1. Navigate your map to a location and view what you want shown in your scene.

2. Click the Add Scene button on the Power Map Ribbon.

3. Navigate to another location, focusing on another aspect of your map.

4. Repeat Steps 2 and 3 until you build a collection of scenes that tell a story.

Configuring scenes

After adding your scenes, each scene is shown as a thumbnail in the Tour task panel. You need to configure each scene to define the duration of the scene, the transition effect, and the animation during the scene. Power Map uses your defined scene settings to create a cinematic animation that seamlessly transitions from one scene to another.

Double-click each scene to see the Scene Options in the Layer Manager task pane (see Figure 6-23). The settings under Scene Options are as follows:

➤ **Scene Duration:** Specify how long, in seconds, a particular scene is in focus. By default, the duration of each scene is 6 seconds. You can boost this up to 30 minutes.

➤ **Scene Name:** Give the scene a friendly name.

➤ **Transition Duration:** Dictate how many seconds a particular transition effect takes to complete its animation. Set the Transition Duration to 0 to get a "cut"-style transition from one scene to the next.

➤ **Effect:** By default, the transition effect is set to Station; meaning no motion. You can alter this setting to use other transaction effects, including Fly-Over, Push-In, Dolly, Figure 8, and Circle. Effects last for the duration of the scene. For example, if you select the Circle effect, the camera goes in a circle in that scene until the scene ends.

➤ **Effect Speed:** Increase or decrease the speed the camera moves. Note that depending on the duration of the scene versus the effect speed, your transition effect may or may not fully complete before the scene ends and transitions to the next scene.

➤ **Time settings:** The settings in the Time section determine how the time-based animations in your tour are handled during a scene. You can choose to limit the range of time that plays in the scene. You can also define how quickly time animation goes from the defined start date to the end date.

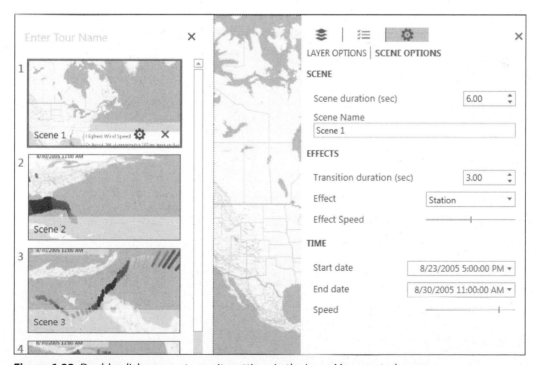

Figure 6-23: Double-click a scene to see its settings in the Layer Manager task pane.

Playing and sharing a tour

After configuring your scenes, you can play the entire tour by clicking the Play Tour button on the Power Map Ribbon.

You can also share your cinematic tour by creating a video. Click the Create Video button on the Power Map Ribbon. Power Map asks you to specify the desired video quality and location to output the final video. After a few minutes of processing, you get an MP4 file, which you can publish to SharePoint, Facebook, YouTube, and other sites.

Sharing screenshots

Power Map makes it easy to share screenshots of your Power Map analysis. Navigate your map to the location and view that you want shown in your screenshot, and then click the Capture Screen button on the Power Map Ribbon. From there, you can paste the screen capture to Word, PowerPoint, Outlook, and so on.

Using the Power Query Add-In

In This Chapter

- Installing Power Query
- Learning about Power Query basics
- Understanding transformation actions
- Connecting to a wide array of data sources
- Creating and using Power Query functions

In information management, ETL refers to three separate functions:

➤ **Extraction:** Reading of data from a specified source and extracting a desired subset of data.

➤ **Transformation:** Cleaning, shaping, and aggregating of data to convert it to the desired structure.

➤ **Load:** Importing or writing of the resulting data to a target location.

You've probably been manually performing ETL processes for years — although you might not think of it that way. Whenever you pull data from a source location, manipulate that data, and integrate it into your reporting, you're performing ETL.

In an attempt to develop robust and reusable ETL processes, Microsoft released the Power Query Add-In. Power Query enhances the ETL experience by offering a mechanism to extract data from a wide variety of sources, perform complex transformations on that data, and then load the data into a workbook or the internal Data Model.

In this chapter, you see how the Power Query Add-In works and discover some of the innovative ways you can use it to help save time and automate the steps needed to ensure that clean data is imported into your reporting models.

Installing and Activating the Power Query Add-In

The Power Query Add-In does not come with Excel out of the box. Your administrator might have installed it for you. If you see the Power Query tab on the Ribbon — look ahead to Figure 7-1 — you already have it. If you don't see it, you need to download and install Power Query.

Downloading the Power Query Add-In

As of this writing, the Power Query Add-In is only available if you have one of the following editions of Office or Excel:

Office 2010 Professional Plus: Available for purchase through any retailer

Office 2013 Professional Plus: Available through volume licensing only

Office 365 Pro Plus: Available with an ongoing subscription to Office365.com

Excel 2013 Stand-alone Edition: Available for purchase through any retailer

If you have one of these editions, you can install and activate the Power Query Add-In. Type **Excel Power Query Add-In** into your favorite search engine to find the free installation package. Note that Microsoft offers Power Query for both Excel 2010 and Excel 2013 in both 32- and 64-bit platforms. Be sure to download the version that matches your version of Excel as well as the platform your PC is running.

After it's installed, you need to activate the add-in by following these steps:

1. Choose File ➜ Options.

2. Select the Add-Ins option on the left, select COM Add-Ins from the Manage drop-down list, and click Go.

3. Look for Power Query for Excel in the list of available COM Add-Ins. Select the check box next to each one of these options and then click OK.

4. Close and restart Excel.

The Power Query tab is now on the Ribbon, as shown in Figure 7-1.

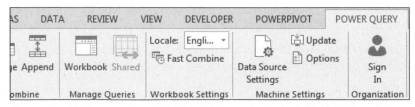

Figure 7-1: The Power Query Add-In is on its own tab on the Ribbon.

Power Query Basics

The first step in using Power Query is to extract data from a wide variety of sources — the extraction part of ETL. For example, you might want to know how many radio stations in Maryland are dedicated to sports. You can find this data by pulling data from the Web through Power Query.

Searching for source data

To start searching for data, follow these steps:

1. Click the Power Query tab.

2. On the Get External Data group, click the Online Search button.

    There are many types of external data sources you can choose here (you can find out about them in the section "Power Query Connection Types" later in this chapter). Searching online is a basic feature of Power Query, so for now, click the Online Search button to pull data.

    Power Query opens the Online Search pane, where you can enter a search term.

3. Enter your search term.

    For example, if you're interested in the number of radio stations that cover sports, you enter **Maryland radio stations**. Power Query presents a list of Web sources that match your search term (see Figure 7-2).

4. Hover your mouse over a result to get a preview of the data shown on the left.

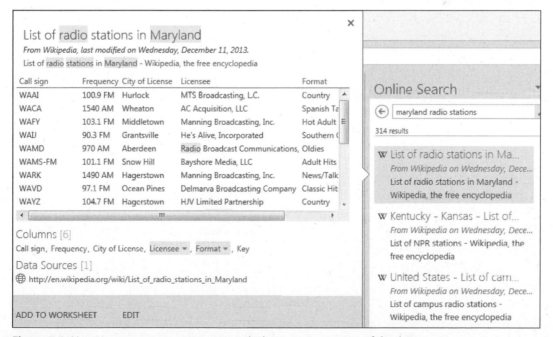

Figure 7-2: Hovering your mouse over any result shows you a preview of the data.

5. When you find a data source that contains what you need, click Edit at the bottom of the preview window.

   The Query Editor window opens at this point, which allows you to select options (see the next section).

Tip

Whether connecting to a Web site, a database, or any other data source, Power Query always starts you off with a dedicated pane that shows the available data sources. You can hover your mouse over any data source to preview the contents. You can then click Edit at the bottom of the preview window to transform the data.

Shaping the selected source data

When you choose to edit a data source, Power Query opens a Query Editor window that contains its own Ribbon; a preview pane on the left, which shows a preview of the data; and a Query Settings pane on the right (see Figure 7-3). This is your primary workbench. Here, you can apply certain actions to shape, clean, and transform the data to suit your needs — the transform part of ETL.

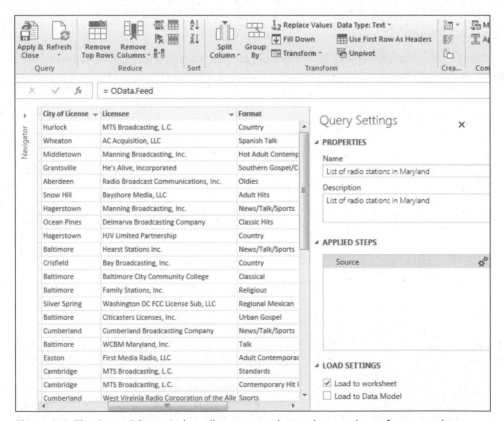

Figure 7-3: The Query Editor window allows you to shape, clean, and transform your data.

The idea is to work with each column shown in the Query Editor, applying the necessary actions that leave you with the data and structure you need.

1. Right-click any column and choose an action.

   We cover all the actions you can take in the section "Understanding Column and Table Actions" later in this chapter. For now, right-click the Format column and select Remove Other Columns to find out how many sport stations are in Maryland.

   Now only one column (the Format column) in the date preview is showing.

2. Right-click the Format column and select Insert Custom Column.

   An additional column is added.

   The Insert Custom Column dialog box shown in Figure 7-4 opens.

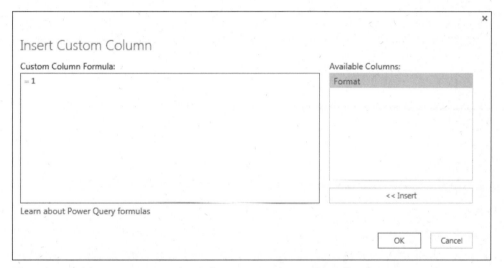

Figure 7-4: Add a new custom column that contains the number 1 for all rows.

3. Type **1** in the Custom Column Formula box, and click OK.

   Each row in the new column is now tagged with a 1, specifying that each row counts as one station. You can now aggregate the data to sum your newly created custom column for each station format.

   You now see the two columns shown in Figure 7-5.

Tip

> **The default name given to any new column you add is Custom. You can rename your newly inserted columns by right-clicking the column header and selecting Rename.**

4. Right-click the Format column and select Group By.

   The Group By dialog box opens, as shown in Figure 7-6.

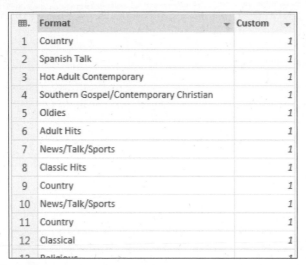

▦.	Format	Custom
1	Country	1
2	Spanish Talk	1
3	Hot Adult Contemporary	1
4	Southern Gospel/Contemporary Christian	1
5	Oldies	1
6	Adult Hits	1
7	News/Talk/Sports	1
8	Classic Hits	1
9	Country	1
10	News/Talk/Sports	1
11	Country	1
12	Classical	1

Figure 7-5: Power Query adds your custom column specifying that each row counts as one station.

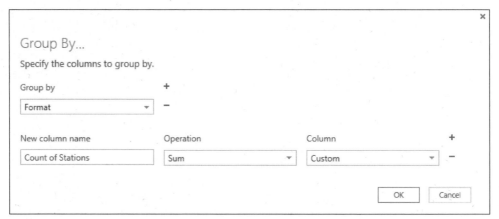

Figure 7-6: Group by the Format column and sum the Custom column into an aggregate column called Count of Stations.

5. Select Format from the Group By drop-down menu, enter **Count of Stations** in the New Column Name box, select Sum from the Operation drop-down menu, and select Custom from the Column drop-down menu. Click OK when you're done.

   Power Query then groups by the Format column and sums the Custom column into an aggregate column called Count of Stations.

   Now there is one row for each radio station format. Each row shows the count of radio stations.

6. Click the Sort command on the Query Editor Ribbon to sort by the Count of Stations column.

   You get the results shown in Figure 7-7.

Now you know how many radio stations Maryland has dedicated to sports: 9.

⊞.	Format	Count of Stations
1	Country	16
2	Sports	9
3	Religious	7
4	News/Talk/Sports	6
5	Contemporary Christian	6
6	Public Radio	6
7	Variety	5
8	Oldies	4
9	Adult Album Alternative	4
10	Hot Adult Contemporary	4
11	Adult Contemporary	3

Figure 7-7: The final table after grouping shows that Maryland has nine radio stations dedicated to sports.

Understanding query steps

With a few clicks, you searched the Internet, found some base data, and manipulated that data to suit your needs. This is what Power Query is all about — it enables you to easily pull, filter, and reshape data without the need for any programmatic coding skills. Power Query does all the legwork using its own formula language (also known as M language). Each action you take when working with Power Query results in a line of code that is written into a query step. Query steps are embedded M code that allow your actions to be repeated each time you refresh your Power Query data. The query steps are listed in the Applied Steps section of the Query Settings pane (see Figure 7-8). Each query step represents an action you took to get to a final data table.

The M code for the selected step.

✓	*fx*	= Table.Group(InsertedCustom, {"Format"}, {{"Count", each List.Sum([Custom]), type number}})	⌄

⊞.	Format	Count
1	Country	16
2	Spanish Talk	1
3	Hot Adult Contemporary	4
4	Southern Gospel/Contemporary Christian	2
5	Oldies	4
6	Adult Hits	2
7	News/Talk/Sports	6
8	Classic Hits	3
9	Classical	3
10	Religious	7
11	Regional Mexican	1
12	Urban Gospel	3
13	Talk	3
14	Adult Contemporary	3

Query Settings   ✕

▲ PROPERTIES

Name

List of radio stations in Maryland

Description

List of radio stations in Maryland

▲ APPLIED STEPS

Source
RemovedOtherColumns
InsertedCustom
✕ GroupedRows

Figure 7-8: Check out query steps in the Applied Steps section of the Query Settings pane.

Click any step and the underlying M code appears in the Power Query formula bar.

Tip   If you don't see a formula bar in the Query Editor, click the View tab on the Query Editor Ribbon, then place a check in the Formula Bar check box.

Tip   When you click a query step, the data shown in the preview pane is a preview of what the data looked like up to and including the step you clicked. For example, if you click the step before the GroupedRows step, you see what the data looked like before you applied grouping.

Managing query steps

You can right-click any step to see a menu of options for managing your query steps. Figure 7-9 shows the following options:

➤ **Edit Settings:** Edit the arguments or parameters that define the selected step.

➤ **Rename:** Give the selected step a meaningful name.

➤ **Delete:** Remove the selected step. Be aware that removing a step can cause errors if subsequent steps depend on the deleted step.

➤ **Delete Until End:** Remove the selected step and all following steps.

➤ **Move Up:** Move the selected step up in the order of steps.

➤ **Move Down:** Move the selected step down in the order of steps.

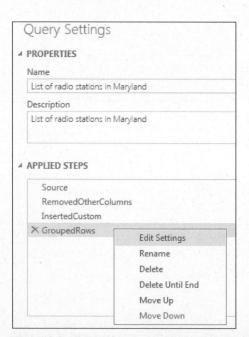

Figure 7-9: Right-click any query step to edit, delete, or move the step.

Viewing the Advanced Editor

Power Query lets you view and edit your query's embedded M code directly. While in the Query Editor window, click the Advanced Editor button on the View tab. The Advanced Editor window opens, as shown in Figure 7-10.

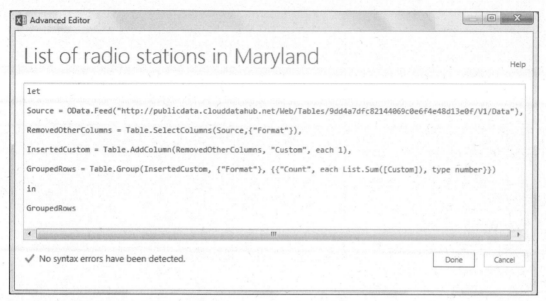

Figure 7-10: The Advanced Editor window.

The Advanced Editor window is little more than a space for you to type your own M code. The M language is a fairly robust one, allowing for many advanced actions that you can't take through the Query Editor. You can directly code your own steps.

Note

If you're interested in learning more about M language and coding your own steps, start with the M Language specification guide by Microsoft. To get it, type **Microsoft Power Query Formula Language Specification** into your favorite search engine.

Outputting your query results

When you've configured your Power Query data, you can output the results. This would be the load part of ETL. At the bottom of the Query Settings pane (see Figure 7-11), choose how you want to output your data:

➤ **Load to Worksheet:** This is the default choice. It outputs the results as a table in a workbook.

➤ **Load to Data Model:** This choice outputs the data to the internal Data Model that you can integrate into a Power Pivot report.

Then click the Home tab and click the Apply & Close button. At this point, the Query Editor window closes, and depending on the location you have chosen, your results are loaded to either an Excel table in the current workbook or the internal Data Model.

Figure 7-11: At the bottom of the Query Settings pane, select whether you want your query to be output to a new worksheet or the internal Data Model.

Refreshing Power Query data

It's important to note that Power Query data is not in any way connected to the source data used to extract it. A Power Query data table is merely a snapshot. In other words, as the source data changes, Power Query does not automatically keep up with the changes. You need to take steps to refresh your query.

Manually refresh a single Power Query output

You can manually refresh your Power Query outputs no matter how you chose to load the results:

➤ **Load to an Excel worksheet:** Find the worksheet that contains your Power Query output, click anywhere within the table, and then click the Refresh button on the Query tab. You can also right-click anywhere inside the table and select Refresh.

➤ **Loaded to the internal Data Model:** Open the Power Pivot window, select your Power Query data, and then click the Refresh button on the Home tab.

Set up automatic refresh

You can configure your data sources to automatically refresh your Power Query data. To do so, follow these steps:

1. On the Data tab, click the Connections button.

   The Workbook Connections dialog box opens.

2. Select the Power Query data connection you want to refresh and click the Properties button.

3. In the Properties dialog box, click the Usage tab.

4. Set the options to refresh the chosen data connection every X minutes or the option to refresh the data connection when the Excel workbook is opened.

    - *Refresh Every X Minutes:* Excel automatically refreshes the chosen data connection a specified number of minutes. This refreshes all tables associated with that connection.

    - *Refresh Data When Opening the File:* Excel automatically refreshes the chosen data connection upon opening the workbook. This refreshes all tables associated with that connection as soon as the workbook is opened.

5. Click OK to confirm your changes.

Managing existing queries

You can see all the Power Query outputs in your workbook by clicking the Workbook button on the Power Query Ribbon. The Workbook Queries pane opens as shown in Figure 7-12.

Figure 7-12: The Workbook Queries pane enables you to edit, delete, and manage the queries in your workbook.

Right-click the desired query to take any one of the following actions:

- ➤ **Edit:** Opens the Query Editor, allowing you to modify the query name, description, and query steps.
- ➤ **Refresh:** Refreshes the data in the query.
- ➤ **Duplicate:** Creates a copy of the query.
- ➤ **Reference:** Creates a new query that references the output of the original query.
- ➤ **Delete:** Deletes the selected query.

➤ **Merge:** Merges the selected query with another query in the workbook by matching specified columns.

➤ **Append:** Appends the results of another query in the workbook to the selected query.

➤ **Share:** Publishes and shares the selected query via a Power BI server, which your IT department sets up and manages.

➤ **Show the Peek:** Shows a preview of the data.

Understanding Column and Table Actions

In the beginning of this chapter, you discovered how to transform data by applying actions to certain columns. Those actions are just a few of the many column-level and table-level transformations you can take. This section lists the various actions available and explains what each does.

Column level actions

Right-click any column in the Query Editor to open a context menu listing the actions you can take (see Figure 7-13).

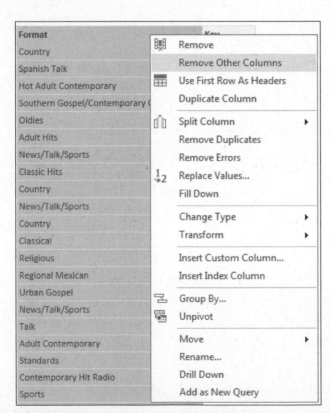

Figure 7-13: Right-click any column to see the column-level actions you can use to transform the data.

Tip

To apply certain actions to multiple columns at one time, select the target columns before right-clicking.

Table 7-1 shows what each action is meant to accomplish, and which actions are available with multiple columns.

Tip

Many of the column actions have corresponding buttons on the Query Editor's Ribbon.

Table 7-1: Column-Level Actions

Action	Purpose	Available When Selecting Multiple Columns
Remove	Removes the selected column from the Power Query data.	Yes
Remove Other Columns	Removes all non-selected columns from the Power Query data.	Yes
Use First Row As Headers	Replaces each table header name by the values in the first row of each column.	No
Duplicate Column	Creates a duplicate of the selected column as a new column placed at the far right of the table. The name given to the new column is Copy of X, where X is the name of the original column.	No
Split Column	Splits the column into multiple columns either by a specified delimiter or by a specified number of characters.	No
Remove Duplicates	Removes all rows from the selected column where the values duplicate earlier values. The row with the first occurrence of a value is not removed.	Yes
Remove Errors	Removes rows containing errors in the selected column.	Yes
Replace Values	Replaces one value with another value in the selected column.	Yes
Fill Down	Fills empty cells in the column with the value of the first non-empty cell above them.	Yes
Change Type	Changes the data type of the selected column to any of these types: Binary, Date, Date/Time, Date/Time/Timezone, Duration, Logical, Number, Text, Time, or Using Locale (localizes data types to the country you specify).	Yes
Transform	Changes the way values in the column are rendered. You can choose from the following options: Lowercase, Uppercase, Capitalize Each Word, Trim, Clean, JSON, or XML. If the values in the column are date/time values, the options are Date, Time, Day, Month, Year, or Day of Week. If the values in the column are number values, the options are Round, Absolute Value, Factorial, Base-10 Logarithm, Natural Logarithm, Power, or Square Root.	Yes
Insert Custom Column	Inserts a new column after the last column of the table. The values in the new column are determined by selecting the type of column to insert: Custom (you define the values) or Index (Power Query adds a sequential list of numbers).	No

continued

Table 7-1: Column-Level Actions *(continued)*

Action	Purpose	Available When Selecting Multiple Columns
Insert Index Column	Adds a column with a sequential list of index numbers starting from 0.	No
Group By	Aggregates data by row values. For example, you can Group by State and either count the number of cities in each state or sum the population of each state.	Yes
Unpivot	Transposes the selected columns from column-oriented to row-oriented, or vice versa.	Yes
Move	Moves the selected column to a different location in the table. You have the choice of moving the column Left, Right, To Beginning, or To End.	Yes
Rename	Renames the selected column to a name you specify.	No
Drill Down	Navigates to the contents of the column. This is used with tables that contain metadata representing embedded information.	No
Add as New Query	Creates a new query with the contents of the column. This is done by referencing the original query in the new one. The name of the new query is the same as the column header of the selected column.	No

Table actions

While in the Query Editor, Power Query allows you to apply certain actions to the entire data table. You can see the available table-level actions by clicking the table icon (see Figure 7-14).

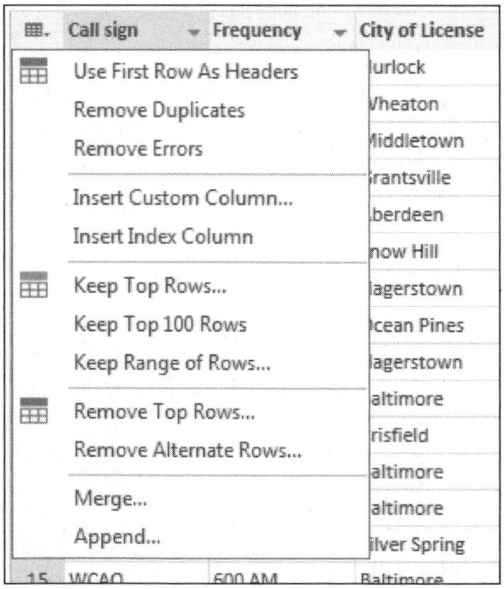

Figure 7-14: Click the table icon in the upper left-hand corner of the Query Editor preview pane to see the table-level actions you can use to transform the data.

Table 7-2 lists each table-level action along with its primary purpose.

Tip

Many of the table actions have corresponding commands on the Query Editor's Ribbon.

Table 7-2: Table-Level Actions

Action	Purpose
Use First Row As Headers	Replaces each table header name by the values in the first row of each column.
Remove Duplicates	Removes all rows from where the values in the selected columns duplicate earlier values. The row with the first occurrence of a value set is not removed.
Remove Errors	Removes rows containing errors in the currently selected columns.
Insert Custom Column	Inserts a new column after the last column of the table. The values in the new column are determined by the value or formula you define.
Insert Index Column	Adds a new column containing a sequential list of index numbers starting from 0.
Keep Top Rows	Removes all but the top N number of rows. You specify the number threshold.
Keep Top 100 Rows	Removes all but the top 100 rows.
Keep Range of Rows	Removes all rows except those that fall within a range you specify.
Remove Top Rows	Remove top N rows from the table.
Remove Alternate Rows	Remove alternate rows from the table starting at first row, specifying the number of rows to remove and the number of rows to keep.
Merge	Creates a new query that merges the current table with another query in the workbook by matching specified columns.
Append	Creates a new query that appends the results of another query in the workbook to the current table.

Power Query Connection Types

Microsoft has invested a great deal of time and resources in ensuring that Power Query has the ability to connect to a wide array of data sources. Whether you need to pull data from an online search, an external Web site, a file, a database system, SharePoint, Facebook, or a big data source such as Hadoop, Power Query can accommodate most, if not all, your source data needs.

The available connection types are in the Get External Data group on the Power Query tab. As shown in Figure 7-15, Power Query offers these categories of connection types:

➤ **Online Search:** Pulls data from a Web source based on a specified search term.

➤ **From Web:** Pulls data from a Web site based on a specified URL.

➤ **From File:** Pulls data from a specified flat file or folder.

➤ **From Database:** Pulls data from a relational database system.

➤ **From Other Sources:** Pulls data from a wide array of inter-company, cloud, and big data sources. This category includes an option to start with a Blank Query in the event you want to write your own M code from scratch.

➤ **From Table:** Pull data from a defined Excel table within the existing workbook.

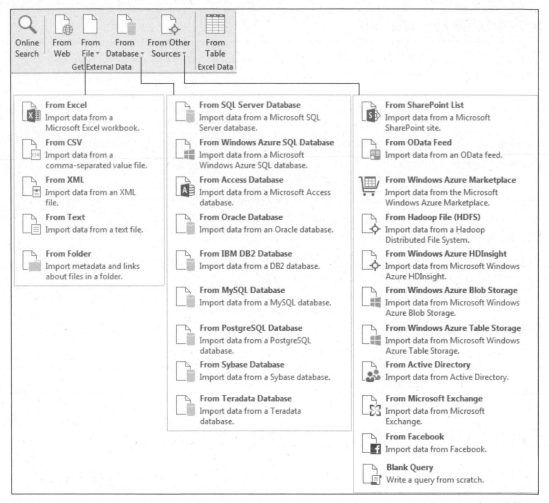

Figure 7-15: Power Query has the ability to connect to a wide array of data sources, from simple text files to big data sources such as Hadoop.

After you select a connection type you enter the parameters Power Query requires in a series of dialog boxes. Such parameters Power Query needs to connect to a data source are file path, URL, server name, and credentials.

Each connection type requires a unique set of parameters, so each of its dialog boxes will be different. Luckily, Power Query rarely needs more than a handful of parameters to connect to any one data source, so the dialog boxes are relatively intuitive and hassle-free.

Power Query saves the data source parameters for each data source connection you have used. You can view, edit, or delete any of the data source connections by clicking the Data Source Settings button on the Power Query tab. In the Data Source Settings dialog box, select any connection and you can edit or delete it; see Figure 7-16.

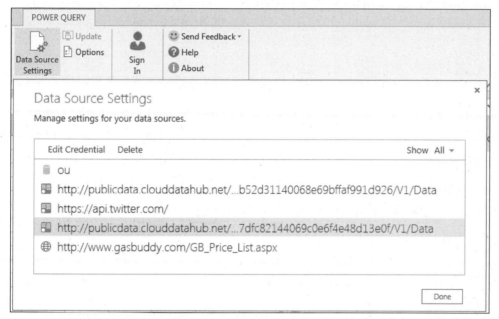

Figure 7-16: The Data Source Settings dialog box enables you to edit or delete previously used data connections.

Note

Deleting a connection does not delete any of its associated data you may have already loaded in your workbook or internal Data Model. However, when you try to refresh the data, Power Query won't have any of the connection parameters (because you deleted them), so it asks you again for the connection parameters.

Creating and Using Power Query Functions

Earlier in this chapter, we discussed how Power Query uses its own formula language known as M. When you connect to a data source and apply transformations to that data, Power Query diligently saves your actions as M code behind the scenes in query steps. This allows for your transformation steps to be repeated when you refresh the data in your query.

With a little knowledge, you can leverage the M language to extend the capabilities of Power Query with your own custom functions. Custom functions come in handy when you frequently need to apply business-specific calculations or perform complex transformations involving conditional testing with If . . . Then . . . Else logic.

In this section we walk you through the basics of building your own custom functions.

Creating and using a basic custom function

When building a custom function for Power Query, you're creating a query and manipulating its M code to return a desired result. That result can be an array, a data table, or a single value.

In this section, you build a basic mathematical function that calculates profit. This function takes a revenue amount and a cost amount and outputs a profit amount using a basic mathematical operation:

```
Revenue &#x2013; Cost = Profit
```

For basic functions such as this one, you can start with a blank query and enter the needed M code from scratch:

1. From the Power Query tab, choose From Other Data Sources ➜ Blank Query.

   The Query Editor window opens.

2. In the Query Editor Ribbon, click the View tab and click the Advanced Editor button.

3. In the Advanced Editor window, replace the starter syntax with the following code in the code box:

```
let Profit = (Revenue, Cost)=>
Revenue-Cost
in Profit
```

The first line tells Power Query that this function needs two parameters: Revenue and Cost. The second line tells Power Query to subtract the Cost parameter from the Revenue parameter. The last line of the code tells Power Query to return the result.

Tip

Power Query doesn't care what you name the functions as long as the names start with a letter and don't include any spaces.

Figure 7-17 shows what the code looks like in the Advanced Editor window.

```
Advanced Editor

Query1

let Profit = (Revenue, Cost)=>
Revenue-Cost
in Profit
```

Figure 7-17: Enter your custom code in the Advanced Editor window.

4. Click Done to close the Advanced Editor window.

5. In the Query Settings pane, change the name of the query in the Name input box.

   Give your function a descriptive name — for example, FunctionProfit — as opposed to Query1.

6. On the Home tab of the Query Editor, click the Apply & Close button.

Power Query creates a seemingly useless table and adds the query to the Workbook Queries pane, as shown in Figure 7-18. Unfortunately, there is no way to create a function without creating an associated table, so as worthless as the table seems, you can't delete it.

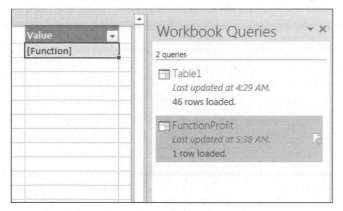

Figure 7-18: Your function is ready to use.

You can now use this function in other queries that contain revenue and cost fields. For example, Figure 7-19 shows a query with a field called Sales Amount and a field called Equipment Cost. You can use your newly created function to calculate profit using these two fields.

⊞.	Product Name	Quantity	Sale Amount	Equipment Cost
1	Slide Door Refrigerator	1	4637	2356.05
2	Garnish Center	7	210	159.285
3	Speed Rail 10 Quart/Liter Bottle Capacity	8	280	69.9
4	Speed Rail 5 Quart/Liter Bottle Capacity	10	240	61.25
5	Commercial Food Processor Mp350Turbo	6	7374	3211.965
6	Commercial Juice Press	5	380	94.5875
7	Vegetable Slicer Spiral	4	864	342.0008
8	Cotton Candy Maker Stainless Steel Whirlwind	8	6592	4352.3752
9	Grill Scraper	5	195	49.225
10	Pizza Humidified Merchandiser	17	16660	12042.3665
11	Press Panini	6	3864	2086.56

Figure 7-19: A table with Sales Amount and Equipment Cost fields.

Right-click any column header and select Insert Custom Column. In the Insert Custom Column dialog box (see Figure 7-20), you can invoke your function by name, passing the Sales Amount and Equipment Cost fields as parameters separated by a comma.

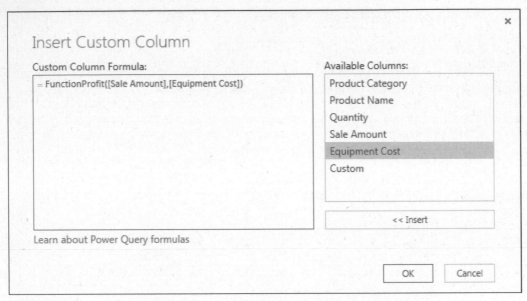

Figure 7-20: Use the Insert Custom Column dialog box to invoke your function.

Click OK, and Power Query triggers the function for each row in the data table. Figure 7-21 shows the newly created Custom column with the returned profit calculation. You can, of course, rename this field to indicate what the numbers represent (right-click the field header and select the Rename option).

	Product Name	Quantity	Sale Amount	Equipment Cost	Custom
1	Slide Door Refrigerator	1	4637	2356.05	2280.95
2	Garnish Center	7	210	159.285	50.715
3	Speed Rail 10 Quart/Liter Bottle Capacity	8	280	69.9	210.1
4	Speed Rail 5 Quart/Liter Bottle Capacity	10	240	61.25	178.75
5	Commercial Food Processor Mp350Turbo	6	7374	3211.965	4162.035
6	Commercial Juice Press	5	380	94.5875	285.4125
7	Vegetable Slicer Spiral	4	864	342.0008	521.9992
8	Cotton Candy Maker Stainless Steel Whirlwind	8	6592	4352.3752	2239.6248
9	Grill Scraper	5	195	49.225	145.775
10	Pizza Humidified Merchandiser	17	16660	12042.3665	4617.6335
11	Press Panini	6	3864	2086.56	1777.44

Figure 7-21: Power Query triggers the function and returns a result for each row in the table.

Note

Power Query functions apply only to the workbook in which they reside. If you start a new workbook, you need to re-create your functions in that new workbook.

Advanced function example: Combining all Excel files in a directory into one table

When building a basic function like a profit function, it's no big deal to start from a blank query and enter all the code from scratch. But for more complex functions, it's generally smarter to build a starter query via Query Editor, and then manipulate the M code to accomplish what you need.

For example, imagine you have a set of Excel files in a directory (see Figure 7-22). These files all contain a worksheet called MySheet that holds tables of data. The tables in each file have the same structure but need to be combined into one file. This is a common task that you've probably faced at one time or another. Without a solid knowledge of Excel VBA programming, this task typically entails opening each file, copying the data on the MySheet tab, and then pasting the data into single workbook.

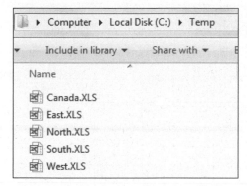

Figure 7-22: Imagine you have the task of combining the data in all the Excel files in this directory into one table.

Power Query can make short work of this task, but it requires a bit of direction via a custom function. It would be difficult for most anyone to start from a blank query and type the M code for the relatively complex function needed for this endeavor. Instead, you can build a starter query via Query Editor, and then wrap the query in a function.

Follow these steps:

1. On the Power Query tab, choose From File ➜ From Excel.

2. Browse to the directory that contains all the Excel files and select one of them.

3. In the Navigator pane (shown in Figure 7-23), select the sheet holding the data that needs to be consolidated and then click Edit to open the Query Editor.

4. Use the Query Editor to apply some basic transformation actions.

    For example, you can designate the first row as a column header and remove any unneeded columns.

5. After you've applied the needed transformations, click the Advanced Editor button on the View tab.

    The Advanced Editor window opens with the bulk of the code for your function already created, as shown in Figure 7-24. Power Query hard-coded the file path and the filename for the Excel file you originally selected. The idea is to wrap this starter code in a function that will pass a *dynamic* file path and filename.

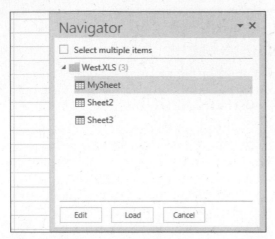

Figure 7-23: Select one of the Excel files in the target directory and navigate to the sheet holding the data that needs to be consolidated.

This part is hard-coded.

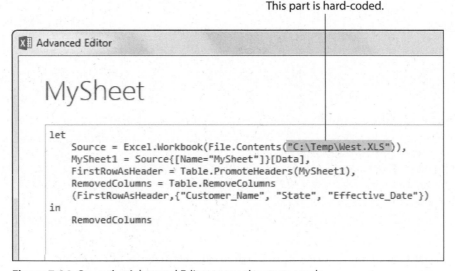

Figure 7-24: Open the Advanced Editor to see the starter code.

6. Wrap the entire block of code with your function tags, specifying that this function requires two parameters: FilePath and FileName.

   The hard-coded file path and filename have been replaced with their respective parameters, as shown in Figure 7-25.

7. Close the Advanced Editor.

8. In the Query Settings pane, change the name of the query in the Name box. Give your function a descriptive name (in this scenario, fGetMyFiles).

This part now includes parameters.

```
X  Advanced Editor

    MySheet

    let GetMyFiles=(FilePath, FileName) =>

    let
        Source = Excel.Workbook(File.Contents(FilePath&FileName)),
        MySheet1 = Source{[Name="MySheet"]}[Data],
        FirstRowAsHeader = Table.PromoteHeaders(MySheet1),
        RemovedColumns = Table.RemoveColumns
        (FirstRowAsHeader,{"Customer_Name", "State", "Effective_Date"})
    in
        RemovedColumns

    in GetMyFiles
```

Figure 7-25: Replace the hard-coded file path and file name with your dynamic parameters.

9. Click the Apply & Close button on the Home tab.

   At this point, you can use the custom function on all the files in the target directory.

10. On the Power Query tab, choose From File ➜ From Folder to start a connection to the directory that contains all the Excel files.

11. In the From Folder dialog box, provide Power Query with the file path of the target directory.

    The Query Editor window opens to show you a table similar to the one in Figure 7-26. This table contains a record for each file in the chosen directory. The Folder Path and Name columns supply the function with the needed FilePath and FileName parameters.

✓ ƒx	= Folder.Files("c:\Temp")				

▦.	Content	Name	Extension	Attributes	Folder Path
1	Binary	Canada.XLS	.XLS	Record	c:\Temp\
2	Binary	East.XLS	.XLS	Record	c:\Temp\
3	Binary	North.XLS	.XLS	Record	c:\Temp\
4	Binary	South.XLS	.XLS	Record	c:\Temp\
5	Binary	West.XLS	.XLS	Record	c:\Temp\

Figure 7-26: Create a new query using the From Folder connection type to retrieve a table of all the files in the target directory.

12. Right-click any column header and select Insert Custom Column.

13. In the Insert Custom Column dialog box (see Figure 7-27), invoke the function and pass the Folder Path and Name fields as parameters separated by a comma. Click OK.

    Power Query triggers the function for each row in the data table. The function itself grabs the data from each file and returns a table array. Figure 7-28 shows the newly created Custom column with a returned table array for each file.

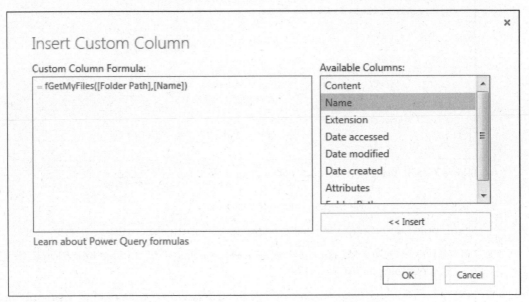

Figure 7-27: Use the Insert Custom Column dialog box to invoke the function.

		fx	= Folder.Files("c:\Temp")

▦.	Content	Name	Extension	Attributes	Folder Path	Custom
1	Binary	Canada.XLS	.XLS	Record	c:\Temp\	Table
2	Binary	East.XLS	.XLS	Record	c:\Temp\	Table
3	Binary	North.XLS	.XLS	Record	c:\Temp\	Table
4	Binary	South.XLS	.XLS	Record	c:\Temp\	Table
5	Binary	West.XLS	.XLS	Record	c:\Temp\	Table

Figure 7-28: Power Query triggers the function and returns a table array for each file in the directory.

14. Click the Custom column header to see a list of fields included in each table array (see Figure 7-29). Select which fields in the table array to show, click the Expand radio button, and then click OK.

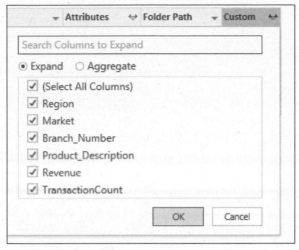

Figure 7-29: Click the Custom column header to expand the table arrays.

With each table array expanded, Power Query shows the columns pulled from each Excel file and adds the detailed records to the data preview. Figure 7-30 shows the data preview for the final combined table.

15. Click the Apply & Close button to output the combined table.

Folder Path	Custom.Region	Custom.Market	Custom.Branch_Num...	Custom.Product_Description
c:\Temp\	NORTH	NEWYORK	801211	Fleet Maintenance
c:\Temp\	NORTH	NEWYORK	804211	Facility Maintenance and Repair
c:\Temp\	SOUTH	NEWORLEANS	801607	Facility Maintenance and Repair
c:\Temp\	WEST	PHOENIX	201714	Fleet Maintenance
c:\Temp\	NORTH	NEWYORK	804211	Green Plants and Foliage Care
c:\Temp\	WEST	PHOENIX	201714	Facility Maintenance and Repair
c:\Temp\	SOUTH	NEWORLEANS	801607	Fleet Maintenance
c:\Temp\	SOUTH	NEWORLEANS	601310	Green Plants and Foliage Care
c:\Temp\	WEST	PHOENIX	201714	Green Plants and Foliage Care

Figure 7-30: The final combined view.

Note

Don't lose track of the fact that this relatively complex task was facilitated by a custom function. For all the steps required to accomplish this task, very little effort was actually expended on writing the code for the function. Power Query wrote the code for the core functionality, and you simply wrapped that code into a function.

Leveraging SQL for Business Intelligence

Essential SQL Server Concepts

8

In This Chapter

- Understanding SQL Server
- Setting up databases
- Working with tables and views
- Understanding SQL Server security
- Importing and exporting data

SQL Server is an enterprise-grade database platform designed to handle large datasets and intensive data processing. Microsoft has positioned SQL Server at the center of its BI Stack, enabling it with powerful features and add-ons specifically designed for business intelligence and analytics. It is critical for you to be familiar with SQL Server if you deal with datasets that are too large for standard desktop tools to handle. The data stored inside SQL Server can be integrated in a variety of front-end tools such as Excel, Access, and advanced reporting and dashboarding tools.

SQL Server Components

SQL Server is an extensive platform with dozens of components. In this section we focus on two of those components:

➤ SQL Server Relational Database Engine

➤ SQL Server Management Studio

SQL Server Relational Database Engine

The SQL Server Relational Database Engine is a stand-alone service that can be installed on a personal computer or a dedicated server or cluster of servers. The specifications of the computer hardware required to run this service depend on the performance requirements. As your dataset size and your data processing requirements grow, your hardware requirements grow accordingly.

Tip

Start your development on your desktop and migrate to a larger machine for your production environment.

There are many benefits to having a dedicated environment for running the SQL Server Relational Database Engine, including:

- ➤ Controlling access to the server
- ➤ Protecting your data
- ➤ Allowing concurrent access
- ➤ Improving performance
- ➤ Making administration easier

SQL Server Management Studio

After the SQL Server Relational Database Engine component is installed, it stays mostly behind the scenes and interactions to that component occur via SQL Server Management Studio.

As shown in Figure 8-1, SQL Server Management Studio is a client tool that can be installed on your computer to enable you to perform several functions on the database service, including:

- ➤ Connecting to a database service
- ➤ Creating and managing databases
- ➤ Configuring security
- ➤ Creating tables, stored procedures, and views
- ➤ Developing SQL queries
- ➤ Creating indexes and performance tuning
- ➤ Importing and exporting data

SQL Server Management Studio allows you to interact with your SQL Server database. With Management Studio, you can manage tables, create queries, pass commands to the database, and receive returned query results.

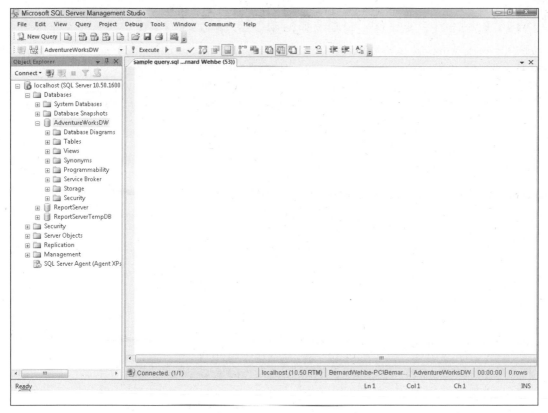

Figure 8-1: SQL Server Management Studio.

There are two views in SQL Server Management Studio that you will primarily use:

➤ The **Object Explorer** allows you to browse objects that have been created on the service, such as databases, tables, and other objects.

➤ The **Query** window allows you to write and execute SQL. The Query window returns data and messages from the service based on the SQL that you execute.

Structured Query Language (SQL) is the primary language for interacting with your SQL Server service (we cover the basics of SQL in Chapter 9). You can use SQL to perform administrative functions on the service, create objects, or query and manipulate data. Performing all these tasks via SQL gets pretty challenging. Luckily, you do not have to memorize all the SQL functions to be able to use SQL Server. Microsoft has built user interfaces for performing most of the functions that you may need to build your data structure, administer your databases, and even perform some data analysis.

Note

You do need to learn SQL basics to get the most out of your installation. The good news is that the learning curve for SQL is not very steep.

Connecting to a Database Service

Microsoft has made it very easy to connect to an SQL Server Relational Database Engine service. Just follow these steps:

1. Open SQL Server Management Studio.

2. Click Connect in the Object Explorer window.

3. Select Database Engine from the Server Type drop-down menu.

   The Connect to Server dialog box shown in Figure 8-2 opens.

Figure 8-2: Connecting to an SQL Server Relational Database Engine service.

4. Choose the appropriate server name and authentication method.

   If you don't know the authentication method to use, contact the administrator.

5. Click Connect.

Now that you have connected to the service, you can expand the databases folders in the Object Explorer window to see if there are any databases created on the service. By default there aren't any.

SQL Server Security

SQL Server security is quite extensive and complex to master. The full scope of security capabilities are beyond the scope of this book, but we'll tell you how to get up and running with your analytics system. At a very high level, there are three levels of access that you should be concerned with: Server, Database, and Database Objects.

Server access

Server access security has two aspects: login and server roles (see Figure 8-3).

Find your login and server roles.

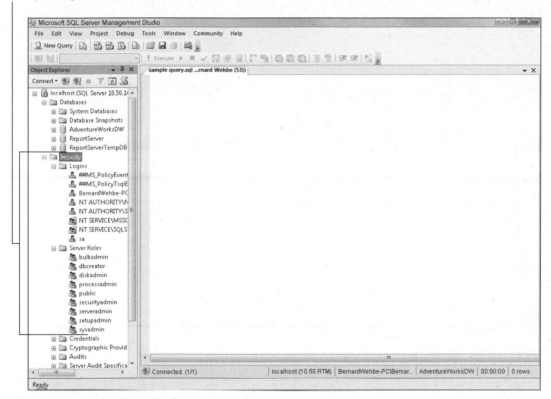

Figure 8-3: Logins and server roles.

Login roles are the named users or groups that are allowed to access to the server. Groups are benefi-cial, instead of individual logins, because group logins allow you to manage everyone in that group in your organization's Active Directory. This keeps security centralized as these groups may have access to other applications with related functions.

Add a login by right-clicking the Logins folder and choosing New Login. Work with your corporate security administrators to make sure you're following your organization's security policies and procedures.

Note

The sa **login is the administrative account, which has full access rights to the server. This login is defined during the installation. If you're the one installing SQL Server, make sure to assign a secure password to this account, otherwise you compromise the security of your system.**

Server roles provide overarching permissions to take server-level actions, such as creating a new data-base, and managing server backups and linked objects.

Every login in SQL Server must have at least one associated server role. You can set the login's roles by right-clicking each login in the Logins folder and selecting Properties. In the Login Properties dialog box, click Server Roles to see the available server roles (see Figure 8-4).

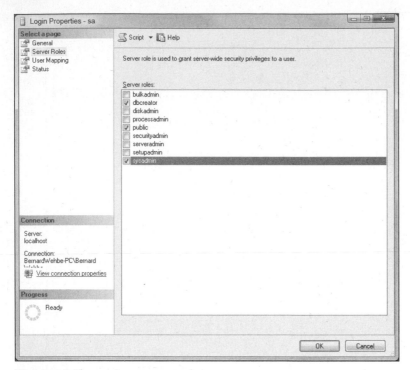

Figure 8-4: Three primary server roles.

A login can be assigned to any number of the available server roles. Each role has a defined set of permissions governing the actions that can be taken on the server. The most commonly used roles are Dbcreator, Public, and Sysadmin:

> ➤ **Dbcreator:** Is able to create new databases on the server and fully control and administer those databases.

> ➤ **Public:** Is allowed access to the server but is not given any server-level capabilities. Typically logins under this role have specific access at the database level.

> ➤ **Sysadmin:** Has full control over the server. You are typically assigned this role if you installed SQL Server yourself or you were given that level of access by another sysadmin.

Database access

After your server-level security has been defined, there is another layer of access control at the database level. You can configure and control this access level in the Security folder of your database in the Object Explorer window. There are two primary aspects to SQL Server's database-level security that are of concern to you: users and database roles (see Figure 8-5).

Find your user and database roles.

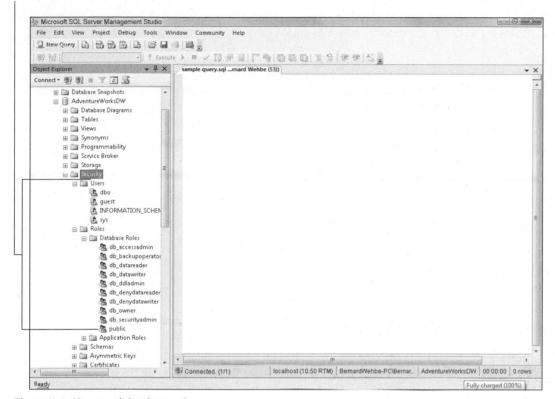

Figure 8-5: Users and database roles.

Add a database user by right-clicking the Users folder in the Object Explorer window and selecting New User. The Database User – New window opens, where you can add a new database user. Every database user must have a server login. To simplify security admin, give the database user the same name as the server login.

After naming the user and assigning the proper server login, you have to define the user's database access level. There are two primary approaching to defining access level:

➤ **Database Role:** Gives the user general database access, making it easier for you to administer security because you do not have to specifically declare access for each object in your database.

➤ **Database Object Access:** Allows you fine control over your database security. This is discussed in detail in the next section.

There are three primary database roles that are important to you (see Figure 8-6):

➤ **Db_datareader:** Is able to read data from all the database tables that are created by other users in the database. Use this role if you want simple security access and you do not have sensitive data.

➤ **Db_datawriter:** Is allowed to edit (insert, update, and delete) data in all the database tables created and populated by other users. This access is typically given to your team members who would be helping with data analysis, and not to the general public. If you give everyone this level of access, you risk losing control of your data and not being able to guarantee the integrity of your system.

➤ **Db_owner:** Has full control over the database and all the objects within it. You should avoid giving this level of access to other users unless they are trusted members of your team with functions that require it.

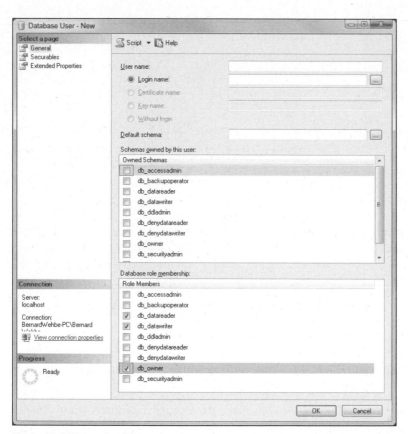

Figure 8-6: Three database roles.

Note

Database users do not have to be assigned any database roles. If you want granular control over a user's access, grant him specific control over the various database objects.

Database object access

SQL Server allows for complete control over your security. If you do not want to give general access at the database level, you can control access on an object-by-object level for each of your users. You can do so on the Securables tab in the Database User window (see Figure 8-7).

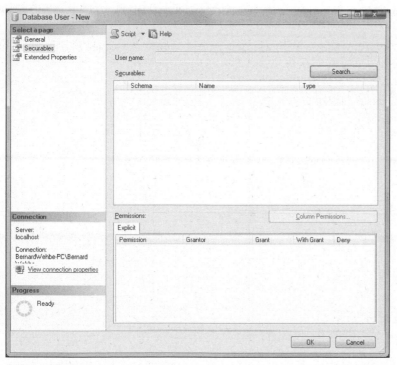

Figure 8-7: Database user securables.

1. Click the target database you're working with. From Object Explorer, click Security and then Users. Then right-click the target user and choose Properties.

2. Click the Search button.

    The Add Objects dialog box opens, as shown in Figure 8-8.

Figure 8-8: Add Objects options.

3. Select the All Objects of the Types option and then click OK.

   The Select Object Types window opens, with a large number of database objects to choose from (see Figure 8-9).

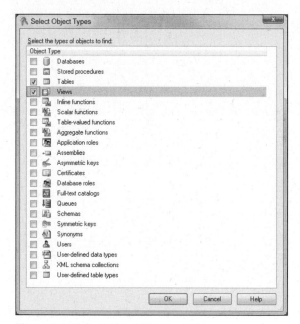

Figure 8-9: Select Object Types window.

4. Select the Tables and Views object types and click OK.

   In most situations, those are the two object types you grant access to.

   Now in the Database User window, the Securables and Permissions areas are populated with objects and permission options, respectively (see Figure 8-10).

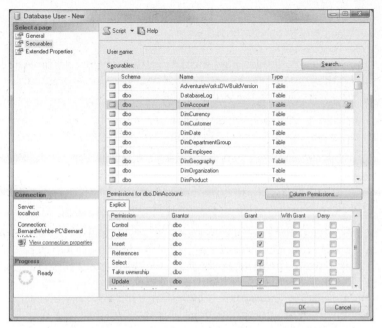

Figure 8-10: Database User window with populated securables.

When you click a specific object in the Securables area (refer to Figure 8-10), you see the specific permissions that you can control for that object in the Permissions area. For tables and views, you should be aware of four primary permission types:

➤ **Delete:** Allows the user to remove data from a table.

➤ **Insert:** Allows the user access to append data to the table, either directly with SQL or by using an application.

➤ **Select:** Gives the user access to read the data by writing SQL against the table or via a reporting or dashboarding tool.

➤ **Update:** Is a combination of a Delete and an Insert on existing data in a table.

Typically you allow Select access to most clients. Use Insert, Delete, and Update for team members assisting you with creating analytics. The one exception to this rule is a lookup table that you want clients to maintain. Lookup tables typically contain business rules or attributes that clients control; for example, a lookup table to maintain unit cost.

Working with Databases

Creating a database is typically done by your system administrator. If you have to perform this function yourself, you need to know some basics about how SQL Server works on a server or your personal computer. The first thing you need to think about is disk configuration. The recommended best practice for SQL Server installation is to segregate the various types of files and databases into separate drives. This allows you to better control the performance and administration of your server. There are four functional areas you need to be concerned with:

➤ **Data files:** As the name implies, these files store the data loaded in your user tables. The size of these files depends on the amount of data and type of data you store in your tables. The larger the number of rows and columns, the larger the files.

➤ **Log files:** These files are used by SQL Server to guarantee data integrity while SQL Server performs the work necessary when SQL statements are submitted by the users. Their size depends on the database setup (we discuss this in a later section) and the transactions submitted.

➤ **Temp DB:** This database is used by SQL Server as a temporary work space for processing user SQL statements. Its use may be explicit by the user or implicit by the SQL Server optimizer. The files of this database can be very large on a server with a high level of activity.

➤ **Backup files:** It is recommended that you back up your SQL Server database on a regular basis to allow you to recover data in case it becomes corrupted. The size of these files depends on the databases being backed up, the frequency of backup, and the number of backups saved.

If you're using a server for your installation, your system administrator should configure SQL Server to automatically point the different files to the appropriate drive when you create a new database. Otherwise, you have to do that configuration yourself.

Creating a database

To create a new database, right-click the Databases folder in the Object Explorer window and select New Database. The New Database window opens, allowing you to define the database (see Figure 8-11).

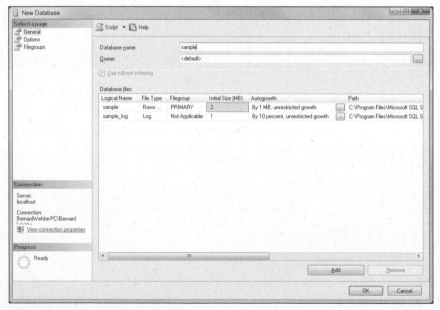

Figure 8-11: New Database window.

There are several options and configurations available to you when creating a database:

➤ **Database name:** Give careful thought to selecting your database name. You can change it; however, it might impact queries and applications that reference that name.

➤ **Owner:** In general, leave this field selected to Default. By default, SQL Server assigns all objects in the database to DBO. For more complex databases, you might consider setting multiple owners in your database to organize objects under them.

➤ **Database files:** Refer to the previous section for best practices on setting up these files.

➤ **Options:** Clicking Options in the Select a Page pane. That takes you to the Options tab in the New Database window (see Figure 8-12). Select Simple from the Recovery Model drop-down list, as shown in Figure 8-12. This option keeps your log file under control.

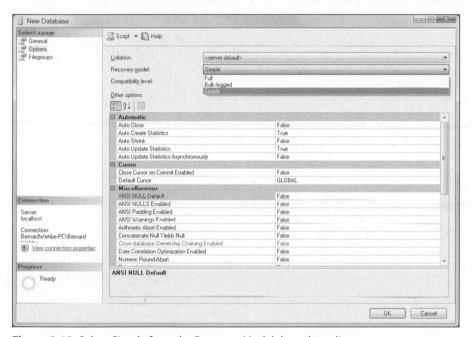

Figure 8-12: Select Simple from the Recovery Model drop-down list.

Database maintenance

SQL Server database maintenance involves several aspects, including backup, index rebuilding, and statistics updates. The full scope of database maintenance is traditionally handled by the system administrator. If you're managing the system yourself, it's helpful to know how to back up a database. Follow these steps for the easiest way to back up your database:

1. Right-click your database, and choose Tasks ➜ Back Up.

   The Back Up Database window opens, which allows you to select the options for the backup you want to perform (see Figure 8-13).

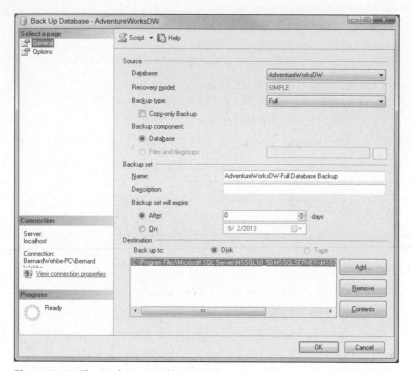

Figure 8-13: The Back Up Database window.

2. In the Name box, enter an appropriate name for the backup.

   Usually it is best to include the date and time as part of the name you give to your backup. This allows you to easily recognize when the backup was taken.

3. Select a location for the backup.

   If your system has multiple drives, make sure you select the drive that is designated for backup.

4. Click the Options page on the left margin of the Back Up Database window and then select the Overwrite All Existing Backup Sets option (see Figure 8-14).

5. Click OK.

Backing up databases allows you to recover data in case data becomes corrupted. Data corruption could occur due to a human error or in the very unlikely event of SQL Server system corruption. To restore a database, right-click the database, choose Tasks ➜ Restore ➜ Database. Follow the instructions to restore the database from the appropriate backup — which is usually the last backup that included valid data.

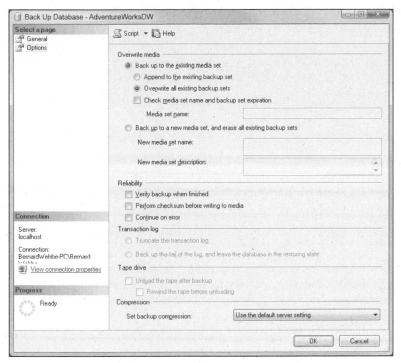

Figure 8-14: Configure backup options.

Working with Tables and Views

Tables represent the core of your analytics system. This is where all your data is stored to be used for generating reports and value-adding analysis. *Views,* as the name implies, don't hold any data, but instead reflect views of the data contained in the underlying tables. Views give you the ability to join several tables together into one dataset.

There are several design considerations that should be taken into account when building tables and views:

➤ **Data model:** The data model refers to the organization of your data elements into tables and columns. The approach you should take for the design depends on the functional area of the database. Typically, analytics data models follow what is referred to as a denormalized model, which focuses on making reporting and analysis efficient as opposed to optimizing data inserts and updates.

➤ **Data size:** It is important to set the data types of sizes of your columns properly. Each column should be set according to the data you expect to load in it, such as integers or characters. For characters and decimals, you need to specify the size of the data.

Note

Be aware of the number of rows you're loading into each table. Managing hundreds of millions of rows requires a lot more care than managing one or two million.

➤ **Data relationships:** If you're storing data in multiple tables, you need to carefully plan how to join the tables together. It is recommended that you design your joins to be based on columns that are integers or smaller.

Caution

Avoid joining on character-based columns, as it may lead to slower performance.

➤ **Data update:** A big consideration in your system is your approach to data updates. As you acquire new data from source systems or third parties, you need to update that data into your system. That may involve appending existing data or doing a complete reload, depending on the strategy you've chosen. Following an append strategy is more complicated, but it leads to faster update performance and helps you avoid changing historical results.

➤ **Reporting and analysis requirements:** This is the main driver behind your analytics system and should be your starting point of the design. Everything you do in your system should be based on the outcomes you are seeking. Spend adequate time thinking through those requirements and make sure your system can meet them.

Creating a table

To create a table in SQL Server, follow these steps:

1. Right-click the Tables folder in the Object Explorer window and choose New Table.

   The table view appears in the Query window, as shown in Figure 8-15.

2. Enter your column name, choose a data type, and specify whether you want to allow nulls in your column.

Note

Nulls in SQL Server are handled in a special way. You cannot join on null columns; if you're looking for nulls, use the `Is Null` clause in your query.

3. Click the X in the top-right corner of the Query window.

   A message box opens asking if you want to save the table.

4. Click Yes, enter the table name, and your table is created.

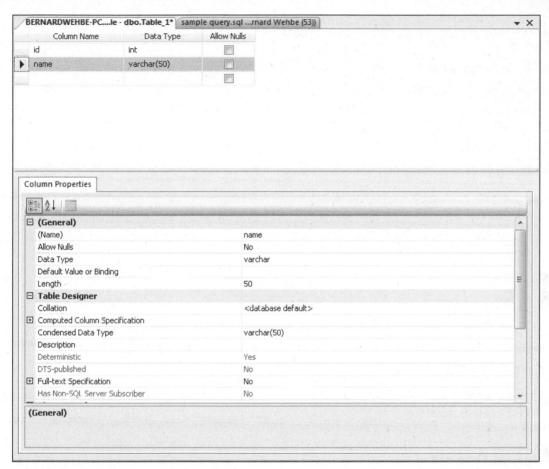

Figure 8-15: A table view.

Figure 8-15 shows a table called *sample* that includes two columns. To see the data and structure of the table, right-click its name in the Object Explorer window and choose Select Top 1000 Rows. A Query window appears (see Figure 8-16).

The top of the New Query window includes the SQL query that returns the top 1,000 rows in the sample table. No data is loaded in the table, so the bottom part of the window shows the table columns but returns no data rows.

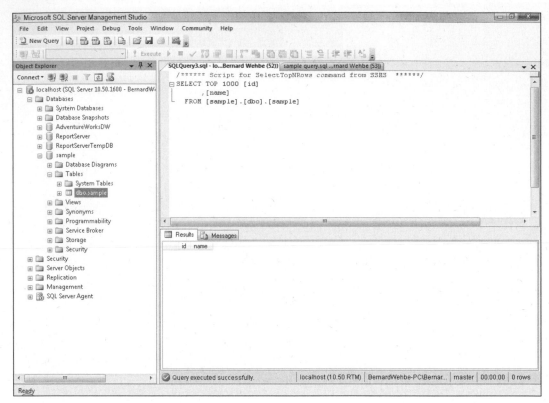

Figure 8-16: A sample table.

Creating a view

To create a view in SQL Server, follow these steps:

1. Right-click the Views folder in the Object Explorer window and select New View.

   The Add Tables dialog box opens, as shown in Figure 8-17, so you can add tables to your view.

   We're using the AdventureWorksDW database for the purposes of these steps.

2. Select the tables you want to add to your view and click the Add button.

   In this case we selected the `DimCustomer`, `DimDate`, `DimGeography`, and `FactInternetSales` tables. SQL Server automatically brings the selected tables in the relationship window and shows the resulting SQL below it.

3. Click the columns that you want to add to your view.

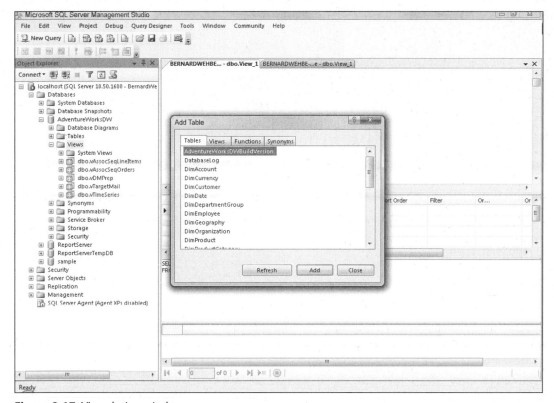

Figure 8-17: View design window.

The columns are automatically added to the SQL statement (see Figure 8-18).

4. After you have finished selecting all the columns and tables you want to add, click the Save icon on the menu bar.

5. Enter the view name.

Make sure to follow a standard naming convention to make it easier to maintain the system. Here are some common conventions for naming objects in SQL server:

- Limit the name to approximately 50 characters (the shorter the name, the better).

- Avoid using spaces in the name. Instead, use *camel case* (using uppercase for the first letter of each word, as in SalesAmount).

- Avoid using numbers and underscores in the name.

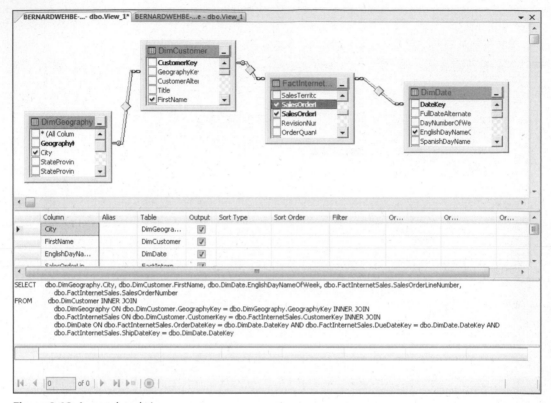

Figure 8-18: A completed view.

So far, you've created the objects you need in your system. In Chapter 9, you discover how to harness the full power of SQL Server with SQL. However, you can get a taste of SQL by right-clicking the view that you created, hovering your mouse over Script Views As, and then choosing Create To ➜ New Query Editor Window. A New Query Editor window opens, as shown in Figure 8-19.

Management Studio automatically creates the syntax needed to replicate the creation of this view. Although you may not fully understand the syntax, it's relatively easy to see what the code is doing. As you become more familiar with SQL, you can leverage Management Studio's ability to create scripts as a starting point for when you want to create your own custom SQL scripts.

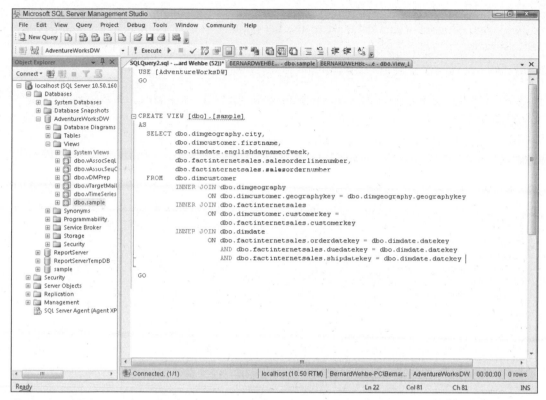

Figure 8-19: The script view output.

Data Importing and Exporting

Most analytics systems include some sort of external data. That data could be in the form of flat file feeds from source systems, or it may be a replicated copy of a source system database. You should carefully consider the data integration needs of your analytics system and work with your system administrators to secure your data feeds.

An important and useful function of SQL Server is its ability to support data integration through SQL Server Integration Services (SSIS). SSIS is a sophisticated and market-leading Extract Transform and Load (ETL) tool. SSIS includes advanced features that allow you to manage complex data integration requirements. In this section we cover some simple functionality to enable you to easily import and export data from and to your SQL Server database. This is a simplified SSIS utility that is accessible from the Microsoft SQL Server Management Studio and includes the ability to connect to multiple types of sources and targets.

Importing and exporting data are functionally the same, with the only difference being the source and target. Taking data out of your database to another target is called *exporting* and bringing data in is called *importing*.

To import data into your SQL Server database follow these steps:

1. Right-click the database in the Object Explorer window, hover your mouse over Tasks, and select Import Data.

   The SQL Server Import and Export Wizard starts.

2. Click Next on the first screen and the Choose a Data Source screen opens, as shown in Figure 8-20.

   You can choose a variety of sources, including flat files, Excel files, ODBC, SQL Server, or other relational databases. We're copying a table from the AdventureWorksDW SQL Server database.

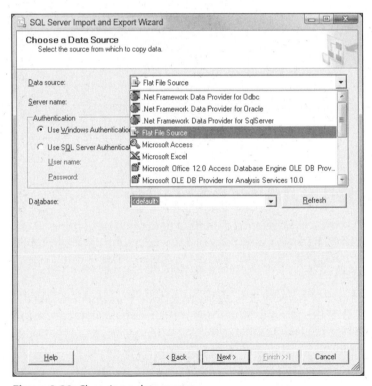

Figure 8-20: Choosing a data source.

3. Choose Microsoft OLE DB Provider for SQL Server as your data source and select the server name and source database. Click Next.

   The wizard presents a new screen where you can choose a destination.

4. Select the right target database, and click Next.

    The Specify Table or Query screen opens, as shown in Figure 8-21. You have two options. You can copy data from other tables or views, or you can write your own query to specify the dataset to transfer over. Use the latter when you want to copy a few columns that are spread over multiple tables in the source system.

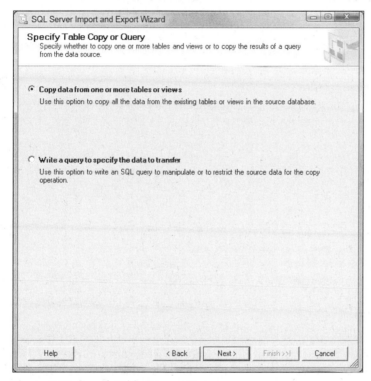

Figure 8-21: Specify Table Copy or Query.

5. Select the Copy Data from One or More Tables or Views option and click Next.

    The Select Source Tables Views screen opens, with a list of tables and views that exist in your source database (see Figure 8-22).

6. Select one or more of those objects and click Next.

7. Choose whether to run the data transfer immediately or save the transfer steps as a package that can be run on demand. Click Next.

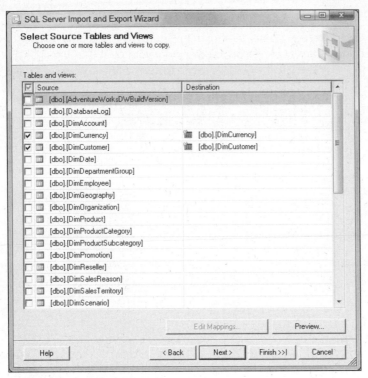

Figure 8-22: Select Source Tables and Views.

8. Click the Finish button.

If you chose to run the data transfer immediately, Management Studio starts the data transfer and displays a progress indicator showing the number of records transferred. If you chose to save the transfer steps as a package, Management Studio creates the package file.

Introduction to SQL

9

In This Chapter

- Starting off with SQL basics
- Going further with advanced SQL concepts

Standard Query Language (SQL) is an industry-standard, fourth-generation programming language designed for working with databases. Most database vendors, including SQL Server, have adopted this language into their implementations, making it easier for data analysts to work on different platforms.

You'll use SQL on a frequent basis. A lot of times that occurs through a reporting interface that translates your requests into SQL. This makes it important for you to at least learn the basics of SQL. Understanding SQL allows you to go beyond the canned reports available to you and develop your own queries directly against the various databases that may exist in your organization.

SQL Basics

Learning SQL is easy after you understand the basic structure of the language. In this section we cover the SQL statements that allow you to retrieve data and then group and filter it.

The Select statement

At its core, SQL revolves around the `Select` statement. This statement enables you to retrieve records from a database table. The basic syntax of a `Select` statement is:

```
Select 'Hello World'
```

To see the `Select` statement in action, open a Query window in Microsoft SQL Server Management Studio with the AdventureWorkdsDW database loaded and run the `Hello World` statement.

 Note Use a single quote in SQL to indicate the beginning and end. Numeric values are entered without quotes in an SQL statement.

The statement returns one row in the result set with the words `Hello World`.

The From clause

The `Select` statement is most often used with the `From` clause. The `From` clause allows you to specify the tables and views you would like to retrieve data from. Here's how you use a `From` clause with a `Select` statement:

```
Select    AccountType, Operator
From    dbo.DimAccount
```

After you add a `From` clause in your `Select` statement, you can call out specific columns you want to return in the output and ask for all columns using the * wildcard:

```
Select    *
From    dbo.DimAccount
```

Note

You can mix columns and constants in your `Select` statement to produce more sophisticated outputs. You can also give aliases to columns or constants by adding a name after each one. Here `Hello World` is repeated in each row in your output and the name of that column is `MyAlias`. The column `Operator` is also renamed to `OperatorName`.

```
Select    AccountType, Operator OperatorName, 'Hello World'
  MyAlias
From    dbo.DimAccount
```

Joins basics

The `From` clause in your query can be extended and made more sophisticated with joins. Joins allow you to bring data from multiple related tables in your database and gives you fine control over how to relate those tables together. There are several types of joins in SQL; in this section we go over the three basic ones:

➤ **Inner:** This is the most often-used join type and, as shown in Figure 9-1, it returns the intersections of two tables or datasets.

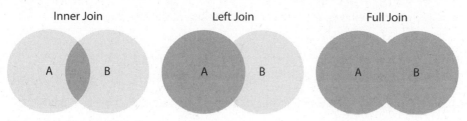

Figure 9-1: Three basic joins.

➤ **Left:** A left join returns all the records in the table on the left of the join and only those related records from the right. You may also perform a right join if you want the opposite outcome. You can stick to a left join to keep things simpler. All you have to do is switch the order of the tables in the left join to achieve the same outcome as a right join.

➤ **Full:** Returns the union of two tables or datasets.

Note

> In the case of a left join or full join, you may get Null columns back for rows that do not have a relationship in the non-primary table or dataset.

When you define a join, you need to also specify the join criteria in your SQL statement. You accomplish this by using the On keyword. To simplify your SQL statement, use an Alias in the join.

```
Select    da.AccountType, da.Operator, ff.Amount
From    dbo.DimAccount da
Join    dbo.FactFinance ff
On    da.AccountKey = ff.AccountKey
```

This query returns two columns from DimAccount and one from FactFinance. The alias given to each table can be specified before every column in your Select statement. (You can skip qualifying a column with an alias if that column name is unique in all the tables in your join.) As a best practice, you should always pre-qualify your columns with the proper alias and use a standard abbreviation to define those aliases.

The Where clause

Use a Where clause in the Select statement to filter the result set and conditionally return specific records. The Where clause is always used in combination with an operator, such as = (equal), <> (not equal), > (greater than), < (less than), >= (greater than or equal to), <= (less than or equal to), Between (within general range).

This SQL statement returns only records with account types equal to Assets.

```
Select    da.AccountType, da.Operator, ff.Amount
From    dbo.DimAccount da
Join    dbo.FactFinance ff
On    da.AccountKey = ff.AccountKey
Where    da.AccountType='Assets'
```

This SQL statement returns only records with amounts greater than or equal to 10.

```
Select    da.AccountType, da.Operator, ff.Amount
From    dbo.DimAccount da
Join    dbo.FactFinance ff
On    da.AccountKey = ff.AccountKey
Where    ff.Amount >=10
```

Grouping

Grouping is a useful SQL feature for analytics. It allows you to aggregate your result set and perform advanced filtering. You perform grouping on your result set by using the `Group By` clause in your `Select` statement. The `Group By` clause is often used with an `Aggregation` function and/or a `Having` clause. Here's a basic `Group By` clause:

```
Select    da.AccountType, sum(ff.Amount) AmountTotal, avg(ff.Amount)
   AmountAverage
From    dbo.DimAccount da
Join    dbo.FactFinance ff
On    da.AccountKey = ff.AccountKey
Group By    da.AccountType
```

This `Select` statement returns a list of values in `AccountType` along with the total amount for each value. This example uses the `Sum` (sum of records) and `Avg` (average of records) `Aggregation` functions. SQL includes several `Aggregation` functions that can be used with a `Group By` clause, including `Count` (count of records), `Min` (minimum value), and `Max` (maximum value).

You can set an advanced filter on a query using the `Having` clause:

```
Select    da.AccountType, sum(ff.Amount) AmountTotal, avg(ff.Amount)
   AmountAverage
From    dbo.DimAccount da
Join    dbo.FactFinance ff
On    da.AccountKey = ff.AccountKey
Group By    da.AccountType
Having    sum(ff.Amount)>=10
```

This `Select` statement returns the `AccountType` records that have a sum of an amount greater than or equal to 10. The difference between this example and a filter applied using the `Where` clause is that the filter is applied after the aggregation.

The Order By clause

The `Order By` clause allows you to set the order of the returned records in your result set. The default sort order in SQL is ascending; you can change that to descending. Here's a basic `Order By` example:

```
Select    da.AccountType, sum(ff.Amount) AmountTotal, avg(ff.Amount)
   AmountAverage
From    dbo.DimAccount da
Join    dbo.FactFinance ff
On   da.AccountKey = ff.AccountKey
Group By    da.AccountType
Having    sum(ff.Amount)>=10
Order By    da.AccountType Asc, sum(ff.Amount) Desc
```

You can specify the Order By clause by referencing the specific column names or the column ordinal as it is listed in the Select clause:

```
Select    da.AccountType, sum(ff.Amount) AmountTotal, avg(ff.Amount)
   AmountAverage
From    dbo.DimAccount da
Join    dbo.FactFinance ff
On   da.AccountKey = ff.AccountKey
Group By    da.AccountType
Having    sum(ff.Amount)>=10
Order By    1 Asc, 2 Desc
```

Selecting Distinct records

The Distinct keyword allows you to return the unique occurrences of the values in your record set without using a Group By clause. This example uses a Distinct keyword in the Select statement.

```
Select    Distinct da.AccountType
From    dbo.DimAccount da
Join    dbo.FactFinance ff
On   da.AccountKey = ff.AccountKey
```

Without the Distinct keyword, AccountType is repeated for every row in FactFinance (that is related to DimAccount). However, with Distinct you would only get the unique occurrences of AccountType.

Tip

A common use of the Distinct keyword is to validate the unique key of a dataset or a table to make sure your understanding of the data matches what exists in your database. Take the DimDate table in the AdventureWorksDW, for example. FullDateAlternateKey is defined, according to the name of the column, as the alternate key for that table. Therefore, running the distinct set of FullDateAlternateKey produces a record count equal to Count (*) on the table (see Figure 9-2). Examining the results in the Results pane of the Query window, you can validate this is true.

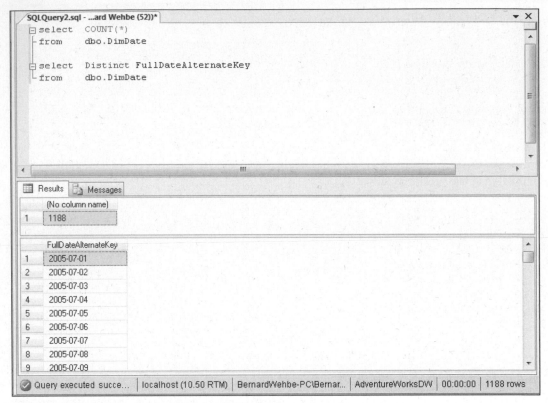

Figure 9-2: Using the Distinct keyword to validate uniqueness.

Selecting Top records

Use the `Top` expression in the `Select` statement (or other data manipulation statements) to allow you to restrict the result set to a number or percent of rows.

This SQL statement returns the top 10 records in the `DimAccount` table:

```
Select    Top 10 AccountType
From    dbo.DimAccount
```

This SQL statement returns the top 10 percent of records in the `DimAccount` table:

```
Select    Top 10 Percent AccountType
From    dbo.DimAccount
```

Advanced SQL Concepts

Now that we've covered the basics, we review some of the more advanced functions in SQL, including data manipulation statements.

The Union operator

As the name implies, the Union operator allows you to combine the result set of two Select statements into one output. There are two variations on this operator: Union and Union All. The difference between the two is that Union returns a distinct output of the result set. Here's how to use the Union All operator:

```
Select    'First Row'
Union All
Select    'Second Row'
Union All
Select    'Third Row'
```

The Select statements with Union or Union All operators can include all the options available to regular Select statements. The only restriction is that the result set in each Select statement must have the same structure.

Case expression

The Case expression is referred to as a Scalar function in SQL. There are several other useful functions in this category and they all follow a similar concept — they are applied on a single value in your result set (or the data you are querying) to manipulate that value. Here's the basic structure of a Case expression:

```
Case
When    <condition>
Then    <output>
Else    <output>
End
```

You can use the Case expression in the Select statement in various places, including the columns list, the join, or the Where clause. This query changes the values of AccountType from Balances to Balance and leaves all other values the same.

```
Select    Case
When AccountType='Balances'
Then    'Balance'
Else    AccountType
   End    ModifiedAccountType
From    dbo.DimAccount
```

Like operator

The Like operator is a versatile SQL function that allows you to perform sophisticated string pattern searching in your query. Here's a basic Like operator:

```
Select    AccountType
   From   dbo.DimAccount
Where    AccountType Like  'Balances'
```

This query returns only records where the AccountType value is exactly equal to Balances. So far this does not seem like anything special; you can achieve the same results using an = (equal) operator. However, the power of the Like operator stems from the use of wildcard characters. SQL Server includes four wildcard characters.

See Table 9-1 for how to use wildcards.

Table 9-1: Examples of Wildcard Characters

Wildcard Character(s)	What It Does	Used with Like	Result
%	Indicates any string	Like 'Ba%' Like '%a%'	Returns all rows where AccountType starts with Ba Returns all rows where AccountType includes the letter a
_	Indicates any single character	Like '_alances'	Returns all rows where AccountType is composed of 8 letters that end with alances
[ ]	Indicates any single character within a specified range	Like '[a-k]alances' Like '[abc]alances'	Returns all rows where AccountType starts with a letter between a and k and ends with alances Returns all rows where AccountType starts with the letter a, b, or c and ends with alances
[^]	Indicates any single character not within a specified range	Like '[^c-k]alances' Like '[^cdf]alances'	Returns all rows where AccountType does not start a letter between c and k and ends with alances Returns all rows where AccountType does not start with the letter c, d, or f and ends with alances

Wildcard Character(s)	What It Does	Used with Like	Result
[ ] and %	Indicates any single character within a specified range combined with any string	Like '[a-k]%'	Returns all rows where AccountType starts with a letter between a and k
[^] and %	Indicates any single character not within a specified range combined with any string	Like '[^abc]%'	Returns all rows where AccountType does not start with the letter a, b, or c

Subqueries

Just as the name implies, a subquery is a query within a query. It can be nested anywhere an SQL expression can be used. In most cases, you can accomplish your objective without the use of subqueries, but they tend to be a style preference. In the following sections, we show you when you'd use a subquery.

In a From clause

The subquery in this example returns all the records that exist both in FactFinance and DimScenario.

```
Select    da.AccountType, sub.ScenarioName, sum(sub.Amount)
From    dbo.DimAccount da
      Left Join (
Select    ff.Amount, ff.AccountKey, ds.ScenarioName
        From    dbo.FactFinance ff
           Join dbo.DimScenario ds
              On ff.ScenarioKey=ds.ScenarioKey
        ) sub
        On da.AccountKey=sub.AccountKey
 Group By    da.AccountType, sub.ScenarioName
```

The result set is left joined to DimAccount. The final output returns all rows from DimAccount and only those rows that match from the subquery.

Correlated subqueries

A correlated subquery means that the subquery runs once for every row in the main query. You can put correlated subqueries in several places inside a Select statement. This subquery runs once for every row in FactFinance and is restricted by the relationship on ScenarioKey with the outer query.

```
Select    Distinct
     ff.AccountKey,
   (
Select    ds.ScenarioName
From    dbo.DimScenario ds
Where    ff.ScenarioKey=ds.ScenarioKey
)
From    dbo.FactFinance ff
```

Note   This query can be much more simply achieved by putting DimScenario in the From clause and creating an inner join on ScenarioKey. The output would be exactly the same. Always avoid making your SQL more complicated whenever possible.

Advanced joins

When you start working in SQL, basic joins work fine for you. However, as you start getting into advanced SQL and sophisticated analytics requirements, you may find you need to go beyond the basics to accomplish your objectives. Depending on your situation, you may need to use one or more of the advanced joins described in this section.

Cross join

A cross join allows you to perform a Cartesian product between two tables returning all combinations of rows. You may want to use this type of join when you're trying to create a list of data combinations to use in a lookup table or on a specialized report. For example, this query results in the unique list of all combinations of AccountTypes and ScenarioNames.

```
Select    Distinct da.AccountType, ds.ScenarioName
From    dbo.DimAccount da
Cross Join    dbo.DimScenario ds
```

Self join

In an SQL statement you may join the same table to itself using different aliases to facilitate a self join. This is mostly used when you have a parent-child relationship in a table. A common example is a hierarchy of some sort (for example, an organization hierarchy). This self join example unravels one level in the parent-child hierarchy in the DimAccount table. To unravel all the levels, you must keep self joining once for every level, restricting the first level to the top-most parent in the hierarchy.

```
Select Distinct a1.AccountDescription, a2.AccountDescription
From   dbo.DimAccount a1
     Join dbo.DimAccount a2
        On a1.AccountKey=a2.ParentAccountKey
Order by 1,2
```

Inner joins

An inner join is not just limited to an equality relationship. Several situations in analytics require you to go beyond that basic relationship and into more advanced ones. This requires a strong ability to visualize data. A common example occurs in what is referred to as a *Type II* dimension. This type of dimension shows a point-in-time snapshot of the data. Take the example of an organization hierarchy. In certain views you may want to see the organization metrics based on how the organization hierarchy looked at the point that metric was taken. In that case, you have to use a between join in your query.

Advanced grouping

SQL includes a very powerful grouping functionality. These functions are most commonly used in analytics and allow you to perform things such as ranking or partitioning your result set. Following is the basic construct of these functions:

➤ **Over Clause:** Used to determine how the dataset should be partitioned and ordered. Inside the `Over Clause`, use the `Partition By` or `Order By` clauses to define the columns involved and the output:

```
Over (Partition By col1, col2, col3)
```

➤ **Window Functions:** The `Over Clause` is used with Window Functions such as `Rank` or `Row_Number`, or with an `Aggregation` function:

```
Select   SalesTerritoryKey, ProductKey,
Sum(OrderQuantity) Over(Partition By SalesTerritoryKey)
SalesTerritoryOrderQuantitySum
From   dbo.FactInternetSales
```

The output of this query returns the sum of `OrderQuantity` by `SalesTerritoryKey` and repeats those numbers for all `ProductKeys` in that `SalesTerritoryKey` (see Table 9-2).

Table 9-2: Over Clause Output

SalesTerritoryKey	ProductKey	SalesTerritoryOrderQuantitySum
9	562	13345
9	482	13345
9	574	13345
9	541	13345
9	535	13345
9	214	13345
9	538	13345
9	537	13345
9	528	13345
6	483	7620
6	477	7620
6	479	7620
6	222	7620
6	480	7620
6	539	7620

Manipulating data

You can perform three basic types of data manipulation activities on your analytics system. After you have learned the basics, you can get more sophisticated with your data updates by combining the other SQL components in this chapter with data manipulation commands to fulfill the requirements.

Insert

An `Insert` statement appends or adds data to a table. There are three primary ways to insert data into a table:

➤ **Insert with values:** This consists of providing a list of values (a single row) that you want to insert into specific table columns:

```
insert into dbo.sample (id, name)
values(1,'sample')
```

➤ **Insert with a `Select` statement:** This involves inserting the result set (multiple rows) of a `Select` statement into a table. This is a fast way to insert large amounts of data into your table:

```
insert into dbo.sample (id, name)
select 1, 'sample'
```

➤ **Using a Select Into statement:** This is used to create and fill a table based on the result set of a Select statement.

```
select 1 id, 'sample' name
into sample
```

Note

The Select **statement can be as sophisticated as you need to accomplish the required transformation.**

Delete and Update

Delete and Update statements allow you to remove or modify rows in a table that fit certain specified conditions. They can get pretty sophisticated and allow you fine control over your data manipulation.

```
Delete
From    dbo.sample
Where   name like 's%'
```

```
Update   dbo.sample
Set    name='testing'
Where    name='test'
```

You can expand the capabilities of your Delete and Update statements by adding joins in the From clause to base your change on values in other tables. We go over some advanced data manipulation patterns specific to analytics in the next chapter.

Creating and Managing SQL Scripts

10

In This Chapter

- Design concepts

- Working with SQL scripts

- Indexing and performance considerations

- SQL solutions to common analytics problems

Analytics systems must procure data from various sources, often in formats that are not necessarily suited for analytics. These data feeds have to be integrated and manipulated to make the output suitable for analytics consumption. In this chapter we go over key concepts and tools to guide you in building an analytics system that is scalable and maintainable.

Design Concepts

Building a successful analytics system requires careful design that stems from experience and lessons learned from prior mistakes. Luckily the industry has now a couple of decades of experience in building these systems. This had led to established best practices to help you avoid the mistakes of the past. In this section we summarize these best practices and give you a foundation to start off on the right foot.

Note

The concepts in this section become important as your system complexity and data volumes grow. When you start your design, you have to assess the scope of your system and decide the level of design sophistication that is necessary to meet your needs.

Stay organized

The most common mistake beginners make when building an analytics system is not being organized. Preparing your data for analytics should be divided into multiple stages. Each stage performs a special purpose in the data preparation process leading up to the final output.

To illustrate the concept, consider the example of a restaurant. You would not put the kitchen equipment where the food preparation occurs in the dining room where customers eat, would you? You want your customers to enjoy their meal without the clutter of the kitchen operations. Inside the kitchen you would separate the area by function to improve efficiency. The same concept is true for your analytics system.

Note

You want to build an analytics system that is easy to reuse. Typically that involves building the data structure and updating the data within it on a regular basis. The data inside that structure can be used to build reoccurring reports or to run *ad hoc* **queries. Once built, these systems are not completely static in terms of their structure and must continuously evolve to keep up with the business changes.**

We recommend separating the tables and scripts into various stages and delineating those stages using a specific naming convention. For a simple system, organize your system in three stages:

➤ **Data extraction:** This stage includes the tables, files, and scripts that are involved in extracting data from the various source systems. Keep this stage simple and light on business logic. For most of your extract, you can rely on a change data capture (CDC) date that outlines the changed data in your system. Otherwise you always have to pull all source data upon every extract, which makes your system slow and degrades performance over time as data sizes grow.

➤ **Data preparation:** This stage includes the tables and scripts that are involved in preparing the data to be inserted in the final output. Most of the system's business logic is in this stage. The final step in this stage is to prepare the incremental data set to be loaded into each table in the final output. So, you should have a mirror table on each Final Output table. Think of this as plating the dishes and setting them out to be picked up by the waiters and delivered to the customers. It may seem like a redundant step to stage your data in a mirror table to your final destination, but there are good reasons for doing so, including data validation, data integrity, consistency, and reusability.

➤ **Data delivery:** This stage includes the tables and scripts that are involved in the final delivery of the data in the analytics system. The delivery steps typically involve updating existing records and inserting new ones. If you completely reload your system every time, you would obviously not have any records to update. We recommend you follow an incremental update strategy to maintain system scalability.

Complex systems require additional categories and phases and more sophisticated processes compared to what we have just outlined. As you feel more comfortable with your analytics system, you can expand on this foundation.

Following a logical organization when building your system can make a big difference in the long run and help keep it maintainable and efficient.

Move data in one direction

The data coming through your analytics system should move from the source systems on down the various phases that you have outlined (see Figure 10-1).

Figure 10-1: Move data in one direction.

Following this principle allows you to ensure data integrity every time you run your script and makes maintenance and troubleshooting easier.

You should also set up your script to run all the components of every phase together. This keeps your design simple and allows you to avoid building tables with incomplete data. Think of each circle in Figure 10-1 as a gateway or checkpoint. The data stops after each of those points and waits for the rest of the data points in that phase to come in. After that is done, you move on to the next phase.

Divide data according to metrics and attributes

When you first build an analytics system, you may be tempted to organize all your data into one large table. At first glance, this may seem like the way to go, but as you get deeper into the process you'll find that this approach has two main limitations:

➤ **Bad performance:** A large table approach leads to bad performance. This is due to several reasons, including unnecessarily repeating data, having to redundantly update that data when changes occur, and increasing the size of data on disk. Performance problems may not show up on day one, but they will creep up as your data volumes increase.

➤ **Lack of flexibility:** Advanced analytics often require multiple metrics that are not always at the same granularity; for example, order count versus order item count. When you lump all the metrics together, you limit your analytics capabilities because you are artificially fitting metrics into one structure.

A more optimal approach is to organize your metrics and attributes separately according to granularity and relationships. Here are two high-level guidelines to follow:

➤ **Separate attributes from metrics.** Attributes are generally strings such as names or descriptions. There is no need for them to be lumped in with metrics. You can put them in their own tables and reference a key relationship to the table that contains your metrics. Figure 10-2 contains a flat reporting table. It's a single table that has the product information, the customer details, and the orders. Figure 10-3 organizes the data into three tables according to relationships. Consider that the Product Name has a misspelling in it and needs to be corrected.

You'd have to update every row in the flat reporting table for the orders that have that product as opposed to one row in the Product table. The impact on performance is massive between the two operations.

Flat Reporting Table
Product Key
Product Name
Product Category
Product Price
Customer Name
Customer Address
Order Count

Figure 10-2: A flat reporting table.

Product
Product Key
Product Name
Product Category
Product Price

Customer Order
Product Key
Customer Key
Order Key
Order Count

Customer
Customer Key
Customer Name
Customer Address

Figure 10-3: Tables organized according to metrics and attributes.

➤ **Organize metrics according to granularity.** Not all metrics have the same granularity. When you're working through your design, consider the various metrics you need in your analytics and take the time to organize them properly. An order can have many order items. If you go the route of a single reporting table (refer to Figure 10-2), you have two choices: Expand the grain of the table down to Order Item, or keep the table as is and add Order Item Count to it. Both options have disadvantages. The first option forces you to allocate Order Count among all the order items, and the second option forces you to lose the ability to see the order items details. The recommended approach to this problem is to break out order item into its own table, as shown in Figure 10-4.

Consider data volumes up front

A common pitfall when designing analytics systems is ignoring future data growth from the start. You must consider the long term when designing your system, because it will typically be around for many years. The primary principles to consider when handling large data volumes are

➤ **Follow an incremental update strategy:** If you want your system to perform well, avoid redundant work. If you run the system today and update all the data up to this point, you don't want to repeat that step the next day if you can avoid it. Updating the system incrementally involves only appending new data that came in since your last update. If done properly, this should speed up data loads and allow you to handle increased data volumes during a short processing window.

Product	Customer Order	Customer
Product Key	Product Key	Customer Key
Product Name	Customer Key	Customer Name
Product Category	Order Key	Customer Address
Product Price	Order Count	

Customer Order Item
Product Key
Customer Key
Order Key
Order Item Key
Order Item Count

Figure 10-4: Adding a Customer Order Item table allows for the addition of granularity to the data.

➤ **Properly index your tables:** A key consideration in analytics is query performance. You may have reports that are hitting your system live. You do not want those reports to perform poorly, because that would lead to a bad user experience. Indexing is the most effective tool you have in SQL for speeding up queries running against large tables. We review indexing concepts in a later section of this chapter.

➤ **Keep your tables narrow:** SQL Server (and relational databases in general) store each row in your table in one location on disk. Therefore, the larger the row, the longer it takes for SQL Server to read or update it. For this reason, keep the tables that have many rows in them narrow. This enables SQL Server to read and write data from these tables much faster and leads to better system performance.

Consider full data reload requirements

Another important factor to consider in your design is the frequency and need for full reloads. Full reloads are not common, but they do occur. Your objective is to minimize them, but if you have a business or technical requirement to support a full reload, your design needs to able to handle such a request. Two primary concerns are related to this:

➤ **Full reload performance:** You can design a system that performs relatively quickly when you're doing incremental updates, but you may find that it's slow when it comes to full reloads. This may be an issue if you have a limited window to perform full reloads. There are several factors to consider when performing a full reload, but the primary one is indexing. Loading a table with multiple indexes is slow in a relational database. The most optimal approach is to drop and re-create your indexes before and after a full reload.

➤ **Source system data changes:** The key question here is, will your system produce the same data after a full reload? That may or may not be the case, depending on the behavior of your source system. Keep in mind that every source system has some data that is overwritten. You have to check your data elements and identify those attributes that cannot be overwritten and avoid doing full reloads on those attributes.

It is not uncommon for analytics systems to have two different scripts — one for incremental load and one for full reload. Take these issues into consideration in your design to avoid painful surprises.

Set up logging and data validation

To make your analytics system robust, you must add some logging and validation capabilities to it. We go over some simple approaches related to these concepts in this section. Think of this as an auditing and quality assurance function.

➤ **Logging:** The purpose of logging is to keep track of your system runs. There are several components to logging in your analytics system. Keep a simple table of your system runs and add initial and modified dates on your tables. Logging can help you look at your system and understand:

- When a run occurred

- How long it took

- What it updated

➤ **Validation:** A key factor in the success of your analytics system is reliability. If you have reports going to various users, including top management, the last thing you want to do is to send them bad numbers. It is in your best interest to do everything you can to increase the reliability of your output. Adding validation steps can help you catch mistakes before they go out for general consumption. Validation involves adding queries to check for the reasonableness of your output. That could take several forms, including:

- Comparing a value against a running average

- Checking a summary of update counts manually or automatically

- Trapping and flagging bad data (data that falls outside a certain range or that violates a certain rule)

Working with SQL Scripts

SQL scripts are automated procedures you develop to tell SQL Server to perform changes to your system. They can be saved in files or stored on the server in the form of stored procedures. These scripts can then be executed on demand or according to a schedule.

We give you an overview of SQL scripting in this section, including outlining scripting patterns that are most commonly used in analytics systems.

The data structure we use in this section involves three SQL Server databases — Orders, Billing, and RevenueAnalytics. Orders and Billing are two source system databases, and RevenueAnalytics is the analytics system. The tables from the source system include Customer, Order, and Product from the Orders system and Payment from Billing, as shown in Figure 10-5. Here is how the three tables work together:

➤ Customer is related to Order via CustomerKey and Product via ProductKey.

➤ Customer and Product are the parents of Order.

➤ The keys to the three tables from the Orders system are also transferred over the ReoccurringPayment table in the Billing system.

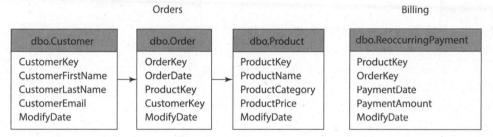

Figure 10-5: Source systems data model.

This example is based on a business that sells products with reoccurring monthly billing — one order results in multiple billings for each customer. The desired output of this system is to produce analytics on reoccurring revenue, including:

➤ Pivoting the data by OrderDate and showing a crosstab of those dates by payment period (defined as the days' difference between OrderDate and PaymentDate divided by 30).

➤ Showing a running cumulative payment amount.

Looking at these requirements, you can outline a simple model for the Data Delivery phase that allows you to produce the required outputs. The model is outlined in Figure 10-6.

Note **Deliver.PaymentPeriod and Deliver.OrderDate do not have load and modify dates because they are static tables loaded one time from Excel or a flat file.**

Data extraction scripting

The data extraction phase should be kept simple and pull in data changes only. All objects in this section should be stored under the same schema in the database. The name of this schema is Extract. Figure 10-7 outlines the tables.

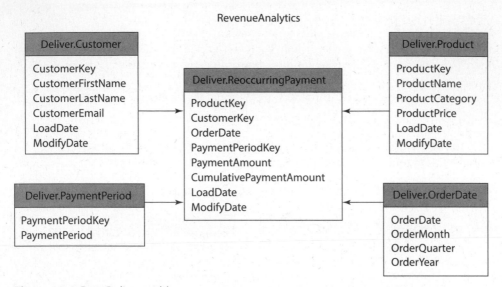

Figure 10-6: Data Delivery tables.

RevenueAnalytics

Extract.Customer	Extract.ReoccurringPayment	Extract.Product
CustomerKey	ProductKey	ProductKey
CustomerFirstName	OrderKey	ProductName
CustomerLastName	OrderDate	ProductCategory
CustomerEmail	CustomerKey	ProductPrice
	PaymentDate	
	PaymentAmount	

Figure 10-7: Extract tables.

The structure of this phase mirrors the source system almost exactly. The only exception is Extract. ReoccurringPayment. The OrderDate is needed because you need to use that column to produce the two analytics requirements outlined in the example definition.

Listing 10-1 shows the data extraction script. It starts by defining a `From` and `To` incremental window of time for updating your system. This window must be maintained in your logging table and updated at the end of each run. Notice that the target table is truncated prior to insert.

Tip   **You can make this step more robust by adding a unique constraint on the Extract. Customer table if you are concerned about data integrity.**

Listing 10-1: Data Extraction

```
Declare    @FromDateTime as datetime,
   @ToDateTime as datetime

--You must set the @FromDateTime and @ToDateTime from the logging table

Truncate Table Extract.Customer

Insert Into Extract.Customer
Select    CustomerKey, CustomerFirstName, CustomerLastName, CustomerEmail
From    Orders.dbo.Customer
Where    ModifyDate Between @FromDateTime and @ToDateTime
```

Listing 10-2 shows a more complicated extract script for ReoccuringPayment. In order to produce the required analytics related to the table in this example, you need the OrderDate and the full payment history for an order. To accomplish this, you make two passes against the ReoccurringPayment table — first to get all the orders that had new or changed payments, and second to grab all of those orders payments.

Listing 10-2: A Complex Data Extraction

```
Declare    @FromDateTime as datetime,
   @ToDateTime as datetime

--You must set the @FromDateTime and @ToDateTime from the logging table

Truncate Table Extract.ReoccurringPayment

Insert Into Extract.ReoccurringPayment
Select      p1.ProductKey, p1.OrderKey, o.OrderDate, o.CustomerKey,
   p1.PaymentDate, p1.PaymentAmount
From    Orders.dbo.Order o
   Join Billing.dbo.ReoccurringPayment p1
      On o.OrderKey=p.OrderKey
   Join (
Select Distinct OrderKey
   Join Billing.dbo.ReoccurringPayment
   Where      ModifyDate Between @FromDateTime and @ToDateTime
            ) p2
   On p1.OrderKey=p2.OrderKey
```

Note

This example makes the extract script more complex in order to handle the required business rules. An alternative approach would be to keep the extract layer simpler, but expand the prepare layer or add a new layer to the system to keep a permanent copy of the source data that you can use to perform the required calculations. In this case, that approach works well because the source systems are replicated to the analytics server and there is no risk of overloading the transactional system.

Data preparation scripting

The objective of the data preparation phase is to set up all the scripts that are necessary to perform the core business functionality of the system and land the desired data into staging tables ready for final merge into the Data Delivery phase tables. The objects in this phase are organized in the Prepare database schema. The tables required mimic the Data Delivery tables, but may also include some intermediate or temporary tables depending on what is necessary to get all the transformations done. Not all the tables in the Data Delivery phase require a step in this phase. Target tables that look very similar to the Extract tables can skip this step or views can be used to put in a logical placeholder for those objects. Figure 10-8 shows the model for this phase. (The Prepare.Customer and Prepare. Product are not included because the target is exactly like the Extract tables; they're for informational purposes only.)

RevenueAnalytics

~~Prepare.Customer~~	Prepare.ReoccurringPayment	~~Prepare.Product~~
~~CustomerKey~~	ProductKey	~~ProductKey~~
~~CustomerFirstName~~	CustomerKey	~~ProductName~~
~~CustomerLastName~~	OrderDate	~~ProductCategory~~
~~CustomerEmail~~	PaymentPeriodKey	~~ProductPrice~~
	PaymentAmount	
	CumulativePaymentAmount	

Figure 10-8: Prepare tables.

There is no typical script for this step because the structure depends on the work required. There are two special business rules required for this example — calculating the PaymentPeriod and and the CumulativePaymentAmount. Listing 10-3 shows the PaymentPeriod calculation. The Cumulative PaymentAmount is illustrated in a later section in this chapter.

Listing 10-3: Data Preparation

```
Truncate Table Prepare.ReoccurringPayment

Insert Into Prepare.ReoccurringPayment
Select   ProductKey,
CustomerKey,
OrderDate,
   Ceiling(DateDiff(dd, OrderDate, PaymentDate)/30.0) PaymentPeriodKey
PaymentAmount,
0 CumulativePaymentAmount --placeholder
From   Extract.ReoccurringPayment
```

Note

The PaymentPeriodKey in this example is calculated using a simple algorithm. The algorithm uses DateDiff to calculate the number of days between the OrderDate and the PaymentDate, and divides that difference by 30 (30.0 is used to make SQL Server output a decimal). The Ceiling function is added to force SQL Server to round up. The resulting output is an integer that represents the period number where a period is 30 days.

Data delivery scripting

In general, during data delivery you follow two common script patterns — append and update, or load an empty table.

Append and update. For an incremental update, there is a specific scripting pattern to follow, as shown in Listing 10-4. Always run your updates before adding new data. If you add new data to your target table first, you end up updating that table again. The pattern involves matching the source and target tables on the business key of the data and checking to see if any attributes have changed for those records that matched. Data is updated for any changes from the source. The second step is to look for all records that do not exist in the target and load them from the source.

Listing 10-4: Append and Update Data

```
Update  t
Set   CustomerFirstName=s.CustomerFirstName,
   CustomerLastName=s.CustomerLastName,
   CustomerEmail=s.CustomerEmail,
   ModifyDate=GetDate()
From   Deliver.Customer t
   Join Prepare.Customer s
      On t.CustomerKey=s.CustomerKey
Where   CustomerFirstName<>s.CustomerFirstName
   Or CustomerLastName<>s.CustomerLastName
   Or CustomerEmail<>s.CustomerEmail


Insert Into Deliver.Customer
Select   s.CustomerKey,
s.CustomerFirstName,
   s.CustomerLastName,
   s.CustomerEmail,
   LoadDate=GetDate(),
ModifyDate=GetDate()
From   Prepare.Customer s
   Left Join Deliver.Customer t
      On t.CustomerKey=s.CustomerKey
Where    t.CustomerKey Is Null
```

Tip

You can use a `Merge` statement to accomplish an append and update to your data, as well.

Load an empty table. You might perform a full data load into a target table, as shown in Listing 10-5. That could occur upon first load or a reload. In those cases, you need to follow a specific scripting pattern to make sure you're performing an efficient load. It involves truncating the table, dropping any indexes, inserting new data, and reloading the indexes.

Listing 10-5: Fulling Loading Data

```
Truncate Table Deliver.Customer

--Check if index exists
If Exists (Select *
From sys.indexes
Where Object_id = Object_Id(N'Deliver.Customer')
And name = N'Indexname')
--Drop index
Drop Index IndexName on Deliver.Customer

Insert Into Deliver.Customer
Select    s.CustomerKey,
s.CustomerFirstName,
    s.CustomerLastName,
    s.CustomerEmail,
    LoadDate=GetDate(),
ModifyDate=GetDate()
From    Prepare.Customer s

--Reload indexes
--Check if index exists
If Exists (Select *
From sys.indexes
Where Object_id = Object_Id(N'Deliver.Customer')
And name = N'Indexname')
    --Create index
Create clustered Index IndexName on Deliver.Customer
    (
    CustomerKey
    )
```

Error handling

Error handling is an important part of your system. Without this function you may end up with bad data loaded into your target tables. There are two primary reasons for error handling:

> ➤ Trapping unexpected errors when they occur and raising an alert to users

> ➤ Handling errors raised purposefully in case specified conditions occur

The primary mechanism for handling errors in SQL Server is using the Try and Catch syntax, as shown in Listing 10-6.

Caution

Without a Try and Catch statement, SQL Server keeps executing any additional steps in your script until all of them are completed.

Listing 10-6: Try and Catch for Error Handling

```
BEGIN TRY
    --Raise error if you are trying to trap a condition or skip this line if you
are not
    RAISERROR('Customer Error',16,1)
END TRY

/****** Error Handling ******/
BEGIN CATCH
    DECLARE @ErrorMessage NVARCHAR(4000);
    DECLARE @ErrorSeverity INT;
    DECLARE @ErrorState INT;

    SELECT @ErrorMessage - ERROR_MESSAGE(),
        @ErrorSeverity = ERROR_SEVERITY(),
        @ErrorState = ERROR_STATE()

    RAISERROR
    (
      @ErrorMessage,
      @ErrorSeverity,
      @ErrorState
    )
END CATCH
```

Beyond Try and Catch, always design your scripts to be restartable to avoid corrupting your system in case it was accidentally run more than once or to allow repopulation of incremental data in case of source system data corruption.

Creating and altering stored procedures

Stored procedures are SQL scripts that are stored in SQL Server. The benefit of using them for loading your analytics system is mostly for organization and ease of maintenance. Once built, you can call stored procedures from other SQL Server components, such as SQL Server Agent Jobs (for scheduling purposes) or by other procedures or applications. To create a stored procedure, follow these steps:

1. Open SQL Server Management Studio and expand the Programmability folder in your database.
2. Right-click the Stored Procedures subfolder and choose New Stored Procedure.

    A Query window opens with a default stored procedure structure, as shown in Figure 10-9.

3. Insert your SQL scripts in between the Begin and End blocks and change the information in between <> according to your needs.
4. When done, click Execute to create the stored procedure.

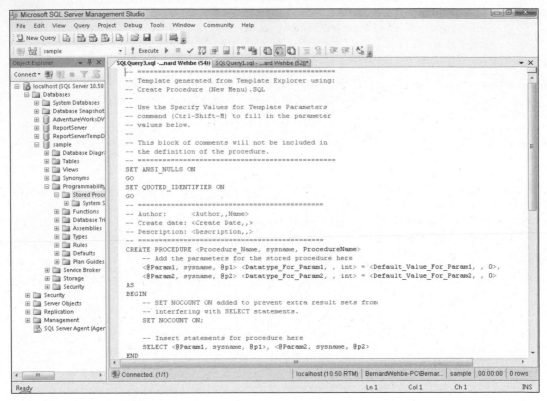

Figure 10-9: Stored Procedures query.

You can see it in the Object Explorer window by refreshing the Stored Procedures folder.

Tip

> You can alter a procedure by right-clicking the procedure and selecting Modify. Make the changes you need and then click Execute.

Indexing and Performance Considerations

Analytics systems performance has two aspects: load performance and query performance. Your objective when building the system should be to optimize both. We delve into the factors involved in achieving that goal in this section.

Understanding index types

Indexing is a very important factor in improving database performance. Indexing helps the database get to the data faster when you're retrieving data in your query. The types of indexes in SQL Server that are important for an analytics system are

➤ **Clustered:** This type of index sorts the data in a table according to the key specified in the index. It is advisable to use a clustered index on your tables and to keep that index as small as possible. Single column integers work best for these types of indexes. You can only have one clustered index in a table.

➤ **Nonclustered:** This type of index builds a pointer to the clustered index of the table if one exists. You can have multiple nonclustered indexes in a table, and you should build these for columns that are used in query joins and search criteria.

➤ **Unique:** A unique index is a constraint that you can place on a column or a group of columns to force SQL Server to allow only unique values or combinations of values in that index.

You should assess the queries in your system and add necessary indexes on your table to optimize performance.

Creating an index

To create an index, follow these steps:

1. Expand the table you're adding the index to in SQL Server Management Studio. Right-click the Indexes folder and choose New Index.

   A New Index window opens, as shown in Figure 10-10.

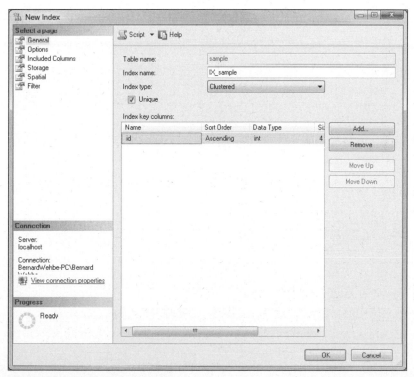

Figure 10-10: Adding a new index.

2. Add a name in the Index Name box, choose the type from the Index Type drop-down list, and specify if the index is unique by selecting the Unique check box.

3. Click the Add button and select the column or columns that should be part of the index.

4. When finished, click OK.

   SQL Server creates your new index on the table. Creating indexes may take some time on large tables.

Dropping an index

You can view your indexes by expanding the Indexes folder in SQL Server Management Studio. If you want to delete an index, right-click it and choose Delete. The Delete Object window opens, as shown in Figure 10-11.

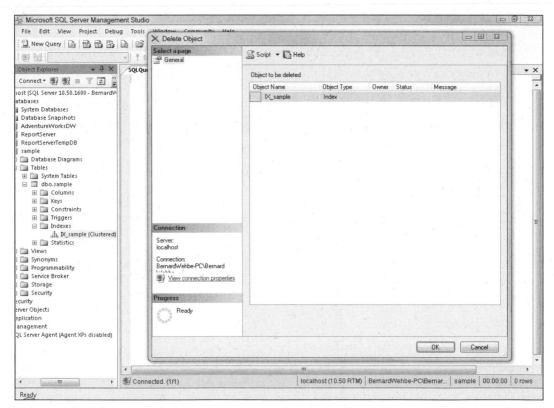

Figure 10-11: Deleting an index.

Make sure the window lists the index you want to delete, and then click OK.

Additional tips and tricks

Several other factors are involved in performance optimization:

➤ **Temp DB usage:** As the name indicates, Temp DB is a temporary database that the SQL Server database engine uses for performing database operations. It's important to understand the role this database plays in queries and SQL scripts, because it impacts your system performance. For example, if you have a large query with a `Union` operator, SQL Server may create a temp table for that operation. If the `Union` is used in an `Insert` operation, you can easily achieve the same result by breaking your `Insert` statement into two.

➤ **Break up complex queries:** Avoid building very complex queries in one SQL statement. Generally, the SQL Server optimizer is quite advanced and can handle a large number of joins in a query; however, it helps to break things down into multiple steps if you notice slow performance. Find the statements that are performing badly and experiment by breaking them into several scripts.

➤ **Avoid multiple passes:** Avoid updating the same table over and over in the same script. For example, if a table has several columns that need to be updated, a common approach beginners take is to write five update statements for each column. Following this approach means you're deleting and inserting the data in the same table five times (because each update is effectively a delete and an insert). When you have situations like these, take a step back and consider a more streamlined design.

SQL Solutions to Common Analytics Problems

As you start diving into using SQL for building analytics, you'll find a lot of requests and questions have a similar pattern. Business users often want to spin the data in similar ways to slice and dice the output and tease out answers that can result in better business decisions. We outline some of the more common questions in this section and describe how you can answer them using SQL.

Creating an Active Members Report

The value of a company often depends on the number of active members it has. Take the example of a social media site. Analysts always talk about monthly active members on the site and the growth, reduction, or flattening out of that figure.

Producing an Active Members Report may seem like an easy undertaking on the surface, but that is not the case. Things get even more complex if you want that report to show a running count of active members over time. To produce this type of report, it's necessary to effectively take a count of active members every day and store that number somewhere. Luckily there is a solution to this problem using SQL.

For the purposes of this example, consider the table shown in Figure 10-12. It represents a table of all the members in the system with the MemberKey along with the StartDate and CancelDate. A Cancelled flag also indicates if the member is active.

Figure 10-12: Members table.

If you think about the data in the Members table, you can deduce that you don't have an entry for each member for each day. Therefore, your query needs to simulate that action. To accomplish that, you have to add a CalendarDate table that has an entry for every day that you want to produce the report for (see Figure 10-13). This table can be created manually in Excel and copied into SQL Server.

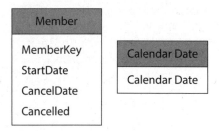

Figure 10-13: CalendarDate table.

When you have the tables set up, you can write the query to produce the Daily Active Member Report (shown in Listing 10-7).

Listing 10-7 A Daily Active Member Report

```
Select    c.CalendarDate, Count(*) DailyActiveMembersCount
From    Member m
      Join CalendarDate c
        On c.CalendarDate between m.StartDate
and Case
When m.Cancelled=1
Then m.CancelDate
Else '12/31/9999'
        End
Group By c.CalendarDate
Order By c.CalendarDate
```

The query in Listing 10-7 is a `Between Join` query that creates additional rows for every row in the CalendarDate table.

Creating a Cumulative Amount Report

Another common analytics request is creating a Cumulative Amount Report. If you take the case of a billing system, for example, the revenue generated from each customer is usually stored at the billing transaction level. However, in many cases, analytics requirements may force you to turn that amount into a running cumulative amount over the lifetime of the customer. Take the example of the reoccurring payment table shown in Figure 10-14.

ReoccurringPayment
ProductKey
CustomerKey
OrderDate
PaymentPeriodKey
PaymentAmount

Figure 10-14: Reoccurring Payment table.

Going from PaymentAmount to CumulativePaymentAmount over the PaymentPeriodKey requires making several passes at the table to aggregate PaymentAmount over every PaymentPeriodKey in sequential order.

The query for solving this problem is a Self Join back into the ReoccurringPayment on the keys of the table; see Listing 10-8.

Listing 10-8: A Cumulative Amount Report

```
Select   r1.ProductKey,
r1.CustomerKey,
r2.PaymentPeriodKey,
Sum(r1.PaymentAmount) CumulativePaymentAmount
From   ReoccurringPayment r1
     Join ReoccurringPayment r2
        On r1.ProductKey = r2.ProductKey
        And r1.CustomerKey = r2.CustomerKey
Where   r1.PaymentPeriodKey<=r2.PaymentPeriodKey
Group By r1.ProductKey, r1.CustomerKey, r2.PaymentPeriodKey
Order By r1.ProductKey, r1.CustomerKey, r2.PaymentPeriodKey
```

The query in Listing 10-8 is a less than or equal to query that simulates running through every combination of ProductKey and CustomerKey, and carries the amount from one PaymentPeriodKey to the next to create the cumulative report.

Creating a Top Performers Report

You may need to create a Top Performers Report related to customers or salespeople. For example, who are your top 10 customers in terms of revenue? Answering this question is relatively easy with SQL. A Group By query works.

If you take the ReoccurringPayment table, you can produce the Top Performers Report using the query shown in Listing 10-9.

Listing 10-9: A Top Performers Report

```
Select   Top 10 CustomerKey,
Sum(PaymentAmount) TotalPaymentAmount
From   ReoccurringPayment
Group By CustomerKey
Order By Sum(PaymentAmount) Desc
```

Creating an Exception List Report

An example of an Exception List Report could be: Who are your customers with a total revenue amount greater than $1,000? You use the ReoccurringPayment table. The SQL query to produce this report is shown in Listing 10-10.

Listing 10-10: A Exception List Report

```
Select   CustomerKey,
Sum(PaymentAmount) TotalPaymentAmount
From   ReoccurringPayment
Group By CustomerKey
Having   Sum(PaymentAmount)>1000
Order By CustomerKey
```

Calling Views and Stored Procedures from Excel

In This Chapter

- Importing Views from SQL Server databases
- Running SQL Server stored procedures from Excel
- Creating dynamic connections with VBA
- Creating a data model with multiple SQL data objects
- Loading SQL Server stored procedures directly into Power Pivot

In Chapter 10, we introduced you to SQL Server databases and discovered how to pull data from SQL Server by creating views and stored procedures.

As you start working with SQL Server views and stored procedures, you'll quickly find the need to bring that data into your reporting models. Luckily, Excel 2013 vastly improves your ability to connect to SQL Server data by providing several methods for integrating external data into your Excel BI solutions.

Importing Data from SQL Server

The option to pull data from SQL Server has been available in Excel for many versions; it was just buried several layers deep in somewhat cryptic menus. This made getting SQL Server data into Excel seem like a mysterious and tenuous proposition for many Excel analysts. With the introduction of the Ribbon in Excel 2007, Microsoft put the Get External Data group of commands right on the Ribbon on the Data tab, making it easier to import data from SQL tables and views.

Using the Get External Data group in Excel allows you to establish an updatable data connection between Excel and SQL. Follow these steps:

1. On the Data tab, select From SQL Server from the From Other Sources drop-down list.

   The Data Connection Wizard opens, as shown in Figure 11-1. You use the wizard to configure your connection settings so Excel can establish a link to the server. The first step is to provide Excel with authentication information.

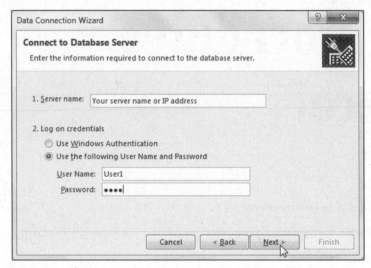

Figure 11-1: Enter your authentication information.

2. Enter the name of your server and username and password. Select the Use Windows Authentication radio button if you use Windows authentication. Click Next when you're done.

   Note the two inputs needed in Figure 11-1:

   - *Server Name:* This is the name of the server that contains the database you want to connect to. You get this from your IT department when they give you access. Your server name will be different from the one shown in Figure 11-1.

   - *Log on Credentials:* These are your login credentials. Depending on how your IT department gives you access, you select either Windows Authentication or SQL Server Authentication. Windows Authentication means that the server will recognize you by your Windows login. SQL Server Authentication means that the IT department created a distinct username and password for you. If you're using SQL Server Authentication, you need to provide a username and password.

   The next step is to select the database with which you are working, as shown in Figure 11-2. Every SQL Server can contain multiple databases. You'll need to have your IT department give you the name of the one you're interested in.

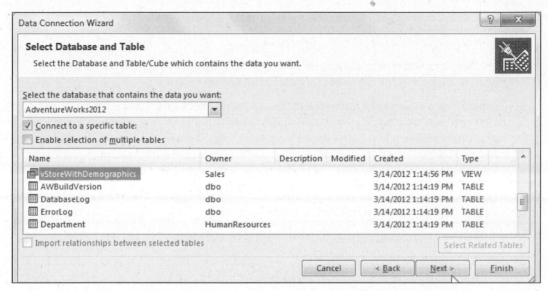

Figure 11-2: Specify your database and then select the table or view you want to analyze.

3. Select the database that contains the data you're using from the drop-down list at the top of the screen. Select the table or view you want to analyze from the box at the bottom. Then click Next.

The next screen in the wizard, shown in Figure 11-3, allows you to enter descriptive information about the connection you've just created.

Figure 11-3: Edit descriptive information for your connection.

4. (Optional) Enter descriptive information for the connection.

   The fields that you use most often are the following:

   - *Friendly Name:* The Friendly Name field allows you to specify your own name for the external source. Enter a name that is descriptive and easy to read.

   - *Save Password in File:* Select the Save Password in File check box if you want your username and password to be stored in the workbook. This allows your connections to remain refreshable when being used by other people. There are obviously security issues with this option, as anyone can view the connection properties and see your username and password. Only use this option if your IT department set you up with an application account; that is, an account created specifically to be used by multiple people.

5. Click Finish to finalize your connection settings.

   The Import Data dialog box opens, as shown in Figure 11-4.

Figure 11-4: Choosing how and where to view your SQL Server data.

6. Choose PivotTable Report to import your data.

7. Click OK.

When the connection is finalized, you can start building your PivotTable.

Note

In most cases, you set up the data connection one time and update it when needed. You can even record an Excel macro to update the data on some trigger or event, which is ideal for automating the transfer of data from SQL Server.

Managing external data properties

When you import external data into a table, you can control a few adjustable properties, which you can find in the Properties dialog box. Click the target table and then click the Properties button on the Data tab to open the External Data Properties dialog box.

Take a moment to familiarize yourself with some useful options in this dialog box:

- **Include Row Numbers:** This property is deselected by default. Selecting this property creates a dummy column that contains row numbers. The first column of your dataset will be this row number column upon refresh.

- **Adjust Column Width:** This property is selected by default, telling Excel to adjust the column widths each time the data is refreshed. Deselecting this option will cause the column widths to remain the same.

- **Preserve Column/Sort/Filter/Layout:** If this is selected, the order of the columns and rows of the Excel range remains unchanged. This way, you can rearrange and sort the columns and rows of the external data in your worksheet without worrying about blowing away your formatting each time you refresh. Deselecting this property will make the Excel range look like the query.

- **Preserve Cell Formatting:** This is selected by default, telling Excel to keep the applied cell formatting when you refresh.

- **Insert Cells For New Data, Delete Unused Cells:** This is the default setting for data range changes. When data rows decrease, you may have errors in adjacent cells that reference your external range. The cells these formulas referenced are deleted, so you will get a #VALUE error in your formula cells.

- **Insert Entire Rows for New Data, Clear Unused Cells:** When the unused cells are cleared instead of deleted, the formula may no longer return an error. Instead, it continues to reference cells from the original range — even though some of them are blank now. This could still give you erroneous results.

- **Overwrite Cells For New Data, Clear Unused Cells:** The third option should be the same as option two when rows decrease as unused cells are cleared.

Passing Your Own SQL Statements to External Databases

If you're a seasoned analyst who is proficient at writing your own SQL queries, you can use the connection properties to write your own SQL statements. This gives you more control over the data you pull into your Excel model, and allows you to perform advanced actions like running SQL Server stored procedures.

Manually editing SQL statements

After you're connected to your external database, you can edit that connection's properties so that it uses use your own SQL statements. Follow these steps:

1. Click the Connections button on the Data tab of the Ribbon.

    The Workbook Connections dialog box opens.

2. Select the connection you want to edit and then click the Properties button.

    The Connection Properties dialog box opens, as shown in Figure 11-5.

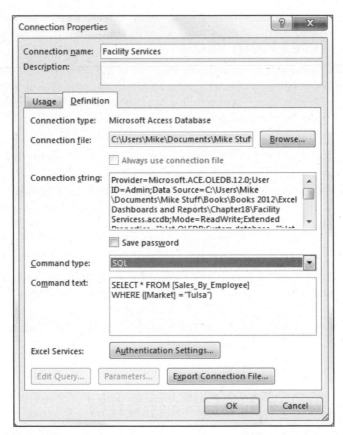

Figure 11-5: On the Definitions tab, select the SQL command type and enter your SQL statement.

3. Click the Definition tab and select SQL from the Command Type drop-down list.

4. Enter your SQL statement in the Command Text box.

    The statement you enter here will typically be a `Select` statement that pulls specific data from one or more tables.

5. Click OK in the Connection Properties dialog box to confirm your change, and then click the Close button on the Workbook Connections dialog box.

Excel automatically connects to the data source and runs your newly added SQL statement. If all goes well, you see your updated data. If Excel encounters an error, a message box opens describing what went wrong.

Note

It's generally a good idea to test your SQL statement before entering it into Excel. This simply means running the SQL statement on the database server to ensure you get the expected results. See Chapter 9 for a refresher on how to create and run SQL statements on the database server.

Running stored procedures from Excel

In Chapter 10, you discovered the benefits of creating stored procedures in SQL Server. The ability to manually enter your own SQL statements into a connection enables you to call a stored procedure right from Excel! For example, the SQL statement in Figure 11-6 executes the SP_MarketSummary stored procedure.

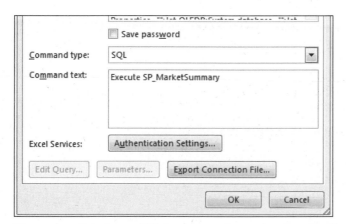

Figure 11-6: Running an SQL Server stored procedure from Excel.

Some stored procedures require parameters (criteria inputs) to run successfully. If your stored procedures require parameters to run, you can simply include them in your SQL statement. Figure 11-7 shows a stored procedure with two parameters: one that passes the required market name, and one that passes the required quarter.

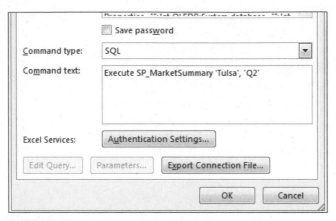

Figure 11-7: Running an SQL Server stored procedure with parameters.

Using VBA to create dynamic connections

You may have noticed that the last few examples have hard-coded the criteria in the SQL statements. For example, in Figure 11-7, Tulsa is specified directly into the SQL statement `Where` clause. This obviously would cause the data being returned to always be data for Tulsa.

But what if you want to select a market and have the SQL statement dynamically change to respond to your selection? Well, you can use a bit of Excel VBA (Visual Basic for Applications) to change the SQL statement on-the-fly. Follow these steps:

1. Designate a cell in your worksheet that will catch the dynamic selection for your criteria.

   For example, in Figure 11-8, cell C2 is where users can select a market. You typically give users a way to select criteria with either a Combo Box or a Data Validation list.

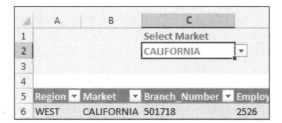

Figure 11-8: Designate a cell that will trap the criteria selection.

2. Click the Connections button on the Data tab.

   Take note of the name for the connection you want to dynamically change.

3. Close the Workbook Connections dialog box and press Alt+F11.

   The Visual Basic Editor opens.

4. Choose Insert ➜ Module.

5. Enter the following code in the newly created module:

```
Sub RefreshQuery()

ActiveWorkbook.Connections("Facility Services").OLEDBConnection.
   CommandText = _
"SELECT * FROM [Sales_By_Employee] WHERE [Market] = '" & _
 Range("C2").Value & "'"

ActiveWorkbook.Connections("Facility Services").Refresh

End Sub
```

This code creates a new macro called RefreshQuery. The RefreshQuery macro points to the correct connection (Facility Services) and specifies the command text for that connection.

The command text is essentially the SQL statement you want the connection to run when triggered. In this example, the command text selects from the `[Sales_By_Employee]` table and sets the criteria for the `[Market]` field to the value in cell C2. The code then refreshes the Facility Services connection.

6. (Optional) Place a button on your worksheet to run your macro.

Click the Developer tab in the Excel Ribbon and select Button Form control from the Insert drop-down list.

7. Select your macro and click OK.

Tip

The Developer tab is hidden by default in Excel. To enable the Developer tab, choose File➔Options➔Customize Ribbon. Select the Developer Tab check box, and click OK. The Developer tab now appears on the Ribbon.

You now have a button that allows for the dynamic extraction of data from your external database based on the criteria you specified (see Figure 11-9).

	A	B	C	D	E
1			Select Market		
2			DENVER	Get Data	
3					
4					
5	Region	Market	Branch_Number	Employee_Number	Last_Name
6	MIDWEST	DENVER	202605	64566	GENZALIS
7	MIDWEST	DENVER	202605	56340	HANKSEN
8	MIDWEST	DENVER	202605	64622	PERKIR
9	MIDWEST	DENVER	202605	64622	PERKIR
10	MIDWEST	DENVER	202605	64566	GENZALIS
11	MIDWEST	DENVER	202605	51345	HANDLE
12	MIDWEST	DENVER	202605	4505	BEALIY
13	MIDWEST	DENVER	202605	4505	BEALIY

Figure 11-9: You now have an easy-to-use mechanism to pull external data for a specified market.

Creating a Data Model with Multiple SQL Data Objects

In Chapter 2, you discovered the internal Data Model, which allows you to analyze multiple data tables in a single PivotTable. That functionality extends to external datasets. This gives you the power to use a normalized set of tables from an external database in an analysis cube. If you're unfamiliar with the internal Data Model, turn to Chapter 2, which gives you the foundation you need.

To understand the benefit of using external data in a Data Model, follow these steps:

1. On the Data tab, select From SQL Server from the From Other Sources drop-down list.

    The Data Connection Wizard opens, as shown in Figure 11-10.

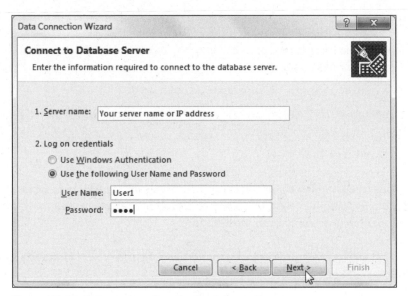

Figure 11-10: Enter your authentication information.

2. Configure your connection settings (server name, username, and password) so Excel can establish a link to the server. Click Next.

    The Select Database and Table screen of the wizard appears, as shown in Figure 11-11.

3. Select the database with which you are working, and then select the Enable Selection of Multiple Tables check box.

4. Select all the tables and views you want imported into the workbook Data Model and then click Next.

    The Import Data dialog box, shown in Figure 11-12, opens.

Figure 11-11: Select the Enable Selection of Multiple Tables check box.

Figure 11-12: Remove the check mark next to Import Relationships Between Tables.

5. Click the drop-down arrow next to the Properties button and remove the check mark next to Import Relationships Between Tables.

   This ensures that Excel does not error out because of misinterpretations of how the tables are related. In other words, you want to create relationships yourself.

6. Select the PivotTable Report radio button and then click OK to create the base pivot.

7. Click the Relationships button on the Data tab.

   The Manage Relationships dialog box opens as shown in Figure 11-13.

8. Create the needed relationships, then click Close.

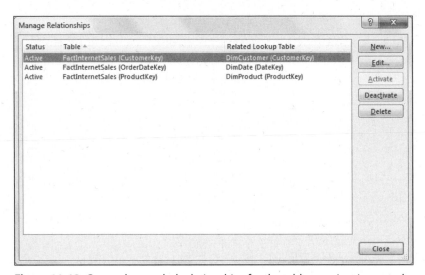

Figure 11-13: Create the needed relationships for the tables you just imported.

In just a few clicks, you've created a powerful platform to build and maintain table PivotTable analysis based on multiple data objects in an SQL Server database (see Figure 11-14).

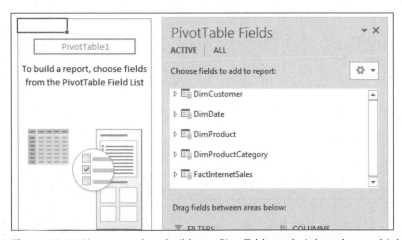

Figure 11-14: You are ready to build your PivotTable analysis based on multiple SQL Server tables and Views.

Note

In addition to pulling from a single SQL Server database, you can add other sources to the Data Model, including Access tables, other SQL Server database tables, Oracle tables, and dynamic text files. If you can create a connection to it, you can add it to the Data Model. The ability to merge disparate data sources into one analytical engine is huge.

Calling Stored Procedures Directly from Power Pivot

In Chapter 4, you explored some of the ways to pull data from SQL Server directly into Power Pivot. This works great for tables and views, but there is no way to call a stored procedure without writing an SQL statement.

Luckily, Power Pivot gives you the option of writing your own SQL statements. Follow these steps:

1. Open the Power Pivot window and click the From Other Sources button on the Home tab.

   The Table Import Wizard opens.

2. Select the Microsoft SQL Server option and click Next.

   The Table Import Wizard asks for all the information it needs to connect to your database (see Figure 11-15).

Figure 11-15: Provide the basic information needed to connect to the target database.

3. Provide the following information to connect to your database:

    - *Friendly Connection Name:* The Friendly Connection Name field allows you to specify your own name for the external source. Enter a name that is descriptive and easy to read.

    - *Server Name:* This is the name of the server that contains the database you're trying to connect to. You get this from your IT department when they give you access.

    - *Log On to the Server:* These are your login credentials. Depending on how your IT department gives you access, you select either the Use Windows Authentication or Use SQL Server Authentication radio button. Use Windows Authentication means that the server will recognize you by your Windows login. Use SQL Server Authentication means that the IT department created a distinct username and password for you. If you're using Use SQL Server Authentication, you need to provide a username and password.

    - *Save My Password:* Select the Save My Password check box if you want your username and password to be stored in the workbook. This allows your connections to remain refreshable when being used by other people. There are obviously security issues with this option, as anyone can view the connection properties and see your username and password. You should only use this option if your IT department set you up with an application account; that is, an account created specifically to be used by multiple people.

    - *Database Name:* Every SQL Server can contain multiple databases. Enter the name of the database you are connecting to. You get this from your IT department when they give you access.

4. After you enter all the pertinent information, click Next.

    The next screen of the wizard (see Figure 11-16) gives you the choice of selecting from a list of tables and views, or writing your own custom query using SQL syntax.

5. Select the Write a Query That Will Specify the Data to Import radio button and click Next.

6. Enter a valid SQL statement into the SQL Statement box (see Figure 11-17).

    Instead of writing a simple `Select` statement, you can take advantage of an existing stored procedure. In this example, we're calling the `SP_GetEmailList` stored procedure.

Tip

You can also enter a friendly name for your custom query. This name becomes the identifier within Power Pivot for the imported data.

7. Click Finish to start the import process.

Once processing is complete, you'll see the results of your stored procedure on a new tab in the Power Pivot window. Like all other connections in Power Pivot, your custom query can be refreshed, effectively triggering the stored procedure to run again and return updated results.

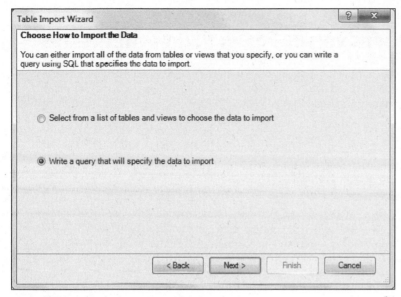

Figure 11-16: Choose to write your own query.

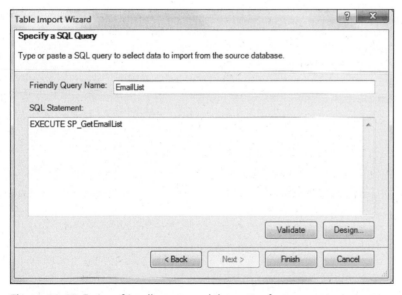

Figure 11-17: Enter a friendly name and the syntax for your custom query.

Excel connections versus Power Pivot connections

In this chapter, you created a connection via the Excel Ribbon interface and the Power Pivot interface. Although they both seem to be doing the same thing, it's important to note that Excel connections and Power Pivot connections are two different things.

Excel connections are used to bring data into the Excel workbook. These connections can exist without ever touching the Power Pivot Data Model. You can edit, update, and fully configure Excel connections.

Power Pivot connections are designed to be used in the internal Data Model and not in the Excel work-book. However, Power Pivot connections must be linked to an Excel connection. This means that when you create a connection using Power Pivot, an Excel connection is automatically generated even though the connection was created for the internal Data Model. Because of this dependence on an Excel connec-tion link, Power Pivot connections cannot be edited or configured. So, for example, if you create a custom query to run a stored procedure in Power Pivot, you cannot change the SQL syntax as you would with an Excel connection. You have to delete the connection and rebuild it.

For this reason, it's often best to create an Excel connection and simply add the connection to the Data Model (versus creating the connection directly in Power Pivot), especially if you're using SQL statements or VBA to dynamically change the connection string. Using an Excel connection enables you to edit and con-figure as needed.

To add an existing Excel connection to the Data Model, click the Connections button on the Data tab. Choose your Excel connection in the Workbook Connections dialog box, click the drop-down arrow next to the Add button, and select Add to the Data Model.

12

Understanding Reporting Services

In This Chapter

- Getting to know Reporting Services

- Building Reporting Services solutions

- Deploying reports

- Managing subscriptions

SQL Server Reporting Services (SSRS) is a robust, flexible, and fully capable enterprise-grade reporting tool. It's important to understand that SSRS is a reporting tool — not a dashboarding tool. *Dashboarding* refers to interactive analytics applications delivered over the Web to your desktop, tablet, or smartphone that allow you to slice and dice predefined data views that represent your most important metrics. *Reporting*, on the other hand, indicates a somewhat static presentation of the data with some parameterized options and minimal navigation functionality between reports. Reporting functionality is geared toward mass consumption in the form of e-mail subscriptions or an on-demand, browser-based review of the data.

This chapter gives you a high-level overview of SSRS and provides a solid understanding of what SSRS can do for you.

Reporting Services Overview

You may find it difficult to comprehend why you should make the leap from Excel reporting to the unfamiliar world of SSRS. The truth is that SSRS has several strengths and advantages that you should consider:

> **Easier build-out of automated SQL reporting:** Because SSRS is closely integrated into the SQL Server environment, you can build automated reporting mechanisms much easier than you can with Excel. Native links between SSRS and SQL Server bypass the need for the management of external data connections, or any sort of VBA scripting. SSRS allows for the

automated processing of stored procedures. This gives your clients the most up-to-date reporting data with on-demand report execution.

➤ **No need for SharePoint and Excel services:** SSRS reports don't require the extra layers of SharePoint server and Excel services. Requiring only a basic SQL Server environment, organizations can build and distribute robust reporting mechanisms without the additional cost of SharePoint.

➤ **No need to install Silverlight:** Power Pivot and Power View both require your clients to install Silverlight (Microsoft's version of Flash) to run properly. SSRS has no such requirement.

➤ **Implementation of dynamic filtering:** Although query filtering can be achieved with Excel data connections, passing dynamic filters takes additional effort in the way of VBA scripting. And because VBA can't be utilized on SharePoint, any Excel report using dynamic filters can't be published to the Web. As a result, most Excel reporting mechanisms extract huge blocks of data from SQL Server databases in order to ensure all the data that will possibly be needed is included. SSRS reports, on the other hand, run in the SQL Server environment where dynamic filtering is supported. This allows your published reports to run faster because they can pull only the data requested by changing filters on the fly.

➤ **Built-in user authentication:** SSRS reports can piggy-back on SQL Server's user logins and database roles. This effectively lets you leverage SQL Server authentication to better manage who can see which reports.

➤ **Ability to export to multiple file formats:** SharePoint and Excel services allow you to export reports only to Excel. SSRS provides multiple export options, including PDF, Excel, CSV, and Text File.

Reporting Services includes four major components: server, development environment, database repository, and Web portal. Each component plays a part in delivering SSRS solutions.

➤ **Server component:** The SSRS server component is the central engine behind the reporting service. Your database administrator typically performs the configuration of the SSRS server component. Most IT departments already have SSRS up and running. You just have to ask for the rights to build and publish SSRS reports.

➤ **Development environment:** SSRS solutions and reports are developed using the SQL Server Business Intelligence Development Studio, which is part of the Microsoft Visual Studio environment. This tool allows you to develop business intelligence applications including SSRS. You need to ask your IT department about installing Microsoft Visual Studio environment.

➤ **Database repository:** SSRS requires an SQL Server instance in order to create the service repository. The repository contains the metadata required to store all the reports and subscription details. The SSRS database repository is named ReportServer by default. Most IT departments running SSRS don't change this name. However, you'll want to confirm the name of the SSRS database with your own IT department.

➤ **Web portal:** SSRS includes a Web portal, which allows you to view reports and manage subscriptions. This portal is the primary user interface for the tool, and it allows you to perform certain administrative functions such as organizing reports into folders, assigning permissions for viewing certain reports, and configuring subscriptions and settings.

Developing a Reporting Services Report

In this section, you explore the mechanics of developing a Reporting Services report from scratch. Follow these steps to start an SSRS project file, define a data source connection, and build a basic layout for your report:

1. Open SQL Server Business Intelligence Development Studio and choose File ➜ New ➜ Project.

2. In the New Project dialog box (see Figure 12-1), select Report Server Project from the list of Visual Studio installed templates, enter a name for your project, and then click OK.

   Visual Studio creates a new SSRS project and opens the Solution Explorer, as shown in Figure 12-2. Here, you see three folders: Shared Data Sources, Shared Data Sets, and Reports.

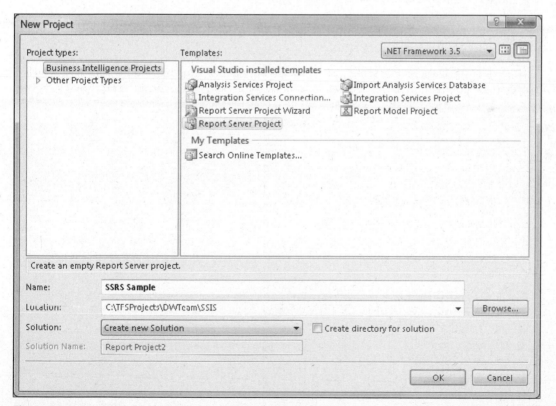

Figure 12-1: Open SQL Server Business Intelligence Development Studio and start a new Report Server Project.

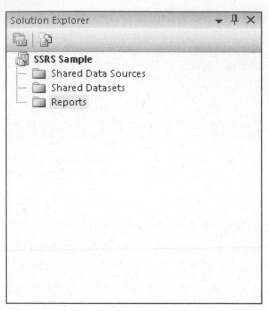

Figure 12-2: The Solution Explorer for your SSRS project.

3. Right-click the Reports folder in the Solution Explorer and choose Add New Report. When the Report Wizard opens, click Next.

The Select the Data Source screen of the wizard appears, as shown in Figure 12-3. Next you'll define the connection to the SQL Server database you plan to use for sourcing the report data.

Figure 12-3: The Select the Data Source screen.

4. Select the New Data Source radio button, enter a name for your connection in the Name box, select Microsoft SQL Server from the Type drop-down list, and click Edit.

   The Connection Properties dialog box shown in Figure 12-4 opens.

Figure 12-4: The Connection Properties dialog box.

5. Enter your server name in the Server Name box and select the database you're connecting to. Click OK when you're done.

   You're taken back to the Select the Data Source screen. (Refer to Figure 12-3.)

6. Select the Make This a Shared Data Source check box and then click Next.

   The Design the Query screen of the wizard appears. Here you can use the Query Builder to build the proper query for your report. (If you're unfamiliar with Query Builder, see Chapter 9.)

7. Click the Query Builder button to open the Query Designer window.

8. In the Query Designer window (see Figure 12-5), choose the tables and views you want to add to your query and select the columns that will appear in the report.

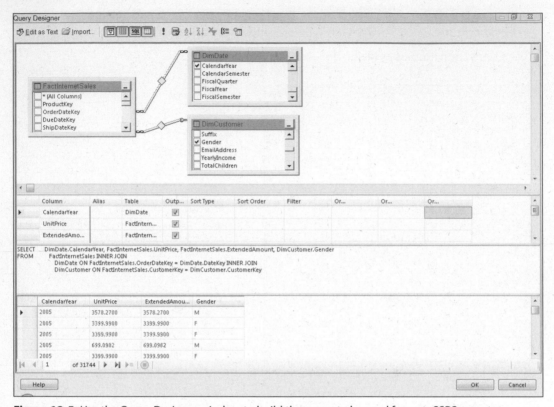

Figure 12-5: Use the Query Designer window to build the query to be used for your SSRS report.

9. Click OK when you're done designing your query. The Click Next in the Report Wizard.

   The Select the Report Type screen of the wizard appears, as shown in Figure 12-6. This screen gives you two options for the layout of your report:

   • *Tabular* produces a report that has columns only.

   • *Matrix* builds a crosstab report that has rows and columns.

10. Choose the appropriate layout for your report and then click Next.

   For this example, we selected the Matrix report type.

   The Design the Matrix screen of the wizard appears, as shown in Figure 12-7.

11. Move the desired fields from the Available fields list box to the Columns, Rows, and Details list boxes. Click Next.

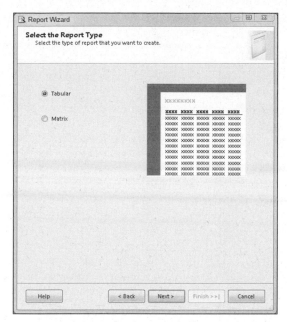

Figure 12-6: The Select the Report Type screen.

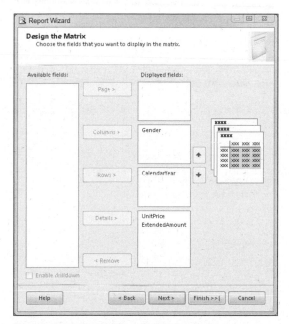

Figure 12-7: The Design the Matrix screen.

12. In the Choose the Matrix Style screen of the wizard (see Figure 12-8), select the style theme for your report and then click Next.

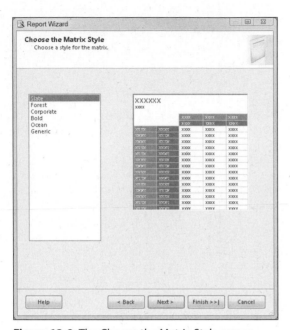

Figure 12-8: The Choose the Matrix Style screen.

13. Check the summary of your configurations and enter a name for your report and click the Finish button.

    Upon completion, you're taken to your SSRS project, where you see a Design tab, as shown in Figure 12-9.

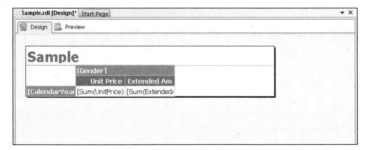

Figure 12-9: The Report Design tab.

14. When you're happy with the report design, click the Preview tab to see the final report outcome. (See Figure 12-10.)

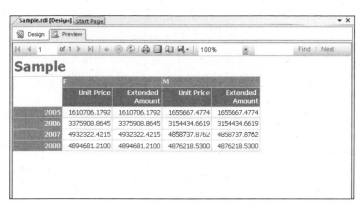

Figure 12-10: You can see a preview of your report by clicking the Preview tab.

The Report Preview window shows the report exactly as it will be presented on the client's browser. You can keep modifying the report in the Design tab and switch to the Preview tab to see your changes in real time.

Defining a shared data source

In the previous section we showed you how to define the data source as a shared data source with the Report Wizard. When you define a data source as a shared data source, you're essentially creating a template of sorts. This template contains all the information for connecting to the specified data source. Any new reports you create within your SSRS project can be pointed to that template (the shared data source).

This way, if you need to make any changes to your data source connection, you can simply make the change in the one shared data source. The change will take effect for all the reports in your project.

To create a new shared data source, follow these steps:

1. Right-click the Shared Data Sources folder in the Solution Explorer window and select Add New Data Source.

2. In the Shared Data Source Properties dialog box (see Figure 12-11), enter a descriptive name, select the type of connection you want, and then click Edit.

   The Connection Properties dialog box opens. (Refer to Figure 12-4.)

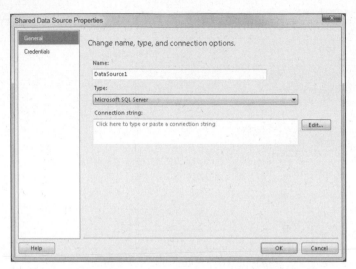

Figure 12-11: Shared Data Source Properties dialog box.

3. Enter the server name and select the database to connect to.

4. Click OK in the Connection Properties dialog box, and then click OK again in the Shared Data Source Properties dialog box.

   The new source is now available under the Shared Data Sources folder in the Solution Explorer window.

Defining a shared dataset

Shared datasets are essentially queries that are defined once in your reporting solutions and used multiple times in the same report or different reports. Similar to shared data sources, a shared dataset can be thought of as a template of sorts that can be used in any new report you create in an SSRS project. Shared datasets come with a couple of advantages:

➤ **Improved performance:** Shared datasets can improve performance because they help avoid sending the same queries to the database multiple times. This can be accomplished by caching the dataset if necessary.

➤ **Improved maintainability:** Shared datasets are defined one time and used in different reports, so any changes required to the query for the dataset only needs to be changed one time.

To create a shared dataset, follow these steps:

1. Right-click the Shared Datasets folder in the Solution Explorer window and select Add New Dataset.

   The Shared Dataset Properties dialog box opens, as shown in Figure 12-12.

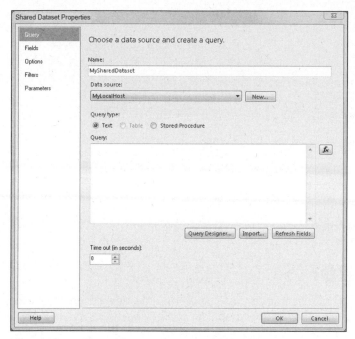

Figure 12-12: Shared Dataset Properties dialog box.

2. Select a query type: Text, Table, or Stored Procedure.

   - *Text:* Allows you to build your own custom SQL statement to get the results you need

   - *Table:* Allows you to point an existing table on the data source

   - *Stored Procedure:* Allows you to use the results from an existing stored procedure

   For this example, we selected Text.

3. Click the Query Designer button to build your query.

   The Query Designer window opens. (Refer to Figure 12-5.)

Tip

You can also enter the query for the dataset directly in the Query box (shown in Figure 12-12) to bypass the Query Designer.

4. In the Query Designer window, choose the tables and views you want to add to your query and select the columns that will appear in the report. Click OK to close the Query Designer window.

5. Click OK in the Shared Dataset Properties dialog box to finalize your new dataset.

   At this point, you can navigate to the Shared Datasets folder in the Solution Explorer to see your newly created shared dataset. (See Figure 12-13.)

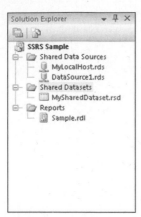

Figure 12-13: A new shared dataset in the Solution Explorer window.

Deploying Reports

Now that the development process of the report is done, you can publish the report to be accessed by your users. In this section, we show you how to start populating the Reporting Services portal with a report. After the report is deployed, you can send a link to the users and assign security access.

The deployment process

Report deployment is managed from SQL Server Business Development Intelligence Studio. Follow these steps:

1. Right-click the solution name and select Properties.

   The Property Pages window opens, as shown in Figure 12-14.

Note

The Property Pages window is named for your specific solution. Figure 2-14 shows the SSRS Sample Property Pages window because our solution is named SSRS Sample.

2. Configure the options for your project, including the following:

   - *TargetDatasetFolder:* This folder holds the shared datasets. You typically want this to be different than the report folder, because only administrators have access to this folder.

   - *TargetDataSourceFolder:* This folder holds the data sources. Again, you typically want this to be different than the report folder, because only administrators will have access to this folder.

   - *TargetReportFolder:* This folder holds your published reports. You may have several folders and subfolders according to how you want to organize your reports. Organize reports by subject area so that you can grant each business function access to only their reports.

   - *TargetServerURL:* This is the URL of the reporting server. The format is as follows: `http://localhost/reportserver`. Replace `localhost` with the exact server name. Replace `reportserver` with the name of the server location where you will publish your SSRS reports.

Figure 12-14: Property Pages window.

3. Click OK.

4. In the Solution Explorer window, right-click the name of your solution and select Deploy.

Your reports and data sources are deployed to the server.

You can open the Reporting Services administrative portal by entering the URL for your reporting services server into your favorite browser. In the Reporting Services portal, you can find your newly published report along with all your previously published reports and data sources. (See Figure 12-15.)

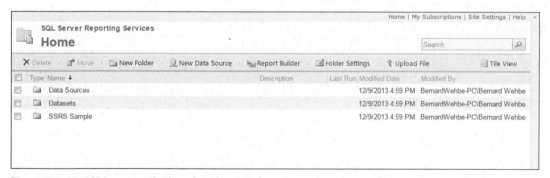

Figure 12-15: SSRS reports deployed to the portal.

Accessing reports

The report can now be accessed by your users. You have the option of allowing anyone in the organization to see your report or restricting access to a specific user or group. We discuss security in the next section. The users can see the report by clicking a URL that you send them. (See Figure 12-16.)

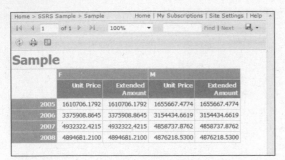

Figure 12-16: Accessing reports in the SSRS portal.

SSRS security

Securing your reports is an important step in the report deployment process. You want to be sure to comply with your organization's security procedures and restrict report access to only those users who are supposed to see that information. The best approach is to set up Active Directory groups for the various business departments in your organization and give those groups access to the reports at the folder level.

To set up security at the folder level, follow these steps:

1. From the Home screen of the SSRS portal, select the folder you want to secure and click the Folder Settings button.

   You are taken to the Security tab (see Figure 12-17).

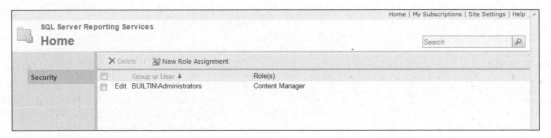

Figure 12-17: SSRS portal folder security.

2. Click the New Role Assignment button. Enter the user or group name in the input box at the top and select the role you want to assign the user. (See Figure 12-18.)

   For example, if you want your business users to only be able to view reports, select the Browser check box.

3. Click OK.

   You now see the new role you added on the Security tab.

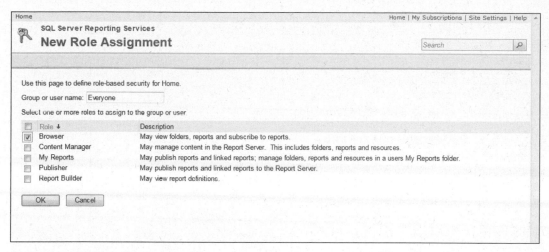

Figure 12-18: Add a role assignment.

Managing Subscriptions

Subscriptions, a powerful feature of SSRS, allow your users to receive any reports that you create via e-mail on a scheduled basis or whenever the underlying data in the report changes. In this section, we walk you through setting up the various types of subscriptions in the SSRS portal and highlight how you can take advantage of this feature.

Before activating subscriptions, you need to specify the credentials to use when the target report is run unattended. That is to say, when the report is automatically run from the system.

Follow these steps to store the credentials used to run the report:

1. Open the Reporting Services administrative portal by entering the URL for your reporting services server into your favorite browser.

2. Click the Data Sources folder and then click the data source for your report.

3. In the Properties window for the selected data source, select the radio button next to Credentials Stored Securely in the Report Server. (See Figure 12-19.)

4. Enter your username and password and select the Use As Windows Credentials When Connecting to the Data Source check box.

5. Click the Test Connection button to make sure you have access. When the test succeeds, click Apply to apply the changes.

After you've ensured that the credentials for the report have been stored, go to the report you want to subscribe to. Hover your mouse over the report and when the drop-down list appears, click Subscribe. (See Figure 12-20.)

✕ Delete   ☞ Move   🔳 Generate Model

Properties

Subscriptions

Dependent Items

Security

Name: MyLocalHost

Description:

☐ Hide in tile view

☑ Enable this data source

Data source type: Microsoft SQL Server   ▼

Connection string: Data Source=localhost;Initial
                      Catalog=AdventureWorksDW

Connect using:

○ Credentials supplied by the user running the report

　　Display the following text to prompt user for a user name and password:

　　Type or enter a user name and password to access the data source

　　☐ Use as Windows credentials when connecting to the data source

● Credentials stored securely in the report server

　　User name: admin

　　Password: ••••••••

　　☑ Use as Windows credentials when connecting to the data source

　　☐ Impersonate the authenticated user after a connection has been made to the data source

○ Windows integrated security

○ Credentials are not required

[Test Connection]

[Apply]

Figure 12-19: Configure the report data source to store credentials on the server.

Home

SQL Server Reporting Services
SSRS Sample

📁 New Folder   📊 New Data Source   📊 Report Builder   📝 Folder Settings   ⬆ Upload File

📄 Sample   ▼

　　　Move
✕　Delete
📊　Subscribe...
📋　Create Linked Report...
　　　View Report History
🔒　Security
　　　Manage
⬇　Download...
📝　Edit in Report Builder

Figure 12-20: Select the Subscribe option.

The Subscription Settings window shown in Figure 12-21 appears. Here, you can apply the following subscription settings:

➤ **Choose a delivery method.** You can choose to have the report e-mailed do you. To enable e-mail delivery, you need to configure the E-Mail Settings in the Reporting Services Configuration Manager. Talk to your system administrator to get the e-mail information details required in this window. Alternatively, you can choose to have the report sent to a specified shared directory as archived PDF or Excel files.

➤ **Define a schedule.** Click the Select Schedule button in the Subscription window to see several options for setting up a schedule. These options are similar to those you see in an Outlook calendar appointment. Set the schedule you would like for receiving the report and then click OK.

➤ **Set parameters for subscriptions.** If your report has parameters, you can specify a value for these parameters in the Subscription window. Parameters allow you more control over what each subscription receives. Using the feature, you can build the report once and use it for different subscriptions by specifying the parameter value for each.

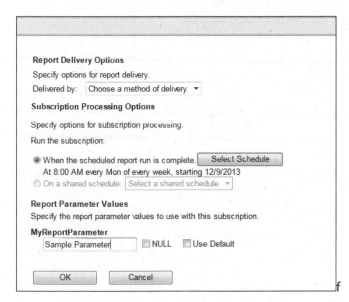

Figure 12-21: The Subscription Settings window.

Reporting Services best practices

As we round out this chapter on Reporting Services, it's worth taking a moment to review some best practices you can follow to ensure successful reporting adoption:

- **Keep it simple.** Complexity is the enemy of user adoption when it comes to information. Always keep your reports simple and easy to understand.

- **Include standard metadata.** Be sure to include metadata and methodology definition in your reports. The best approach is to drive your metadata off a central repository that allows you to define your metrics and attributes once and then reuse them on different reports.

- **Include detailed data to back up your graphs.** Sometimes using graphs makes it easier to spot trends and anomalies; however, most people need the underlying data for further analysis and confirmation. Make it a habit to give users access to graph data in a tabular format to avoid confusion and to increase user adoption.

- **Take advantage of advanced formatting.** SSRS has several advanced formatting options, including multi-axis support for graphs and exception highlighting. Be sure to explore these advanced options and take advantage of them to make your reporting more relevant to users' business needs.

- **Keep text and formatting consistent.** One of the main turnoffs for users is inconsistency with how terms and definitions are presented, as well as an inconsistent approach to building reports. Make sure you adopt strict standards when it comes to building your reports so that they all have the same look and feel even if they're built by different developers.

13

Browsing Analysis Services OLAP Cubes with Excel

In This Chapter

- Understanding Analysis Services OLAP cubes

- Connecting to an OLAP data source

- Creating offline cubes

- Using cube functions

- Adding calculations to your OLAP PivotTables

Since the release of SQL Server OLAP 7.0, Microsoft Analysis Services has proven to be an analytics workhorse that has taken and maintained the lead position in the market for OLAP (online analytical processing) databases. Many of the leading analytics and data visualization tools (including Excel) provide native connectivity with Analysis Services, providing interaction with a very rich and responsive data store via end-user data tools. Most importantly, there is a significant number of Analysis Services installations across businesses that are handling reporting, analytics, budgeting, and planning on a day-to-day basis.

But with all its capabilities, Analysis Services is complex and can present you with a significant learning curve. Though it serves as a back-end data platform for dashboards and PivotTables, Analysis Services is not well understood by many end users, remaining a platform and set of tools best understood by database developers. Even though these tools are mostly used by database developers, you can benefit from learning how they work.

This chapter provides a solid conceptual understanding of what Analysis Services is capable of. This knowledge not only enhances your abilities when it comes to the ongoing, daily analytics tasks you perform, but just as important, it significantly enhances your abilities as a team member or leader of a team focused on business analytics.

On the Web

You can find the example file for this chapter on this book's companion Web site at `www.wiley.com/go/bitools` **in the workbook named** `Chapter 13 Samples.xlsx`.

What Is an OLAP Database and What Can It Do?

The dominant database type in most organizations is the OLTP (online transaction processing) database. Indeed, most of you are probably working some form of an OLTP database. This type of database typically contains many tables, each table usually contains multiple relationships with other tables, and records within any given table can be routinely added, deleted, or updated.

Although OLTP databases are effective in gathering and managing data, they typically don't make for effective data sources for reporting. There are three main reasons for this:

➤ **Complexity:** The large number of tables and relationships that can exist in an OLTP database can leave you wondering exactly which tables to join and how the tables relate to each other.

➤ **Volume:** OLTP databases normally contain individual records; lots of them, too. In order to create any number of aggregate reports and views, you would have to run views that group, aggregate, and sort records on-the-fly. The sheer volume of data in the database could very well inundate you with painfully slow reporting.

➤ **Consistency:** By its very nature, the records in a transactional database are ever-changing. Building a reporting solution on top of this type of database will inevitably lead to inconsistent results from month to month, or even from day to day.

Some organizations avoid these woes by building their reporting solutions on top of OLAP databases. OLAP databases are data islands that are isolated from the hustle and bustle of transactional databases. An OLAP database can help alleviate these problems in the following ways:

➤ **Structured data:** In an OLAP database, all of the relationships between the various data points have been predefined and stored in *cubes*. These cubes contain the hierarchical structures that allow for the easy navigation of available data dimensions and measures. With this configuration, you no longer have to create joins or try to guess how one data table relates to another. All of that complexity is taken care of behind the scenes, leaving you free to develop the reports you need.

➤ **Predefined aggregations:** The data in an OLAP database is not only organized, but it is aggregated. This means that grouping, sorting, and aggregations are all predefined in OLAP databases. In addition, OLAP databases make heavy use of indexes; a technique that allows a database to search for records more efficiently. All of this amounts to reporting solutions that are optimized to provided the reports you need as quickly as possible.

➤ **Consistent results:** OLAP databases contain only snapshots of data. That is, the data in an OLAP database is typically historical data that is read-only, stored solely for reporting purposes. New data is typically appended to the OLAP database on a regular basis, but the existing data is rarely edited or deleted. This allows you to retrieve consistent results when building your reporting solutions.

Understanding OLAP Cubes

The backbone of an Analysis Services database is the OLAP cube. A cube can be thought of as an analytical matrix consisting of dimensional coordinates where each coordinate contains a calculation for every unique intersection. Think of a PivotTable where the data fields in the Rows area and Columns area intersect to calculate the figures in the Values area. In an OLAP cube, the data fields are called *dimensions* and the calculated values are called *measures.*

Understanding dimensions and measures

For an analytic engine like Analysis Services to be useful, it must work with source data that can be measured or quantified in some way, possibly in many different ways. This means that the source data must contain numeric fields that can be summed or otherwise computed using a mathematical aggregate function such as Sum(), Count(), Min(), or Max(). Quantitative columns are *measures,* and there are countless examples of measures in the real world: revenue, cost, quantity sold, and employee count, to name a few.

Descriptive data provides context, meaning, and structure to quantifiable data. Descriptive fields are *dimensions.* There are countless examples of dimensions, but here are a few: date, territory, product, customer, and sales rep.

Note

Dimensions can get more complicated than measures. This is because dimensions not only provide context and meaning to measures, but also behave like glue in terms of making the analytics system feasible. For example, dimensions can relate to measures, to other dimensions, or to themselves.

Understanding hierarchies and dimension parts

While relational databases are primarily concerned with relationships for data integrity, storage, and retrieval purposes, Analysis Services uses the relationships as a set of instructions that indicate how each node in a dimension relates to other nodes in order to form a whole structure. Put another way, Analysis Services uses data and data relationships to build hierarchies.

For example, in a Date dimension, a set of dates falls under a set of months, which falls under a set of years. Analysis Services understands the hierarchy between these nodes from a parent-child perspective, as well as the ordinal positioning of nodes.

Within a hierarchy, each data value serves as a dimension part. Dimension parts are common terms that are applied based on the context of the analysis being performed:

➤ **Member:** A member is any value within a particular dimension. In the example of a Date dimension, some members would be 2012, 2013, January, and February.

➤ **Parent:** A parent is a member that has immediate hierarchical precedence over another member; that is, it is the "hierarchical parent" of another member. For example, 2013 would be the parent of January and February. Likewise, January is shown as the parent of 1/1/2013 and 1/2/2013.

➤ **Child:** A child is the inverse of a parent.

➤ **Level:** A level is a grouping of members that falls under the same parent. In the example of the Date dimension, there is one level for Years, another level for Months, and another level for Dates.

➤ **Ancestor(s):** An ancestor has eventual (not immediate) hierarchical precedence over another member; that is, it is the "hierarchical ancestor" of another member. For example, 2013 is shown as the ancestor of 1/1/2013.

➤ **Descendant(s):** A descendant is the inverse of an ancestor.

Figure 13-1 illustrates the basic structure of a typical OLAP cube.

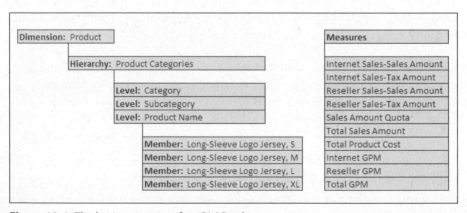

Figure 13-1: The basic structure of an OLAP cube.

Connecting to an OLAP Data Source

Before you can browse OLAP data, you must establish a connection to an OLAP cube. From the Data tab, select From Analysis Services from the From Other Sources drop-down menu.

The Data Connection Wizard starts, shown in Figure 13-2. This wizard allows you to configure your connection settings so Excel can establish a link to the server.

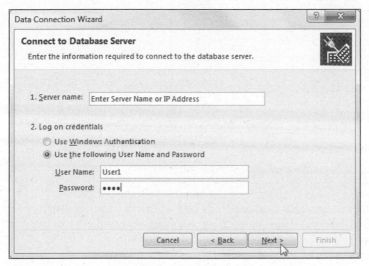

Figure 13-2: Enter your authentication information and then click Next.

Note

The examples you see in this chapter have been created using the Analysis Services Tutorial cube that comes with SQL Server Analysis Services 2012.

Follow these steps to connect to an OLAP cube:

1. Enter the name of your server as well as your username and password, as shown in Figure 13-2. Then click Next.

   If you typically authenticate via Windows authentication, select the Use Windows Authentication option before clicking Next.

2. Select the database with which you are working from the drop-down menu.

   As shown in Figure 13-3, the Analysis Services Tutorial database is selected for these steps.

   Selecting a database causes all the available OLAP cubes to appear in the list of objects below the drop-down menu.

3. Select the cube you want to analyze and then click Next.

4. In the next screen, shown in Figure 13-4, enter descriptive information about the connection you've just created.

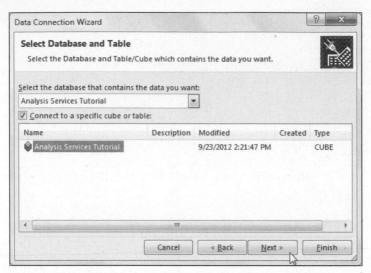

Figure 13-3: Specify your database and then select the OLAP cube you want to analyze.

Note All the fields in the screen shown in Figure 13-4 are optional. You can bypass this screen without doing anything, and your connection will work fine.

Figure 13-4: Enter descriptive information for your connection.

5. Click Finish to finalize your connection settings.

   The Import Data dialog box opens, as shown in Figure 13-5.

6. Select PivotTable Report and then click OK to build your PivotTable.

Figure 13-5: When your connection is finalized, you build your PivotTable.

After building your PivotTable, you see measures (represented by the Sigma icon), dimensions (represented by a table icon), hierarchies, and levels. Figure 13-6 illustrates what the PivotTable Fields list for an OLAP PivotTable might look like.

Measures

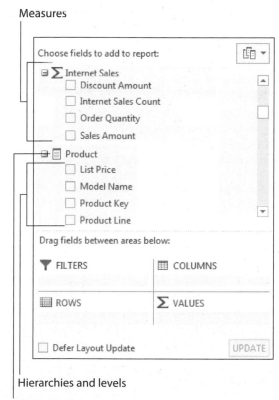

Hierarchies and levels

Dimensions

Figure 13-6: You can navigate through the OLAP cube with ease using your PivotTable Fields list.

Understanding the Limitations of OLAP PivotTables

For the most part, PivotTables that are based on OLAP data sources look, feel, and act like standard PivotTables.

Note

An OLAP data source is ultimately controlled by the database administrator, who is responsible for maintaining the Analysis Services server. That control encompasses every aspect of the OLAP cube's behavior, from the dimensions and measures included in the cube to the ability to drill into the details of a dimension. As the consumer of the OLAP data source, you have limited control on how the OLAP cube ultimately looks and feels.

This limited control translates into some limitations to the actions you can take with your OLAP-based PivotTables. You should take these limitations into account before moving forward with an OLAP-based reporting solution.

When your PivotTable report is based on an OLAP data source

➤ You cannot place any field other than measures into the Values area of the PivotTable.

➤ You cannot change the function used to summarize a data field.

➤ The Show Report Filter Pages command is disabled.

➤ The Show Items with No Data option is disabled.

➤ The Subtotal Hidden Page Items setting is disabled.

➤ The Background Query option is not available.

➤ Double-clicking in the Values field returns only the first 1,000 records of the pivot cache.

➤ The Optimize Memory check box in the PivotTable Options dialog box is disabled.

Creating Offline Cubes

With a standard PivotTable, the source data is typically stored on your local drive. This way, you can work with and analyze your data while disconnected from the network. However, this is not the case with OLAP PivotTables. With an OLAP PivotTable, the pivot cache is never brought to your local drive. This means that while you're disconnected from the network, your PivotTable is out of commission. You can't even move a field while disconnected.

Offline cubes are files that locally store portions of the source data found in an OLAP data source for browsing while you're disconnected from the network. These types of cubes are useful when you need to distribute reporting solutions to clients who do not have access to your network, or clients for whom network access is extremely slow.

To create an offline cube, start with an OLAP-based PivotTable and follow these steps:

1. Position your cursor anywhere inside the PivotTable and, from the OLAP Tools drop-down menu on the PivotTable Tools Analyze tab, select Offline OLAP.

2. From the Offline OLAP Settings dialog box, click the Create Offline Data File button.

3. In the Create Cube File Wizard, click Next.

4. Select the dimensions and levels you want included in your offline cube; see Figure 13-7. Then click Next.

   This is the data you want to import from the OLAP database. Select only the dimensions that you need available to you while disconnected from the server.

Caution   **The more dimensions you select, the more disk space your offline cube file takes up.**

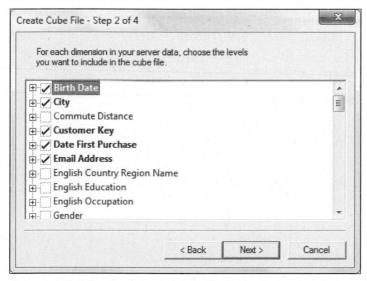

Figure 13-7: Select the dimensions and level you want included in your offline cube.

5. Filter any members or data items you do not want to include; see Figure 13-8. Then click Next.

   For example, the Extended Amount measure is not needed, so deselect that check box. This ensures that this measure will not be imported and will not take up unnecessary disk space.

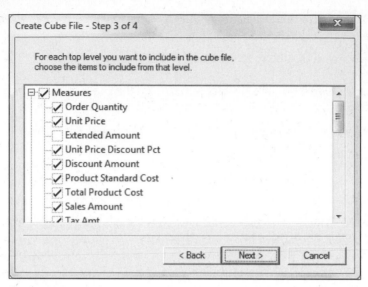

Figure 13-8: Deselect any members you do not need to see offline.

6. Specify a name and location for your cube file. Click Finish when you're done.

   The file extension for all offline cubes is `.cub`. In Figure 13-9, the cube file is named `MyOfflineCube.cub`, and it's placed in your chosen directory.

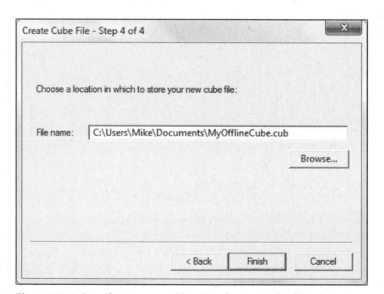

Figure 13-9: Specify a name and location for your cube file.

After a few moments of crunching, Excel outputs your offline cube file to your chosen directory. Double-click the file and the Excel workbook opens that is linked to the offline cube via a PivotTable.

After your offline cube file has been created, you can distribute it to others and use it while you're disconnected from the network.

When you're connected to the network, you can open your offline cube file and refresh the PivotTable to get updated data.

Using Cube Functions

Cube functions are Excel functions that can be used to access OLAP data outside a PivotTable object. In pre-2010 versions of Excel, you could find cube functions only if you installed the Analysis Services Add-In. In Excel 2010, cube functions were brought into the native Excel environment.

One of the easiest ways to start exploring cube functions is to allow Excel to convert your OLAP-based PivotTable into cube formulas. Converting a PivotTable to cube formulas is an easy way to create a few cube formulas without doing any of the work yourself. Excel replaces all the cells in the PivotTable with a formula that connects back to the OLAP database. Figure 13-10 shows a PivotTable connected to an OLAP database.

Customer Geography	United States			
Internet Sales-Sales Ar		CY 2003	CY 2004	Grand Total
Accessories				
Bike Racks		$7,680	$9,480	$17,160
Bike Stands		$6,996	$6,519	$13,515
Bottles and Cages		$8,292	$12,738	$21,030
Cleaners		$1,240	$1,590	$2,830
Fenders		$8,880	$12,946	$21,826
Helmets		$31,771	$45,522	$77,293
Hydration Packs		$6,049	$9,073	$15,122
Tires and Tubes		$38,001	$51,520	$89,521
Accessories Total		**$108,909**	**$149,388**	**$258,298**

Figure 13-10: A normal OLAP PivotTable.

With just a few clicks, you can convert any OLAP PivotTable into a series of cube formulas. Place the cursor anywhere inside the PivotTable and select Convert to Formulas from the OLAP Tools drop-down menu on the Analyze tab.

If your PivotTable contains a report filter field, the message box in Figure 13-11 appears. This dialog box gives you the option of converting your filter drop-down selectors to cube formulas. If you select the Convert Report Filters check box, the drop-down selectors are removed, leaving a static formula. If you need to have your filter drop-down selectors intact so that you can continue to interactively change the selections in the filter field, deselect the Convert Report Filters check box.

If you're working with a PivotTable in compatibility mode, Excel automatically converts the filter fields to formulas.

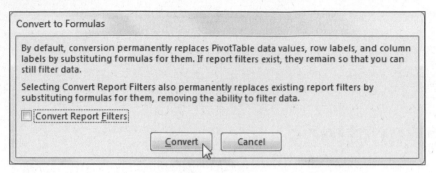

Figure 13-11: Excel gives you the option of converting your filter fields.

After a second or two, the cells that used to house a PivotTable are now homes for cube formulas. Note that, as shown in Figure 13-12, any styles you may have applied are removed. The formula bar tips you off that these cells are now cube formulas: the formulas start with =CUBEVALUE.

C6				f_x	=CUBEVALUE("AdventureWorks OLAP Cube",B1,A3,$B6,C$4)		

	A	B	C	D	E	
1	Customer Geography	United States				
2						
3	Internet Sales-Sales Amount					
4			CY 2003	CY 2004	Grand Total	
5	Accessories					
6		Bike Racks	$7,680.00	$9,480.00	$17,160.00	
7		Bike Stands	$6,996.00	$6,519.00	$13,515.00	
8		Bottles and Cages	$8,292.26	$12,738.04	$21,030.30	
9		Cleaners	$1,240.20	$1,590.00	$2,830.20	
10		Fenders	$8,879.92	$12,946.22	$21,826.14	
11		Helmets	$31,770.92	$45,521.99	$77,292.91	
12		Hydration Packs	$6,048.90	$9,073.35	$15,122.25	
13		Tires and Tubes	$38,001.19	$51,519.83	$89,521.02	
14	Accessories Total		$108,909.39	$149,388.43	$258,297.82	

Figure 13-12: The formula bar shows these cells are now a series of cube formulas.

So why is this capability useful? Well, now that the values you see are no longer part of a PivotTable object, you can insert rows and columns, add your own calculations, combine the data with other external data, and modify the report in all sorts of ways by simply moving the formulas around.

Adding Calculations to Your OLAP PivotTables

In previous versions of Excel, OLAP PivotTables were limited in that you couldn't build your own calculations with the OLAP data. This means you could not add that extra layer of analysis like you could with the calculated fields and calculated items functionality found in standard PivotTables.

Excel 2013 changes that with the introduction of the new OLAP tools: calculated measures and calculated members. With these two new tools, you can add your own analysis by building your own calculations.

In this section you explore how to build your own calculated measures and calculated members.

A word about MDX

When you are using a PivotTable with an OLAP cube, you're sending the OLAP database MDX (multidimensional expressions) queries. MDX is an expression language that is used to return data from multidimensional data sources (that is, OLAP cubes).

As your OLAP PivotTable is refreshed or changed, subsequent MDX queries are passed to the OLAP database. The results of the query are sent back to Excel and displayed through the PivotTable. This is how you can work with OLAP data without a local copy of a pivot cache.

When building calculated measures and calculated members, you need to utilize MDX syntax. This is the only way the PivotTable can communicate your calculation to the back-end OLAP database.

The examples in this chapter use basic MDX constructs to demonstrate the functionality found in Excel 2013. If you need to create complex calculated measures and calculated members, you need to learn MDX.

That said, the topic of MDX is robust and beyond the scope of this book. If after reading this section, you want to learn more about MDX, consider picking up *MDX Solutions: With Microsoft SQL Server Analysis Services 2005 and Hyperion Essbase* by George Spofford (John Wiley & Sons); an excellent guide to MDX.

Creating calculated measures

A calculated measure is essentially the OLAP version of a calculated field. A calculated measure creates a new data field based on some mathematical operation that uses the existing OLAP fields.

Figure 13-13 shows an OLAP PivotTable containing products along with their respective quantities and revenues. It needs a measure that calculates average sales price per unit.

	A	B	C
1	Row Labels	Order Quantity	Sales Amount
2	All-Purpose Bike Stand	249	$39,591
3	Bike Wash	908	$7,219
4	Classic Vest	562	$35,687
5	Cycling Cap	2,190	$19,688
6	Fender Set - Mountain	2,121	$46,620
7	Half-Finger Gloves	1,430	$35,021
8	Hitch Rack - 4-Bike	328	$39,360
9	HL Mountain Tire	1,396	$48,860
10	HL Road Tire	858	$27,971
11	Hydration Pack	733	$40,308
12	LL Mountain Tire	862	$21,541
13	LL Road Tire	1,044	$22,436
14	Long-Sleeve Logo Jersey	1,736	$86,783
15	ML Mountain Tire	1,161	$34,818

Figure 13-13: To show average sales price per unit, you need a calculated measure.

Place your cursor anywhere in the PivotTable and follow these steps:

1. Select MDX Calculated Measure from the OLAP Tools drop-down menu on the Analyze tab.

    The New Calculated Measure dialog box opens, as shown in Figure 13-14.

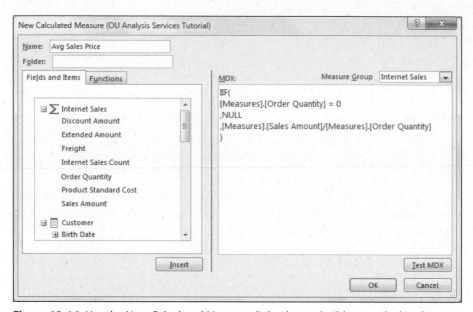

Figure 13-14: Use the New Calculated Measure dialog box to build your calculated measure.

2. Give your calculated measure a name by entering it in the Name text box.

3. Click the Measure Group drop-down menu and select the group you want to place your calculated measure in.

    If you don't choose one, Excel automatically places your measure in the first available measure group.

4. Enter the MDX syntax for your calculation in the MDX text box.

    To save time, you can use the list on the left to select the existing measures you need for your calculation. Double-click the measures needed, and Excel enters them in the MDX text box. In this example, the calculation for the average sales price is `IIF([Measures].[Order Quantity] = 0,NULL,[Measures].[Sales Amount]/[Measures].[Order Quantity])`.

    Tip **Click the Test MDX button to check if your MDX is well formed. Excel lets you know via a message box if there is an error in your syntax.**

5. Click OK.

    Excel builds your defined measure and adds it to the PivotTable Fields list.

6. Select your newly created calculation from the PivotTable Fields list (see Figure 13-15).

Figure 13-15: Add your newly created calculation to your PivotTable via the PivotTable Fields list.

Your calculated measure adds a meaningful layer of analysis to the PivotTable (see Figure 13-16).

	A	B	C	D
1	Row Labels	Order Quantity	Sales Amount	Avg Sales Price
2	All-Purpose Bike Stand	249	$39,591	$159.00
3	Bike Wash	908	$7,219	$7.95
4	Classic Vest	562	$35,687	$63.50
5	Cycling Cap	2,190	$19,688	$8.99
6	Fender Set - Mountain	2,121	$46,620	$21.98
7	Half-Finger Gloves	1,430	$35,021	$24.49
8	Hitch Rack - 4-Bike	328	$39,360	$120.00
9	HL Mountain Tire	1,396	$48,860	$35.00
10	HL Road Tire	858	$27,971	$32.60
11	Hydration Pack	733	$40,308	$54.99
12	LL Mountain Tire	862	$21,541	$24.99
13	LL Road Tire	1,044	$22,436	$21.49
14	Long-Sleeve Logo Jersey	1,736	$86,783	$49.99
15	ML Mountain Tire	1,161	$34,818	$29.99

Figure 13-16: Your PivotTable now contains your calculated measure.

Note

When you create a calculated measure, it exists in your workbook only. You're not building your calculation directly in the OLAP cube on the server. This means no one else connected to the OLAP cube can see your calculations unless you share or distribute your workbook.

Creating calculated members

A calculated member is essentially the OLAP version of a calculated item. A calculated member creates a new data item based on some mathematical operation that uses the existing OLAP members.

Figure 13-17 shows an OLAP PivotTable containing sales information for each quarter of the year. Imagine you want to aggregate quarters 1 and 2 into a new data item called First Half of Year. You also want to aggregate quarters 3 and 4 into a new data item called Second Half of Year.

	A	B	C	D
1	Row Labels ▼	Order Quantity	Sales Amount	Avg Sales Price
2	1	15,425	$7,586,624	$491.84
3	2	17,465	$8,893,345	$509.21
4	3	13,011	$6,009,120	$461.85
5	4	14,497	$6,869,588	$473.86
6	Grand Total	60,398	$29,358,677	$486.09

Figure 13-17: You want to add new calculated members to aggregate the four quarters into First Half of Year and Second Half of Year.

Place your cursor anywhere in the PivotTable and follow these steps:

1. From the Analyze tab, select MDX Calculated Member from the OLAP Tools drop-down menu.

   The New Calculated Member dialog box opens, as shown in Figure 13-18.

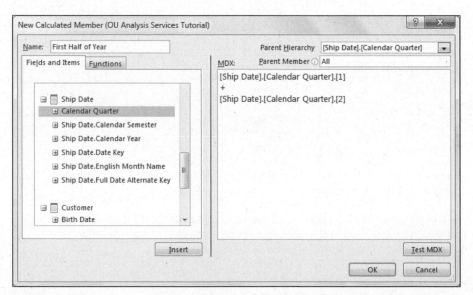

Figure 13-18: Use the New Calculated Member dialog box to build your calculated member.

2. Give your calculated member a name by entering it in the Name text box.

3. Click the Parent Hierarchy drop-down to select the hierarchy for which you are creating new members.

Be sure to leave the Parent Member set to All. This ensures that Excel takes into account all members in the parent hierarchy when evaluating your calculation.

4. Enter the MDX syntax for your calculation in the MDX text box.

   To save time, you can use the list on the left to select the existing members you need for your calculation. Double-click the member needed, and Excel enters them into the MDX text box. In the example shown in Figure 13-18, the MDX is `[Ship Date].[Calendar Quarter].[1] + [Ship Date].[Calendar Quarter].[2]`.

Tip   Click the **Test MDX** button to check if your MDX is well formed. Excel lets you know via a message box if there is an error in your syntax.

5. Click OK.

As soon as you click OK, Excel shows your newly created calculated member in the PivotTable. As shown in Figure 13-19, the calculated member is included with the other original members of the pivot field.

	A	B	C	D
1	Row Labels	Order Quantity	Sales Amount	Avg Sales Price
2	1	15,425	$7,586,624	$491.84
3	2	17,465	$8,893,345	$509.21
4	3	13,011	$6,009,120	$461.85
5	4	14,497	$6,869,588	$473.86
6	First Half of Year	32,890	$16,479,969	$501.06
7	Grand Total	60,398	$29,358,677	$486.09

Figure 13-19: Excel immediately adds your calculated member to your pivot field.

Figure 13-20 shows the calculated members for the Second Half of Year.

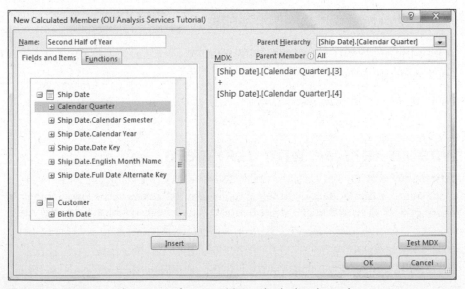

Figure 13-20: Repeat the process for any additional calculated members.

Figure 13-21 shows the result. Excel makes no attempt at removing any of the original members. In this case, you see that quarters 1, 2, and 4 are still in the PivotTable. This may be fine for your situation, but in most scenarios, you'll probably hide these members to avoid confusion.

	A	B	C	D
1	Row Labels ▼	Order Quantity	Sales Amount	Avg Sales Price
2	1	15,425	$7,586,624	$491.84
3	2	17,465	$8,893,345	$509.21
4	3	13,011	$6,009,120	$461.85
5	4	14,497	$6,869,588	$473.86
6	First Half of Year	32,890	$16,479,969	$501.06
7	Second Half of Year	27,508	$12,878,709	$468.18
8	Grand Total	60,398	$29,358,677	$486.09

Figure 13-21: Excel shows your final calculated members along with the original members.

Remember that your calculated member exists in your workbook only. No one else connected to the OLAP cube can see your calculations unless you share or distribute your workbook.

Caution

If the parent hierarchy or parent member is changed in the OLAP cube, your calculated member ceases to function. You'll have to re-create the calculated member.

Managing your OLAP calculations

Excel provides an interface to manage the calculated measures and calculated members in your OLAP PivotTable.

Place your cursor anywhere in the PivotTable and select Manage Calculation from the OLAP Tools drop-down menu found on the Analyze tab.

In the Manage Calculations dialog box shown in Figure 13-22, you see three buttons:

➤ **New:** Create a new calculated measure or calculated member.

➤ **Edit:** Edit the selected calculation.

➤ **Delete:** Permanently delete the selected calculation.

Performing what-if analysis with OLAP data

One final piece of functionality Excel 2013 offers is the ability to perform what-if analysis with the data in OLAP PivotTables. With this new functionality, you can actually edit the values in the PivotTable and recalculate your measures and members based on your changes. You can even publish your changes back to the OLAP cube.

To use the what-if analysis functionality, create an OLAP PivotTable, then on the Analyze tab, choose What-If Analysis ➜ Enable What-If Analysis from the OLAP Tools drop-down menu.

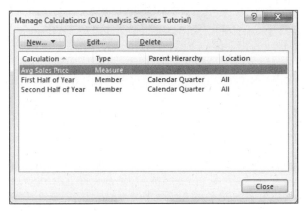

Figure 13-22: The Manage Calculations dialog box allows you to create a new calculation, edit an existing calculation, or delete an existing calculation.

Now you can edit the values in your PivotTable. After you have made your changes, right-click any of the changed values and select Calculate PivotTable with Change (see Figure 13-23). This forces Excel to reevaluate all the calculations in the PivotTable based on your edits; including your calculated members and measures.

	A	B	C	D	E
1	**Row Labels** ▼	**Order Quantity**	**Sales Amount**	**Avg Sales Price**	
2	All-Purpose Bike Stand	249	$39,591	$159.00	
3	Bike Wash	908	$7,219	$7.95	
4	Classic Vest	562	$35,687	$63.50	
5	Cycling Cap	2,190	$19,688	$8.99	
6	Fender Set - Mountain	4,432	$46,620	$21.98	
7	Half-Finger Gloves	1,430			
8	Hitch Rack - 4-Bike	328			
9	HL Mountain Tire	1,396			
10	HL Road Tire	858			
11	Hydration Pack	733			
12	LL Mountain Tire	862			

Value has been changed

Data source value: 2,121 (click to refresh)

Calculate PivotTable with Change

Discard Change

What-If Analysis Settings

Figure 13-23: Select Calculate PivotTable with Change to reevaluate all your calculations.

The edits you make to your PivotTable while in what-if analysis mode are, by default, local edits only. If you want to actually make the changes on the OLAP server, you have to tell Excel to publish your changes.

From the Analyze tab choose What-If Analysis ➜ Publish Changes from the OLAP Tools drop-down menu. This triggers a write back to the OLAP server, meaning the edited values are sent to the source OLAP cube.

Note   You need adequate server permissions to publish changes to the OLAP server. Your database administrator can guide you through the process of getting write access to your OLAP database.

14

Using the Data Mining Add-In for Microsoft Office

In This Chapter

- Installing the Data Mining Add-In
- Leveraging the Data Mining Table Analysis Tools

The Data Mining Add-In for Microsoft Office provides you with a way to leverage the power of Analysis Services from within the familiar Excel interface. With the Data Mining Add-In, you can utilize powerful SQL Server Analysis algorithms to find data patterns, uncover hidden relationships, develop data-based predictions, and perform many more complex analyses.

In this chapter, you discover some of the ways you can use this robust analysis tool to develop analytics and reporting that would have been previously impossible with vanilla Excel.

Installing and Activating the Data Mining Add-In

Open Excel and look for a Data Mining tab on the Ribbon. If you see one, the Data Mining Add-In is already activated. If you don't see the tab, you have to download and install it yourself.

Downloading the Data Mining Add-In

Type **Excel Data Mining Add-In** in your favorite search engine to find the free installation package. Note that Microsoft offers versions for SQL Server 2008 and SQL Server 2012. Be sure to download the version that matches the version of SQL Server your organization is using.

Starting with the sample workbook

A good way to start using the Data Mining Add-In is to practice using the sample workbook that installs with it. The DMAddins_SampleData workbook is used for all the examples in this chapter. Assuming you have installed the Data Mining Add-In on your PC, this workbook is usually located here: `C:\Program Files\Microsoft SQL Server 2012 DM Add-Ins\DMAddins_ SampleData.xlsx`.

After it is installed, follow these steps to activate the add-in:

1. Choose File ➜ Options.

2. Select the Add-Ins option on the left, and select COM Add-Ins from the Manage drop-down menu. Click Go.

3. Select SQLServer.DMClientXLAddIn and SQLServer.DMXLAddIn in the list of available COM Add-Ins. Click OK.

4. Close and restart Excel.

Pointing to an Analysis Services database

Upon restarting Excel, you're automatically walked through a wizard to connect your newly installed Data Mining Add-In to an Analysis Services database (see Figure 14-1). The Data Mining Add-In requires an existing 2008 (or later) Analysis Services database to serve as the engine for processing the analyses you eventually perform with it.

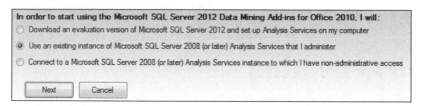

Figure 14-1: The Data Mining Add-In requires a connection to an Analysis Services database instance.

Select the appropriate option and follow the instructions in the setup wizard.

Note   If you inadvertently close the setup wizard, or if you need to point to a different Analysis Services database, you can open the setup wizard by choosing Help ➜ Getting Started on the Data Mining tab.

The full breadth of functionality that comes with the Data Mining Add-In is staggering. There are many features of the add-in you will likely never touch. Instead of focusing on all aspects of the Data Mining Add-In, the remainder of this chapter discusses the features found in the Data Mining Table Analysis Tools.

The Table Analysis Tools is an ideal set of analytical features if you aren't a data mining expert, but you need to perform complex pattern recognition and predictive analytics.

Note

It's important to note that you can use data from almost any source with the Data Mining Add-In. The data does not have to come from SQL Analysis Services. That being said, to use the Table Analysis Tools, you need to convert your data ranges to named Excel tables. Click anywhere inside your data range and press Ctrl+T. In the Create Table dialog box, ensure that the range for the table is correct and then click OK.

Click anywhere inside your named Excel table to see the Table Tools on the Analyze tab (see Figure 14-2).

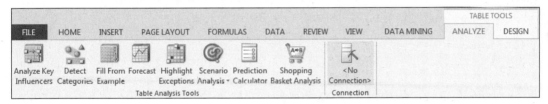

Figure 14-2: Click inside any defined Excel table to see the Table Analysis Tools on the Analyze tab.

➤ **Analyze Key Influencers:** Automatically detect relationships between columns in your input data so that you can understand which factors tend to influence other factors.

➤ **Detect Categories:** Find common characteristics that tend to form clusters within your input data.

➤ **Fill From Example:** Use expert knowledge about underlying data to fill in a few examples, which can be extrapolated by Analysis Services into a pattern to be applied to all of the rows in the input dataset.

➤ **Forecast:** Use a time series algorithm to predict future outcomes based on historical data.

➤ **Highlight Exceptions:** Relying on the same underlying method that is used to build categories, exceptions in your input data can be highlighted to call out erroneous or outlier data points that may need to be filtered out of analyses.

➤ **Scenario Analysis:** Play out goal-seeking or what-if modeling scenarios with your input data to optimize decision-making.

➤ **Prediction Calculator:** Decide whether to proceed with an action that assumes predictive accuracy by using input data to build a predictive model along with cost and profit inputs, which can be arbitrarily assigned.

➤ **Shopping Basket Analysis:** Identify which products tend to be purchased in combination with other products and what the relative amounts of different product bundles spell out from a profitability standpoint.

To work through the tools in the following sections, open the DMAddins_SampleData.xlsx sample workbook. Find the Table Analysis Tools Sample worksheet and select the Excel table. You're ready to use the Table Analysis Tools. This table contains demographic data for individuals and a column indicating whether those individuals purchased a bike (see Figure 14-3).

Marital Status	Gender	Income	Children	Occupation	Home Owner	Cars	Commute Distance	Region	Age	Purchased Bike
Married	Female	40000	1	Skilled Manual	Yes	0	0-1 Miles	Europe	42	No
Married	Male	30000	3	Clerical	Yes	1	0-1 Miles	Europe	43	No
Married	Male	80000	5	Professional	No	2	2-5 Miles	Europe	60	No
Single	Male	70000	0	Professional	Yes	1	5-10 Miles	Pacific	41	Yes
Single	Male	30000	0	Clerical	No	0	0-1 Miles	Europe	36	Yes
Married	Female	10000	2	Manual	Yes	0	1-2 Miles	Europe	50	No
Single	Male	160000	2	Management	Yes	4	0-1 Miles	Pacific	33	Yes
Married	Male	40000	1	Skilled Manual	Yes	0	0-1 Miles	Europe	43	Yes
Married	Male	20000	2	Clerical	Yes	2	5-10 Miles	Pacific	58	No
Married	Male	20000	2	Manual	Yes	1	0-1 Miles	Europe	48	Yes
Married	Female	30000	3	Skilled Manual	No	2	1-2 Miles	Pacific	54	Yes
Single	Female	90000	0	Professional	No	4	10+ Miles	Pacific	36	No
Married	Male	170000	5	Professional	Yes	4	0-1 Miles	Europe	55	No

Figure 14-3: This dataset contains demographic data for a bike company.

Analyze Key Influencers

Generally speaking, a dataset is defined by its "structure" (cells, rows, columns) as well as its relationships with other datasets. But there is another way to think of a defined dataset, and that is the patterns that can be discovered in the data itself, irrespective of the data's structure. A simple example of a data pattern can be shown in the following two number sequences:

Sequence 1: {0, 1, 2, 3, 4}

Sequence 2: {2687, 2696, 2589, 694, 466}

In these two sequences, a pattern can easily be discerned in which the values of Sequence 2 seem to be influenced by the values in Sequence 1 (the higher the value from Sequence 1, the lower the value in Sequence 2). Our brains are relatively good at detecting simple patterns, but more complex patterns and/or larger datasets require CPU power. The Analyze Key Influencers Table Analysis tool does exactly this.

When you use the Analyze Key Influencers tool, a lot of complex work is happening behind the scenes:

1. A temporary mining structure is created on the Analysis Services instance to hold the data in the table that is being analyzed.

2. Using the Microsoft Naïve Bayes algorithm, a mining model is generated that allows each column to be scored in terms of predicting the target column.

3. The results of this scoring process are inserted into a new report, which is added to a new worksheet automatically. Optionally, other reports can be added that further analyze any combination of target column with one input column.

Suppose you want to determine which of the demographic factors are key influencers in any one individual's decision to buy a bike or not. Click the Analyze Key Influencers button on the Analyze tab.

In the Analyze Key Influencers window (see Figure 14-4), select the Purchased Bike column as the column to analyze for key factors and click Run.

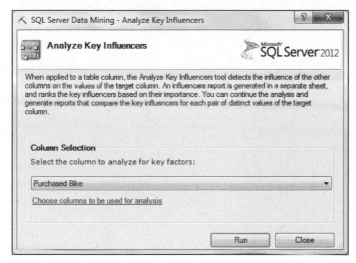

Figure 14-4: Select the column to use as the basis for evaluating key factors.

You get a similar report to the one shown in Figure 14-5.

	A	B	C	D	E	F
1	**Key Influencers Report for 'Purchased Bike'**					
2						
3	**Key Influencers and their impact over the values of 'Purchased Bike'**					
4	Filter by 'Column' or 'Favors' to see how various columns influence 'Purchased Bike'					
5	Column ▼	Value ▼	Favors ▼	Relative Impact ⬛		
6	Cars	2	No			
7	Marital Status	Married	No			
8	Region	North America	No			
9	Cars	0	Yes			
10	Marital Status	Single	Yes			
11	Cars	1	Yes			
12	Region	Pacific	Yes			
13						

Figure 14-5: Results of the Key Influencers report.

The Key Influencers report shows each demographic data point that is likely to influence the purchase of a bike. In this case, the report tells you that cases where 0 cars are owned seems to be the key driver for bike purchases (see where there is a "Yes" in the Favors column). Conversely, cases where 2 cars are owned seems to be a likely indicator that a bike will not be purchased (see where there is a "No" in the Favors column). Following the values from top to bottom of the report, you can clearly see no cars or few cars owned lead to a higher likelihood of bike purchase.

Detect Categories

Another form of pattern recognition that can occur on a dataset is groupings of data based on like characteristics. A simple example of this would be the Detect Categories tool.

Use the Detect Categories tool to categorize records in a dataset based on the attributes of each record. Breaking the data into categories enables you to quickly identify the natural groupings in your data.

For example, if you want to create distinct lead lists from a larger dataset, you can use the Detect Categories tool to help understand the characteristics of your data and possibly identify the most appropriate way to parse your larger dataset into smaller lists for targeted marketing campaigns.

To see the Detect Categories tool in action, click the Detect Categories button on the Analyze tab. In the Detect Categories dialog box, select the columns you want to evaluate to create your distinct categories and click the Run button.

You get a report similar to the one shown in Figure 14-6.

Category Name	Row Count	
Category 1		189
Category 2		141
Category 3		158
Category 4		149
Category 5		126
Category 6		129
Category 7		108

			Category Characteristics	
Filter the table by 'Category' to see the characteristics of different categories.				
Category ⏷	**Column** ⏷	**Value** ⏷	**Relative Importance** ⏷	
Category 1	Income	Very Low:< 39050		
Category 1	Region	Europe		
Category 1	Occupation	Manual		
Category 1	Occupation	Clerical		
Category 1	Commute Distance	0-1 Miles		
Category 1	Cars	0		
Category 1	Children	2		
Category 1	Children	1		
Category 1	Education	Partial High School		
Category 1	Education	High School		
Category 1	Children	3		

Figure 14-6: Results of the Detect Categories report.

After the Detect Categories tool runs, you get a report that tells you how many categories were identified, gives each category a name (Category Name) and tells you how many rows/records are included in each category (Row Count). The report also displays a Category Characteristics section that contains the attribute details of each category.

In the result set shown in Figure 14-6, the Detect Categories tool found seven distinct categories. Category 1 contains the most records. The primary attribute of Category 1 is the Income column. This means that having an annual income of less than $39,050 was the most important driver for this particular category. If you were creating lead lists, Category 1 could be a list targeting low-income customers.

Fill From Example

The Fill From Example tool automatically fills in missing data in a specified column for all rows in the selected table, based on detected patterns in a set of samples you provide, and applies those to the remaining missing values.

Figure 14-7 shows a table where the High Value Customer column is blank for most records. The first ten rows of this column are filled with sample values. Based on the sample values, the Fill From Example tool detects patterns that relate the other column values to the sample information we added to the High Value Customer column, then extends those patterns to all the remaining rows.

Marital Status	Gender	Income	Children	Home Owner	Cars	Commute Distance	Region	Age	High Value Customer
Married	Female	40000	1	Yes	0	0-1 Miles	Europe	42	Yes
Married	Male	30000	3	Yes	1	0-1 Miles	Europe	43	Yes
Married	Female	80000	5	No	2	2-5 Miles	Europe	60	Yes
Single	Male	70000	0	Yes	1	5-10 Miles	Pacific	41	No
Single	Male	30000	0	No	0	0-1 Miles	Europe	36	Yes
Married	Female	10000	2	Yes	0	1-2 Miles	Europe	50	No
Single	Male	160000	2	Yes	4	0-1 Miles	Pacific	33	No
Married	Male	40000	1	Yes	0	0-1 Miles	Europe	43	Yes
Married	Male	20000	2	Yes	2	5-10 Miles	Pacific	58	No
Married	Male	20000	2	Yes	1	0-1 Miles	Europe	48	Yes
Married	Female	30000	3	No	2	1-2 Miles	Pacific	54	
Single	Female	90000	0	No	4	10+ Miles	Pacific	36	
Married	Male	170000	5	Yes	4	0-1 Miles	Europe	55	

Figure 14-7: Start with a column (High Value Customer, in this case) that contains a handful of sample values.

Click the Fill From Example button on the Analyze tab. In the Fill From Example dialog box, select the column you want to use as both sample input and interpolation for filling in values (in this example, the High Value Customer column). Click the Run button and you get a report similar to the one shown in Figure 14-8.

	A	B	C	D	E	F
1				Pattern Report for 'High Value Customer'		
2						
3		Key Influencers and their impact over the values of 'High Value Customer'				
4	Filter by 'Column' or 'Favors' to see how various columns influence 'High Value Customer'					
5	Column	Value	Favors	Relative Impact		
6	Region	Pacific	No			
7	Commute Distance	5-10 Miles	No			
8	Gender	Female	No			
9	Education	Partial High School	No			
10	Education	Bachelors	No			
11	Commute Distance	1-2 Miles	No			
12	Occupation	Professional	No			
13	Commute Distance	2-5 Miles	Yes			
14	Children	5	Yes			
15	Region	Europe	Yes			
16	Home Owner	No	Yes			
17	Education	Partial College	Yes			
18	Children	3	Yes			
19	Cars	2	Yes			
20						

Figure 14-8: Results of the Fill From Example report.

The output is a Pattern Report (see Figure 14-8), which shows column and value states as they relate to the sample values column (High Value Customer). This report orders value states by relative impact. It's useful to consider the results by each factor; for example, by considering the favors "Yes" states separately from the favors "No" states. A quick glance shows you that customers located in Europe with relatively short commute distances (2–5 miles) favors a high value customer status, while for customers in the Pacific, higher commute distances (5–10 miles) or very short commute distances (1–2 miles) do not favor high value customer status. Other factors can quickly be identified.

Forecast

The Forecast tool is similar to the Fill From Example tool, but with two important distinctions:

> ➤ The Forecast tool assumes a time-oriented dataset. The time column could be time of day, date, or a combination of the two (date + time). Why does it matter that one of the columns is specifically a date/time value? Because the underlying algorithm, Microsoft Time Series, is based on a time-ordered dataset.

> ➤ Where the Fill From Example tool fills in missing values for a single column based on relationships detected with other input columns (column-based pattern), the Forecast tool fills in missing rows for multiple columns based on relationships detected in other rows (row-based pattern).

Following is a list of prerequisites for using the Forecast tool:

> ➤ One of the columns must be time-oriented or a unique ordered set of numbers (which could substitute for an actual time/date column).

> ➤ The predictable column must be a continuous value. Bear in mind you will not be predicting values for the time/date column.

> ➤ Before the model is generated, you can provide a hint to specify that your time-oriented data has a cyclical pattern, as would be the case for monthly sales, for example.

The Forecast tool helps you make predictions based on data in an Excel data table or other data source, and optionally view the probabilities associated with each predicted value. For example, if your data contains a date column and a column that shows total sales for each day of the month, you could predict the sales for future days. You can also specify the number of predictions to make. For example, you can predict five days, or thirty.

To see the Forecast tool in action, click the Forecast button on the Analyze tab. In the Forecast dialog box, shown in Figure 14-9, identify the following inputs: Columns to be forecast, Number of time units to forecast, Time stamp (optional), and Periodicity of data (optional). Click the Run button and you get a report similar to the one shown in Figure 14-10.

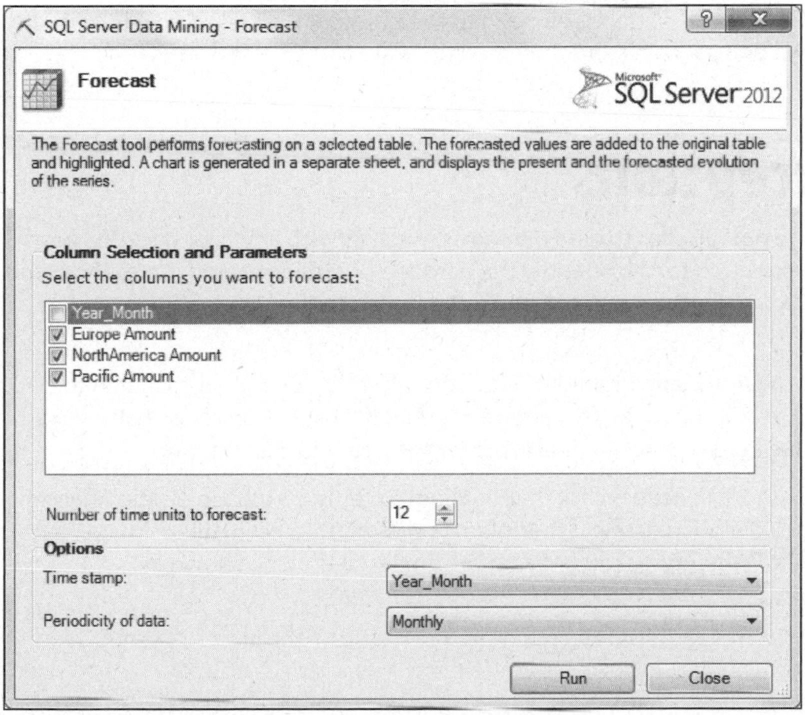

Figure 14-9: Configure the Forecast dialog box as needed.

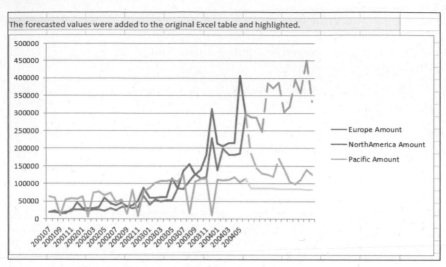

Figure 14-10: Results of the Forecast report.

When the tool completes, it appends the new predictions to the end of the source data table and highlights the new values. The tool also creates a new worksheet named Forecasting Report. This worksheet reports whether the wizard successfully created a prediction. The new worksheet also contains a line graph that shows the historical trends along with the predicted values that were added. The historical values are shown as a solid line and the predictions are shown as a dotted line.

Highlight Exceptions

Because "garbage in = garbage out" applies to data mining as much as with any data-oriented process, a specific tool has been provided to help identify the garbage or outliers in your data. This is the Highlight Exceptions tool, which relies on the Microsoft Clustering algorithm to identify rows with similar characteristics.

The Highlight Exceptions tool analyzes and highlights data rows that do not appear to match the general patterns found in the rest of the table. This not only highlights exception rows, it also highlights the specific column value in each row that is likely to be the cause of the exception.

To see the Highlight Exceptions tool in action, click the Highlight Exceptions button on the Analyze tab. In the Highlight Exceptions dialog box, select the columns you want to evaluate to create your distinct categories and click the Run button. You get a report similar to the one shown in Figure 14-11.

The outlier cells are highlighted in the original table.			
Exception threshold (more or fewer exceptions)	75		
Column	**Outliers**		
Marital Status	0		
Gender	0		
Income	4		
Children	9		
Education	1		
Occupation	3		
Home Owner	0		
Cars	7		
Commute Distance	4		
Region	0		
Age	6		
Purchased Bike	0		
Total	34		

Figure 14-11: Results of the Highlight Exceptions report.

This report provides a threshold that shows 75 exceptions by default (you can change the threshold; the rows in the actual input table will be correspondingly highlighted). The data table shows you two columns, one for each input column where outliers were detected and another showing the number of outliers that were detected. In this report, you can see that there are 9 outliers for the Children input column. If you want to see which values actually constitute these outliers, you can go back to the source table and find them — they're highlighted.

Note

There is no simple way to isolate the outlier values in the input dataset other than sorting the columns (In the event that outliers are at the beginning or end of the value range) or scrolling through the dataset to find the highlighted outliers. For this reason, the Highlight Exceptions tool is not practical for large datasets.

Scenario Analysis

A common data analysis scenario is understanding the impact to other columns given a hypothetical value (or set of values) in an input column that is designated as a target column. The Scenario Analysis tool does exactly this, but it is actually two different tools: Goal Seek Scenario and What-If Scenario.

Using the Goal Seek Scenario tool

The Goal Seek Scenario tool provides the following input options:

➤ **Target:** This is where you select the column that will contain the target values of your goal-seeking scenario. After you select the column, you must specify your target value(s) using one of the following input options:

- *Exactly:* Enter a number that specifies a target value for your target column.

- *Percentage:* Enter a number that will translate into a multiplier of the target column. For example, entering 120 would indicate that your target values should be 120 percent of the input values (or 20 percent higher).

- *In Range:* Enter a low and high value that will constitute a range where your target values should lie.

➤ **What to Change:** Select the column to change to achieve the target value specified in the Target input.

The Goal Seek Scenario tool provides useful recommendations when you know the desired value for a column of the current row (the Target column) and need to know how to change another column (the Change column) to reach that desired value. The recommendations are based on the patterns and rules detected in your table.

Note **In order to use the Goal Seek Scenario tool, your source table must contain at least 50 rows of data.**

In the example shown in Figure 14-12, the Goal Seek Scenario tool determines how many LevelTwoOperators are needed to reduce the ServiceGrade score to between 0 and .05.

	LevelOneOperators	LevelTwoOperators	ServiceGrade	Goal: ServiceGrade between 0 and .05	Recommended LevelTwoOperators
4	2	7	0.03	✓	7
5	2	10	0.12	✓	14
6	3	11	0.14	✓	14
7	1	4	0.08	✗	14
8	2	8	0.09	✗	14
9	3	10	0.08	✗	14
10	3	12	0.16	✗	14
11	1	3	0.04	✓	3
12	2	8	0.12	✗	7
13	3	9	0.1	✗	7
14	3	10	0.16	✗	14
15	1	4	0.13	✗	7
16	2	8	0.1	✗	7
17	3	10	0.06	✗	14

Figure 14-12: Results of the Goal Seek Scenario tool.

When the Goal Seek Scenario tool is run, two new columns are added to the source table: Goal (plus the goal name) and Recommended (plus the changeable column). The goal column shows a simple Yes/No response in the form of red and green status flags, with a green flag indicating the goal is achievable and the red flag indicating it is not. The recommended column provides a specific value that would be required for the input column value in order to achieve the goal.

For example, row 6 is highlighted, showing an example where the ServiceGrade score is 14. Note that the LevelTwoOperators is 11. Goal Seek Scenario predicts that if you add 3 more level two operators for a total of 14, you can meet the ServiceGrade goal of between 0 and 5 percent.

Note

Another way to work with the Goal Seek Scenario tool is to run it for individual rows. Select the row that you want analyzed. Then when running the wizard, select the On This Row option instead of the Entire Table option. When running the tool in this fashion, results display in the message box along with a confidence rating (poor, fair, very good, and so on).

Using the What-If Scenario tool

The What-If Scenario tool provides the following input options:

➤ **Change:** This is where you select the column that will contain the target values of your what-if scenario. This must be a continuous column. After you select the column, you must specify your target value(s) using one of the following input options:

- *To Value*: Enter a number that specifies a target value for your target column.

- *Percentage*: Enter a number that will translate into a multiplier of the target column. For example, entering 120 would indicate that your target values should be 120 percent of the input values (or 20 percent higher).

➤ **What Happens To:** Select the column that will be impacted as a result of changing the values in the Change column.

➤ **Specify Row or Table:** Specify whether you want the what-if analysis to be applied to the entire table or the selected row.

Note

In order to use the What-If Scenario tool, your source table must contain at least 50 rows of data.

In the example shown in Figure 14-13, the What-If Scenario tool determines how many LevelTwoOperators would be needed if you changed your AverageTime expectation to 70.

	LevelTwoOperators	AverageTime	New LevelTwoOperators	Confidenc	Net
4	7	79	7		0
5	10	94	10		0
6	11	92	11		0
7	4	73	3		-1
8	8	58	8		0
9	10	83	10		0
10	12	85	12		0
11	3	68	3		0
12	8	84	7		-1
13	9	79	9		0
14	10	70	9		-1
15	4	76	3		-1
16	8	64	7		-1
17	10	70	9		-1
18	12	81	11		-1
19	6	94	6		0

Figure 14-13: Results of the What-If Scenario tool.

As you can see, two new columns are added to the input spreadsheet: New (plus the adjustable column name) and Confidence. The New column shows the value that would be needed in order to fulfill the AverageTime goal of 70.

If you look at row 7, you'll see that the actual LevelTwoOperators was 4 and the actual AverageTime was 73, which is 3 seconds above the target AverageTime of 70. In this case, the What-If Scenario tool suggests that removing one LevelTwoOperator (Net = -1) would still allow you to hit the goal of AverageTime of 70.

Note Another way to work with the What-If Scenario tool is to run it for individual rows. Select the row that you want to analyze, then select the On This Row option instead of the Entire Table option in the wizard. When running the tool in this fashion, results display in the message box along with a confidence rating (poor, fair, very good, and so on). You can also select a different row while keeping the wizard open and run the analysis again.

Prediction Calculator

We've all heard the quote "You miss 100 percent of the shots you don't take." It's easy to understand that this quote refers to the need to take risks in order to realize gains, but in realistic situations this is an oversimplification because generally speaking, the goal is to take those shots that you predict will lead to a profitable outcome while avoiding those shots that may lead to a loss. But what about the shots that you "should have" taken because they "would have" resulted in a gain? These missed opportunities, called *false negatives* in the Prediction Calculator, can be thought of as conditional or alternative outcomes and represent one of the four possible gain and loss categories to be considered when calculating the profitability of predicted scenarios. The other three — true positives, true negatives, and false positives — are discussed in this section. Using the Prediction Calculator Data Mining Add-In tool, this section discusses an approach for calculating prediction outcomes in the context of these four possible outcomes.

The Prediction Calculator tool allows you to use prior knowledge in the form of a table to ask the question: Should I take *this* shot? The answer to this Yes/No present-tense question is based not only on the statistical relationships in your input table containing historical data, but also the four gain/cost factors you provide. The result is a profit threshold that is either reached or not reached, leading to a go or no-go decision at the individual case level.

The underlying assumption behind the Prediction Calculator is that your input table has historical data points that fit into a regression model that holds the relationships between input columns (and their possible states) with a target predictable column. With this historical-based model, you can use the columns and states, such as `HomeOwner = Yes`, and predict the likelihood of obtaining a desired outcome state, such as `Bike Buyer = Yes`. When using the Prediction Calculator, the underlying algorithm is Microsoft Logistic Regression, which can handle both discrete data types (like Yes/No) and continuous data types (like salary amount).

To see the Prediction Calculator tool in action, click the Prediction Calculator button on the Analyze tab. In the Prediction Calculator dialog box, shown in Figure 14-14, identify the following inputs:

➤ **Target:** Select the column that will contain the target values of your prediction scenario. After you select the column, specify your target by using either the Exactly option (defines a specific value for your target column) or the In Range option (low and high numerical values that constitute a range where your target values should lie).

➤ **Output Options:** Choose to output an Operational Calculator (an interactive sheet where results can be manipulated) or a Printer-Ready Calculator (a single sheet with all results included).

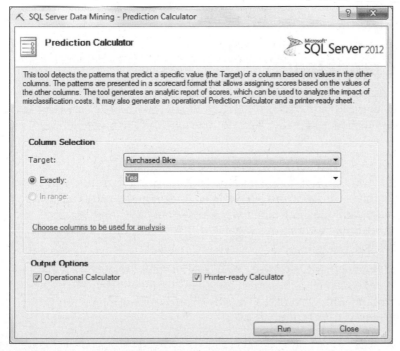

Figure 14-14: Configure the Prediction Calculator dialog box.

Click the Run button when you're done and you get a report similar to the one shown in Figure 14-15.

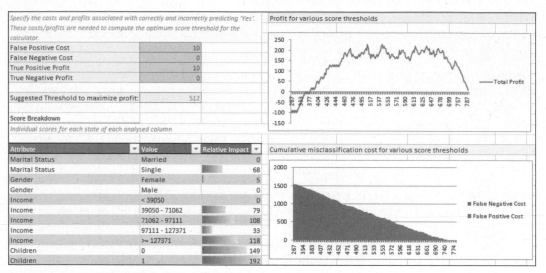

Figure 14-15: Results of the Prediction Calculator report.

The Prediction Calculator report facilitates the high-level scoring system that will be used to score predictions at the individual case level. The relevant question that can be answered by the report is "how high of a score should an individual case have in order to proceed?" The report provides the following components: Interactive cost and profit inputs, Score Breakdown, Data table, Profit for Various Score Thresholds, Cumulative Misclassification Cost for Various Score Thresholds. We discuss each of these in the following sections.

Interactive cost and profit inputs

In the upper left of the Prediction Calculator report (refer to Figure 14-15) you see the base calculation premise that includes values for profits and costs. This section allows you to specify how much profit can be gained from a true prediction, and on the flip side, how much a false prediction will cost.

Profits are associated with correct (true) predictions of the outcome state, which can be positive or negative. As a general rule, a positive outcome state is the desired outcome and leads to direct profit, while a negative outcome state simply means that you did not reach the desired positive outcome state. As expected, profits associated with true predictions vary widely depending on the scenario, which follows naturally when considering the enormous variability in economic profit between different kinds of products and services.

Costs associated with false predictions are called *misclassification costs* and also vary widely. For example, misclassification costs in targeted mail campaigns are probably small compared to misclassification costs associated with loan approvals, which in turn may be very small compared to misclassification costs associated with medical diagnoses.

The values are unique to each type of scenario being analyzed, but generally, there are two cost types and two profit types:

➤ **False positive (FP):** A prediction that targeting this customer would lead to a bicycle purchase was false (a cost was gained by targeting a customer that didn't lead to a sale).

➤ **False negative (FN):** A prediction that targeting this customer would not lead to a bicycle purchase was false (an opportunity cost was gained because the customer would have purchased a bicycle had he been targeted).

➤ **True positive (TP):** A prediction that targeting this customer would lead to a bicycle purchase was true (a sale was made with a realized gain).

➤ **True negative (TN):** A prediction that targeting this customer would not lead to a bicycle purchase was true (the cost of targeting was avoided).

You can update the input values for the Prediction Calculator, which leads to instant updates in the maximum profit chart and suggested threshold. In Figure 14-15, the profits and costs in the Prediction Calculator report as follows: False Positive Cost = $10, False Negative Cost = $0, True Positive Profit = $10, True Negative Profit = $0. These inputs give you a Suggested Threshold to Maximize Profit of 512.

Note

Although there may be significant variability in the input data that is used to build the model, such as some products that produce very high profits and some that produce very low profits, the profits and costs are global factors. This means that a true positive (that is, a sale is predicted and you did make the sale) carries the same value regardless of product cost. To get around this, you can limit the input data to similar cases so that there is more consistency in terms of matching the global profits and costs to the individual cases.

Score Breakdown

Directly below the cost and profit inputs, the Score Breakdown section uses a point system and shaded bars to show the relative impact of each input column (and input column state) in terms of its tendency to lead to the target predicted column state, which in this case is `Purchase Bike = Yes`. By sorting the Relative Impact column by Largest to Smallest, you can see the strongest predictors of purchasing a bike: `Children = 3, Cars = 0`, and so on. Note that these predictive power scores are based on the underlying regression model and do not change when you change the cost and profit inputs.

Data table

Several dozen rows below the Score Breakdown is a data table that is used as an input for the remaining charts to be discussed in the next two sections of this chapter. This data table is automatically built for purposes of simulating a reasonable number of test cases. Each test case (each row in the table) has a number of prediction outcome states (remember that there are four prediction outcome states: false positives, false negatives, true positives, and true negatives). The data table includes columns for predicted Total Cost, predicted Total Profit, and Score. The values in these columns are calculated using our input data and cost/profit factors.

Profit for Various Score Thresholds

This report section to the right of cost and profit inputs uses a line chart to show where the suggested profit maximization threshold falls. The horizontal axis represents all of the possible scores from the Score column in the data table (described in the previous section) and the vertical axis represents the Total Profit column from that same table.

Cumulative Misclassification Cost for Various Score Thresholds

Cumulative Misclassification Cost for Various Score Thresholds section is located below the Profit for Various Score Thresholds chart (refer to Figure 14-15) and shows two area segments to represent both FPs in blue and FNs in red. This example only shows an area plot for FP because there isn't a cost to be associated with FNs.

Shopping Basket Analysis

You're probably familiar with shopping basket algorithms from shopping online. Though not the only weapon in the arsenal for Web storefront businesses, this approach to maximizing customer transactions is simple and has been around for years. The idea is that historical data shows which items customers tend to buy in bundles, and this information can be used in future transactions by suggesting to you other items you should purchase. This targeting is relatively non-intrusive and can even be seen as a helpful reminder to buy something useful (given the other items in the cart) that you would have otherwise forgotten to purchase. From the business perspective, the targeting is a way to maximize the value of each transaction.

To see the Shopping Basket Analysis tool in action, follow these steps:

1. In the `DMAddins_SampleData.xlsx` sample workbook, go to the worksheet called Associate and click inside the Excel table.

2. From the Analyze tab, click the Shopping Basket Analysis button.

3. In the Shopping Basket Analysis dialog box, shown in Figure 14-16, choose the following inputs:

   - *Transaction ID:* This is where you identify a column that represents a transaction ID. This column gives the association algorithm a way to group rows that belong to the same transaction. This column could be called OrderID or something else, as long as it is the identifier of a transaction.

- *Item:* This is where you specify the column that represents the item being sold. Common examples of the kinds of columns used as the Item would be Product Name, Product Category, and Product Type.

- *Item Value:* This is an optional input that allows you to introduce a column of quantitative data. Typical columns used as Item Values are Product Price and Product Count.

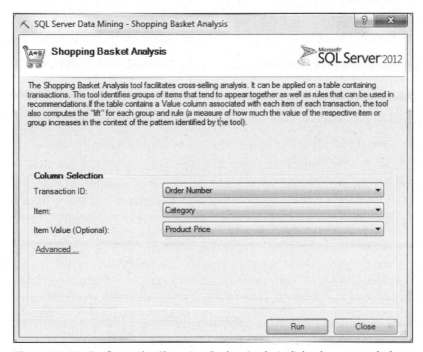

Figure 14-16: Configure the Shopping Basket Analysis dialog box as needed.

4. Click the Run button.

You get a report similar to the one shown in Figure 14-17.

Bundle of items	Bundle size	Number of sales	Average Value Per Sale	Overall value of Bundle
Fender Set - Mountain, Mountain-200	2	438	$2,342	$1,025,783
Mountain Bottle Cage, Mountain-200	2	430	$2,330	$1,001,891
Mountain-200, Sport-100	2	407	$2,374	$966,210
Touring-1000, Sport-100	2	344	$2,438	$838,693
Mountain Bottle Cage, Mountain-200, Water	3	344	$2,335	$803,230
Mountain-200, Water Bottle	2	344	$2,325	$799,793
HL Mountain Tire, Mountain-200	2	314	$2,355	$739,467
Mountain-200, Patch kit	2	209	$2,885	$602,961
Touring-1000, Road Bottle Cage	2	216	$2,393	$516,901
Road-350-W, Sport-100	2	206	$2,497	$514,452
HL Mountain Tire, Mountain-200, Mountain T	3	204	$2,360	$481,436
Mountain-200, Mountain Tire Tube	2	204	$2,325	$474,296
Touring-1000, Road Bottle Cage, Water Bottle	3	195	$2,398	$467,620
Touring-1000, Water Bottle	2	195	$2,389	$465,867

Figure 14-17: Results of the Shopping Basket Analysis.

The final output contains the following columns:

➤ **Bundle of Items:** Each bundle that has been identified in the input table is listed as item 1, item 2, and so on. For example, the bundle in row 8 consists of a Touring-1000 (bicycle) and Sport-100 (helmet), while the bundle in row 13 also lists the Touring-1000 but this time bundled with the Road Bottle Cage.

➤ **Bundle Size:** This column tells how many items are included in the bundle. Although you can determine the bundle size by examining the bundle description that appears in the column to the left, the Bundle Size column proves to be useful in other ways. For example, you can sort the results based on bundle size if you're interested in studying only those bundles that are at least a certain size.

➤ **Number of Sales:** This column tells how many cases (rows) from the input table are included in the bundle. For example, the bundle in row 8 (Touring-1000 bicycle and Sport-100 helmet) resulted in 344 sales transactions, but the bundle in row 13, which also includes a Touring-1000 bicycle, resulted in only 216 transactions.

➤ **Average Value Per Sale:** While the main point of this report is to identify bundles of items, it is even more useful to identify those bundles that tend to produce higher revenues on the whole. Suppose you have two different bundles, Bundle 1 and Bundle 2, which both include a particular item that costs $100 ("Item A"). If Bundle 1 packages Item A with a low-cost item, say $10, while Bundle 2 packages it with a higher-priced item, say $50, you'd prefer Bundle 2 to Bundle 1 because it generates higher sales revenue. The only thing that might stop you from suggesting the item from Bundle 2 when customers put Item A into their carts is data that shows Bundle 2 is not sufficiently likely to occur, which can be determined based on the Number of Sales column. The Average Value Per Sale column helps you make these kinds of decisions by giving you the average price of each bundle. In the report output, you can see that the first bundle resulted in an average bundle price of $2,341. *Note:* The average is used here because some transactions may price the same item differently.

➤ **Overall Value of Bundle:** When it comes to analyzing bundles of items, another useful measure is the overall revenues realized by all instances of a given bundle. Although you could probably do the math, this column does the math for you. In the report output, you can see that the Touring-1000 bicycle and Sport-100 helmet bundle in row 8 resulted in aggregate sales of $838,693, and the Touring-1000 bicycle and Road Bottle Cage bundle in row 13 resulted in sales of $516,901. You should also notice that the rows in the table are sorted by this column in descending order.

In addition to the Shopping Basket bundled items report, the Data Mining Add-In creates a worksheet that provides recommendations on what to do with the bundles. This report output (see Figure 14-18) consists of the following columns:

➤ **Selected Item:** Of the items identified to be commonly included in bundles, each is listed separately in this column. You can think of the values in this column as a starting point; that is, the first item a customer puts into her cart. In the report output, the first item listed is Mountain Tire Tube.

➤ **Recommendation:** If you're focusing on an item as a starting point for a bundle recommendation, this column provides that recommendation. Put another way, this column recommends a second item that should be "hinted" or "suggested" to accompany the first item in the customer's cart. Looking at the report, you can see that if a customer puts a Mountain Tire Tube into her cart, you should suggest the Sport-100.

➤ **Sales of Selected Items:** What is the proof behind the recommendation? The Sales of Selected Items column, along with the next two columns (Linked Sales and % of Linked Sales), provide the proof. The Sales of Selected Items column tells you the aggregate sales volume for the item that appears in the Selected Item column. For example, you had 749 sales that included the Mountain Tire Tube item.

➤ **Linked Sales:** The Linked Sales column represents the power of the relationship between the item in the Recommendation column and the item in the Selected Item column.

Selected Item	Recommendation	Sales of Selected Items	Linked Sales	% of linked sales
Mountain Tire Tube	Sport-100	1782	749	42.03 %
All-Purpose Bike Stand	Patch kit	130	54	41.54 %
Half-Finger Gloves	Sport-100	849	352	41.46 %
Touring-1000	Sport-100	811	344	42.42 %
Touring Tire Tube	Touring Tire	897	507	56.52 %
Road-550-W	Sport-100	618	264	42.72 %
Mountain Bottle Cage	Water Bottle	1201	998	83.10 %
Touring-2000	Sport-100	211	86	40.76 %
Road Bottle Cage	Water Bottle	1005	897	89.25 %
ML Road Tire	Road Tire Tube	533	363	68.11 %
LL Road Tire	Road Tire Tube	608	334	54.93 %
HL Road Tire	Road Tire Tube	463	326	70.41 %
HL Mountain Tire	Mountain Tire Tube	816	552	67.65 %
Touring Tire	Touring Tire Tube	582	507	87.11 %
ML Mountain Tire	Mountain Tire Tube	661	435	65.81 %
LL Mountain Tire	Mountain Tire Tube	499	277	55.51 %

Figure 14-18: The Shopping Basket recommendations report.

PART III

Delivering Business Intelligence with SharePoint and Excel Services

Publishing Your BI Tools to SharePoint

In This Chapter

- Understanding SharePoint and Excel Services
- Publishing an Excel workbook to SharePoint
- Using the Power Pivot Gallery
- Refreshing Power Pivot data connections
- Managing Power Pivot performance

Each version of Microsoft Office has demonstrated a greater ability to integrate with SharePoint. The most exciting aspect of this new paradigm is that you can publish interactive BI solutions to a Web site.

By publishing your Excel reports and dashboards to SharePoint, you can make them available to others in your organization via a browser. This avoids multiple users having separate versions of your workbooks on their computers. This also enables you to make your BI solutions easier to find, share, and use.

In this chapter, you gain a basic understanding of what SharePoint is and how it helps organizations share and collaborate data. You also explore how to publish your Excel reports and dashboards to SharePoint.

Understanding SharePoint

SharePoint is Microsoft's premier collaborative server environment, providing tools for sharing documents and data across various organizations within your company network.

SharePoint is typically deployed on a company's network as a series of intranet sites, giving various departments the ability to control their own security, workgroups, documents, and data. As with any other Web site, a SharePoint site — even an individual page within the site — is accessible through a URL.

SharePoint is most often used to store version-controlled documents, such as Word documents and Excel worksheets. In many environments, documents are passed back and forth between users via e-mail. There is considerable potential for mixing up different versions of the same document. Also, storing multiple copies of the same document takes up a lot of disk space. Because SharePoint provides a single source for storing, viewing, and updating documents, many of these issues are eliminated entirely. Because SharePoint easily handles any type of document, it's frequently used to consolidate and store various types of documentation (such as project drawings, videos, schematics, photographs, and workbooks) required for large projects where multiple teams must collaborate.

Why SharePoint?

Microsoft chose SharePoint as the platform for Excel publishing because of the significant features built into SharePoint, including the following:

➤ **Security:** SharePoint supports users and groups of users. Users and groups may be granted or denied access to various parts of a SharePoint Web site, and designated users may be granted permission to add, delete, or modify the site.

➤ **Versioning:** SharePoint automatically maintains a version history of objects and data. Changes can be rolled back to an earlier state at virtually any time. The ability to roll back changes can be granted to individual users, and DBA support is not required.

➤ **Recycle bin:** Deleted data and objects are held in a recycle bin so that they may be recovered. SharePoint supports an undo feature for its data.

➤ **Alerts:** Users and groups can be sent e-mail when a specific document in SharePoint is added, deleted, or changed. If granted the proper permissions, users can manage their own alerts.

➤ **End-user maintenance:** SharePoint sites are meant to be maintained by their users, without the intervention of IT departments. Although SharePoint pages are not as flexible as typical Web pages, a SharePoint developer can add or remove features from pages; change fonts, headings, colors, and other attributes of pages; create sub-sites and lists; and perform many other maintenance and enhancement tasks.

➤ **Other features:** Every SharePoint site includes a number of features, such as a calendar, a task list, and announcements that users can turn off or remove.

Note

Most IT organizations have already implemented a SharePoint environment, so it's likely that your organization already has SharePoint running on your network. No one user can simply stand up a SharePoint site. If you're interested in using SharePoint, contact your IT department about getting access to a SharePoint site.

Understanding Excel Services for SharePoint

The mechanism that allows for the publishing of Excel documents to SharePoint as interactive Web pages is Excel Services. Excel Services is a broad term that describes the following three components:

➤ **Excel Calculation Services:** Serves as the primary engine of Excel Services. This component loads Excel documents, runs calculations on the Excel sheet, and runs the refresh process for any embedded data connection.

➤ **Excel Web Access:** This component allows users to interact with Excel through a Web server.

➤ **Excel Web Services:** This component is hosted in SharePoint Services and provides developers with an application programming interface (API) to build custom applications based on the Excel workbook.

When you publish a workbook to Excel Services, your audience can interact with your Excel file in several ways:

➤ View workbooks that contain a Data Model and Power View reports

➤ Navigate between worksheets

➤ Sort and filter data

➤ Work with PivotTables

➤ Use slicers and PivotTable report filters

➤ Refresh data for embedded data connections

Limitations of Excel Services

It's important to understand that workbooks on the Web are running in an environment that is quite different from the Excel client application you have on your PC. Excel Services has limitations on the features it can render on the Web browser. Some limitations are due to security issues, while others are simply because Microsoft hasn't had time to evolve Excel Services to include the broad set of features that come with standard Excel.

Limitations include the following:

➤ Data validation does not work on the Web. This feature is simply ignored when you publish your workbook to the Web.

➤ No form of VBA, including macros, runs in the Excel Web App. Your VBA procedures simply do not transfer with the workbook.

➤ Worksheet protection does not work on the Web. Instead, you need to use the options shown in the Browser View Options dialog box (look ahead to Figure 15-2).

➤ Links to external workbooks no longer work after publishing to the Web.

➤ You can use any PivotTables with full fidelity on the Web, but you cannot create any new PivotTables while your workbook is on the Web. You need to create any PivotTables in the desktop version of Excel on your PC before publishing on the Web.

➤ OfficeArt, including Shapes, WordArt, SmartArt, diagrams, signature lines, and ink annotations, doesn't render on the Web.

SharePoint requirements and Office 365

Excel Services is a SharePoint implementation that is available only with SharePoint 2010 or 2013, so you'll want to ensure that your SharePoint site is one of those two versions.

You most likely work in a SharePoint 2010 or 2013 environment. However, if you don't have access to an existing SharePoint environment, hundreds of service providers offer subscription-based SharePoint services. Many of these providers provide volume-based pricing on a subscription model.

In fact, Microsoft offers Office 365, a cloud-based Microsoft environment that gives you a line of collaborative Microsoft Office–like tools that you can access through the Web. Similar to Google Docs or Google Spreadsheets, Microsoft offers Word, Excel, and PowerPoint in Office 365. This means you can use Office 365 to publish and host your Excel solutions.

Subscribing to a commercial SharePoint service provider may be the fastest and most affordable way to host Microsoft Excel solutions on SharePoint. Again, the only caveat is that the commercial service provider you choose must offer either SharePoint 2010 or 2013 with Excel Services implemented.

Publishing an Excel Workbook to SharePoint

In order to take advantage of the functionality afforded by Excel Services, you must have permission to publish to a SharePoint site that is running Excel Services. You'll need to speak with your IT department to obtain access.

When you have access to publish to SharePoint, follow these steps:

1. Choose File ➜ Save As, select Other Web Locations, and then click the Browse button.

   The Save As dialog box opens, as shown in Figure 15-1.

2. Enter the URL address of your SharePoint site in the File Name box and click the Browser View Options button.

   The Browser View Options dialog box opens, as shown in Figure 15-2.

3. Select which parts of your workbook you want to make available on the Web, and then click OK.

   You can choose to show the entire workbook, only certain sheets, or only specific objects (charts, PivotTables, and so on). You can also define parameters to allow certain named ranges to be editable in the Web browser.

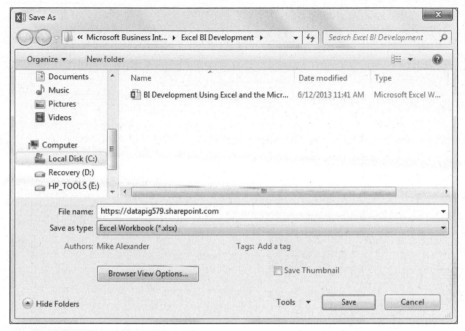

Figure 15-1: Enter your SharePoint URL in the File Name box of the Save As dialog box.

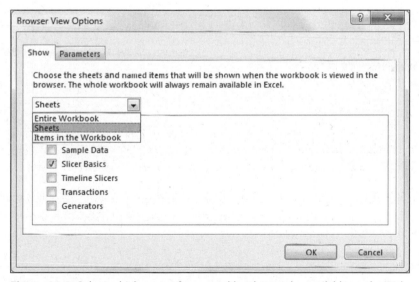

Figure 15-2: Select which parts of your workbook to make available on the Web.

4. Click Save in the Save As dialog box.

   You then connect to the SharePoint site and get a list of the document libraries, as shown in Figure 15-3.

Note

Think of these libraries as folders on the SharePoint site.

5. Enter the name of the file in the File Name box, double-click the library where you want to save your file, and then click Save.

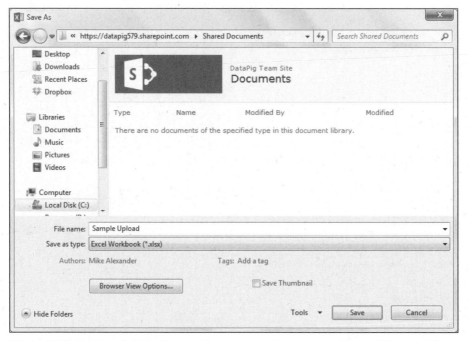

Figure 15-3: Double-click the library where you want to save your file, and then click Save.

After you have published the workbook, you can view it on the Web by going to your SharePoint site and finding the document in the appropriate library. When you open the workbook, it shows in the browser with several menu options (see Figure 15-4):

➤ **Edit Workbook:** Either download the workbook or edit the workbook in the browser.

➤ **Share:** E-mail a link to your newly published workbook.

➤ **Data:** Refresh any external data connections you have in your workbook.

➤ **Find:** Search for specific text in the workbook.

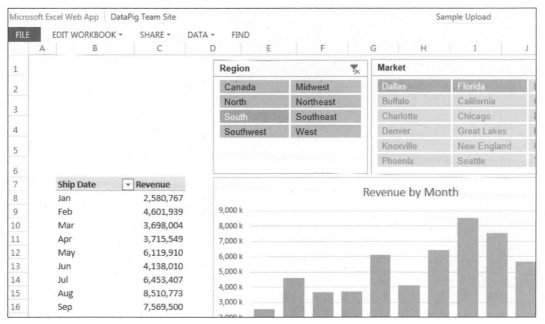

Figure 15-4: A workbook as shown in Excel Services.

Publishing to a Power Pivot Gallery

A Power Pivot Gallery is a type of document library that showcases Power Pivot reports and allows for scheduled refresh cycles.

For your end users, the Power Pivot Gallery provides an attractive portal that serves as a one-stop shop for all the reports and dashboards you publish. For you, the Power Pivot Gallery enables better management of your Power Pivot solutions by allowing you to schedule nightly refreshes of the data in them.

You need to speak with your SharePoint administrator about your organization's SharePoint instance and ask him to consider adding a Power Pivot Gallery to your site. When you have access to a Power Pivot Gallery, you can upload your Power Pivot workbooks using the same steps you took to publish a standard workbook to SharePoint.

Figure 15-5 shows a typical Power Pivot Gallery. Note that each workbook is shown as a thumbnail, providing users with a snapshot of the each report. Clicking a thumbnail opens the report as a Web page.

Note

If you're using an Office 365 SharePoint subscription, you unfortunately have no option for a Power Pivot Gallery, as Office 365 doesn't support it. This may change in the future as Microsoft continues to add improvements to Office 365.

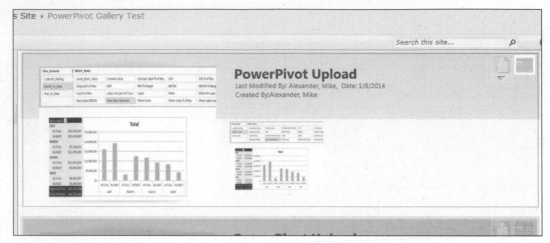

Figure 15-5: A Power Pivot Gallery.

You can manually refresh the data connections within your published Power Pivot report by opening the workbook and selecting the Data drop-down menu, as shown in Figure 15-6. You have the option of refreshing a single selected connection or all connections in the workbook.

FILE	EDIT WORKBOOK ▾	SHARE ▾	DATA ▾	FIND
	A	B	C	

Refresh Selected Connection
Refresh the data connection for the currently selected PivotTable or PivotChart.

Refresh All Connections
Refresh all data connections in the workbook.

Calculate Workbook
Recalculate the workbook.

Figure 15-6: Use the Data drop-down menu to manually refresh data connections.

If you don't want to go through the trouble to manually refresh your connections, you can set a schedule. Click the Manage Data icon in the upper right-hand corner of the target report (see Figure 15-7).

SharePoint opens the Manage Data Refresh window shown in Figure 15-8. The idea is to configure each setting to achieve the desired refresh schedule.

➤ **Data Refresh:** The Data Refresh setting is the On/Off switch for your schedule. Select the Enable check box to make the schedule active. Deselect the check box to stop automatic refreshes.

➤ **Schedule Details:** The Schedule Details section allows you to specify the frequency and intervals of your schedule. In addition to selecting your time intervals, you have the option to refresh as soon as possible. Selecting this option starts a refresh within a minute, letting you test your refresh process and ensure that it runs properly.

Manage Data Refresh

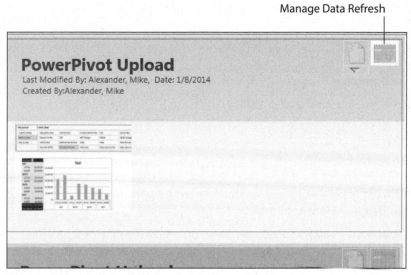

Figure 15-7: Refresh your data with this icon.

Data Refresh Specify if you would like to turn Data Refresh on or off.	☑ Enable
Schedule Details Define the frequency (daily, weekly, monthly or once) and the timing details for the refresh schedule.	◉ Daily ◉ Every `1` day(s) ◯ Weekly ◯ Every weekday ◯ Monthly ◯ On the following days: ◯ Once ☐ Sunday ☐ Monday ☐ Tuesday ☐ Wednesday ☐ Thursday ☐ Friday ☐ Saturday ☐ Also refresh as soon as possible
Earliest Start Time Specify the earliest start time that the data refresh will begin	◯ After business hours ◉ Specific earliest start time: `3` ▾ : `00` ▾ ◉ am ◯ pm
E-mail Notifications Specify e-mail address of the users to be notified in the event of data refresh failures.	Alexander, Mike ; 🖉 📖
Credentials Provide the credentials that will be used to refresh data on your behalf.	◉ Use the data refresh account configured by the administrator ◯ Connect using the following Windows user credentials ◯ Connect using the credentials saved in Secure Store Service (SSS) to log on to the data source. Enter the ID used to look up the credentials in the SSS ID box
Data Sources Select which data sources should be automatically refreshed.	☑ All data sources **Refresh** **Data Source** ☑ vmsqlprod01_sp2010dev SYNOPSIS MARKERS 3

Figure 15-8: Set a schedule to refresh your data.

➤ **Earliest Start Time:** The Earliest Start Time specifies the time of day to run the refresh process.

➤ **E-mail Notifications:** The E-mail Notifications setting lets you specify who should receive an e-mail from SharePoint each time the scheduled refresh is run. Note that individuals specified will receive an e-mail whether the process ran with errors or ran successfully.

➤ **Credentials:** Most data sources require authentication in order to pull data in a refresh process. The Credentials setting specifies how authentication is passed to external data sources. There are three options:

   ● *Use the Data Refresh Account Configured by the Administrator:* This means that a SharePoint system account authenticates to the data source. You typically have to work with your SharePoint administrator to set up this authentication method and ensure that the data source can use SharePoint's system account.

   ● *Connect Using the Following Windows User Credentials:* This enables you to enter a user-name and password for authentication. It's not a good idea to use your own personal username and password here. Instead, this option is best used with an application account — a dummy account created by your database administrators.

   ● *Connect Using the Credentials Saved in Secure Store Service (SSS) to Log On to the Data Source:* This option allows you to refresh data connections without a password. To do so, you need to acquire a Secure Store ID from your SharePoint administrator.

➤ **Data Sources:** This setting lets you define whether all data connections are refreshed, or only specific connections. Deselect the All Data Sources check box to enable the selection of individual connections in your workbook.

Managing Power Pivot Performance

When you publish Power Pivot reports to the Web, you want to give your audience the best experience possible. A large part of that experience is ensuring that performance is not an issue. In terms of applications and reporting, performance is typically synonymous with speed. Speed is how quickly your application performs certain actions, such as opening within the browser, running queries, and filtering.

Because Power Pivot inherently paves the way for large amounts of data with fairly liberal restrictions, it's common to end up with BI solutions that work, but are unbearably slow. And nothing turns your intended audience away from your slick new BI solution faster than sluggish performance.

To help you create the best interactive experience for your users, and ultimately improve user adoption of your published BI solutions, we wrap up this chapter with some best practices for optimizing the performance of your Power Pivot reports.

Limit the number of columns in your Data Model tables

One of the biggest influences on Power Pivot performance is the number of columns you import into the Data Model. Every column you import is one more dimension Power Pivot has to process when loading your workbook. If you're not certain you will use certain columns, don't bring them in "just in case." You can easily add columns if you find you need them later.

Limit the number of rows in your Data Model

This one is simple. More rows mean more data to load, more data to filter, and more data to calculate through. Avoid selecting an entire table if you don't have to. Use a query or a view at the source database to filter for only the rows you need to import. Why import 400,000 rows of data when you can use a simple `Where` clause and import 100,000?

Avoid multi-level relationships

Both the number of relationships and the number of relationship layers have an impact on the performance of your Power Pivot reports. When building your model, it's a best practice to have a single fact table containing primarily quantitative numerical data (facts) and dimension tables that relate to the facts directly. In database-speak, this configuration is called a *star schema* (see Figure 15-9).

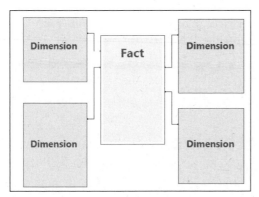

Figure 15-9: A star schema is the most efficient model, with a single fact table and dimensions relating directly to it.

Avoid building models where dimension tables relate to other dimension tables. Figure 15-10 illustrates this configuration, also known as a *snowflake schema*. This configuration forces Power Pivot to perform relationship lookups across several dimension levels. This can be particularly inefficient depending on the volume of data in the model.

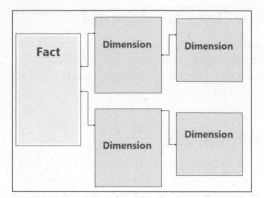

Figure 15-10: Snowflake schemas are less efficient, causing Power Pivot to perform chain lookups.

Let your back-end database servers do the crunching

Most Excel analysts who are new to Power Pivot have the tendency to pull raw data directly from the tables on their external database servers. When the raw data is in Power Pivot, they then build calculated columns and measures to transform and aggregate the data as needed. For example, it's common to pull revenue and cost data, then create a calculated column in Power Pivot to compute profit. So why make Power Pivot do this calculation when the back-end server could have handled it?

The reality is that back-end database systems like SQL Server have the ability to shape, aggregate, clean, and transform data much more efficiently than Power Pivot. Why not utilize their powerful capabilities to massage and shape your data before importing into Power Pivot?

Instead of pulling raw table data, consider leveraging queries, views, and stored procedures to perform much of the data aggregation and crunching work for you. This reduces the amount of processing Power Pivot has to do and naturally improves performance.

Beware of columns with non-distinct values

Columns that have a high number of unique values are particularly hard on Power Pivot performance. Columns like Transaction ID, Order ID, and Invoice Number are often unnecessary in high-level Power Pivot reports and dashboards. So unless they are needed to establish relationships to other tables, leave them out of your model.

Avoid the excessive use of slicers

Slicers are one of the best BI features added to Excel in recent years. With slicers, you can provide your audience with an intuitive interface that allows for interactive filtering of your Excel reports and dashboards.

One of the more attractive benefits of slicers is that they respond to one another, giving you a cascading filter effect. For example, in Figure 15-11, clicking Midwest in the Region slicer not only filters the PivotTable, but also the Market slicer responds by highlighting the markets that belong to the Midwest region. Microsoft calls this behavior *cross-filtering*.

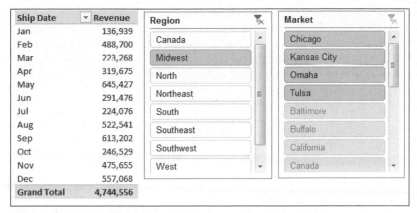

Figure 15-11: Slicers work together to show you relevant data items based on your selection.

As useful as slicers are, they are, unfortunately, extremely bad for Power Pivot performance. Take a moment to think about this. Each time a slicer is changed, Power Pivot must recalculate all the values and measures in the PivotTable. In order to do that, Power Pivot must evaluate each tile in the selected slicer and process the appropriate calculations based on the selection.

Take that a step further and think about what happens when you add a second slicer. Because slicers cross-filter, each time you click one slicer, the other slicer also changes, so it's almost as if you clicked both of them. Power Pivot must respond to both slicers, evaluating each tile in both slicers for each calculated measure in the PivotTable. So adding a second slicer is tantamount to doubling the processing time. Add a third slicer, and you have tripled the processing time.

In short, slicers are bad for Power Pivot performance. However, the functionality slicers bring to Excel BI solutions is too good to give up completely.

The following is a list of actions you can take to mitigate any performance issues you may be having with your Power Pivot reports:

> **Limit the number of slicers in your report.** Remove the slicers one at a time, testing the performance of your Power Pivot report after each removal. You'll often find that removing one of your slicers is enough to correct performance issues.

> **Only create slicers on dimension fields.** Consider building slicers using the fields in smaller dimension tables — not the considerably larger fact tables in your model. Note that slicers with many tiles often cause a larger performance hit than those containing only a handful of tiles. Avoid slicers that contain a large number of tiles, opting instead to use a PivotTable Filter drop-down menu instead.

> **Remove slicers that aren't clicked very often.** Some slicers hold filter values that frankly aren't touched very often. For example, you may have a slicer that allows users to select current year or last year. If the last year view is not often called up, consider removing the slicer or using PivotTable Filter drop-down menu instead.

➤ **Disable the cross-filter behavior for some slicers.** Disabling the cross-filter behavior of a slicer essentially prevents that slicer from changing selections when other slicers are clicked. This prevents the need for Power Pivot to evaluate the titles in the disabled slicer, thus reducing processing cycles. To disable the cross-filter behavior, right-click the target slicer and select Slicer Settings. In the Slicer Settings dialog box, deselect the Visually Indicate Items with No Data check box, as shown in Figure 15-12.

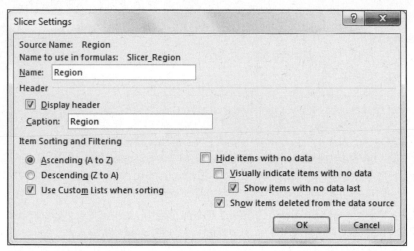

Figure 15-12: Deselect the Visually Indicate Items with No Data check box to disable the slicer's cross-filter behavior.

Leveraging Performance Point Services

In This Chapter

- Accessing the strengths and limitations of PerformancePoint

- Designing a dashboard through the Authoring Dashboard

- Viewing a dashboard with the PerformancePoint dashboard

In this chapter, we discuss the Authoring Dashboard — the tools and concepts that are necessary to create and edit dashboards with Dashboard Designer — and using PerformancePoint — which allows you to interact with your report.

 Note

In this chapter, we use the AdventureWorks Analysis Services Tutorial sample database installed with SQL Server Analysis Services.

The capabilities within PerformancePoint are geared toward someone with knowledge of databases and other relevant technologies. But if you have the appropriate permissions to a SharePoint site with PerformancePoint enabled, you can also leverage many of its capabilities.

Why PerformancePoint?

Over the years, Microsoft consistently releases impressive database software with its SQL Server family of products, while retaining its leadership position in the office productivity category. Somewhere in between these two product families is a specialized data tools vacuum that Microsoft has addressed with PerformancePoint. From the perspective of end users, this specialized area could be described as a Web-based application that facilitates both general reporting of business intelligence data as well as interactive, dashboard-style analytics.

PerformancePoint strengths

PerformancePoint is one of Microsoft's long-standing offerings if you need Web-based, interactive, dashboard-style analytics and reporting. Besides the fact that it's available as part of the SharePoint Enterprise family of applications (check with your IT department to see if it is enabled on a SharePoint site within your organization), here are a few advantages of using PerformancePoint:

➤ **Web-based interface:** PerformancePoint is Web-based, requiring no user installation. This makes it perfect if you need author dashboards that are shared with large groups of users. In fact, one of the biggest strengths of PerformancePoint is how well it can scale to massive user bases.

➤ **Rich interactions:** You've become accustomed to working with data with ultimate flexibility — working with data in the context of drill-downs, ad hoc queries, or a broad range of interactive features. PerformancePoint provides all of the classic business intelligence tool functionality along with a few extra features.

➤ **Great performance:** You don't have to wait for more than a few seconds after each click. PerformancePoint provides good performance in most scenarios.

PerformancePoint limitations

Now that we have discussed the benefits of PerformancePoint, we need to address the cautions that come along with it:

➤ **Limited options for data visualizations:** Dashboards are all about visualizing data, which creates a need for significant flexibility to visualize the same data in many different ways. PerformancePoint focuses on a few well-proven visualizations that work well for all kinds of data (bar charts, area charts, grid, and so on). However, there are one or two surprises, such as the decomposition tree.

➤ **Complicated installation:** Although it probably won't matter much to you, installing and configuring PerformancePoint is not a trivial matter. Furthermore, though PerformancePoint is bundled with SharePoint Enterprise, it's not installed by default and requires some additional setup. Additional server resources may also need to be allocated, depending on the number of projected users and data.

➤ **Learning curve for dashboard authoring:** Though not rocket science, there is enough complexity in PerformancePoint to make it a challenge for beginners, especially when considering some of the advanced features of PerformancePoint such as integrating external Web reports and customizing filter behavior with MDX.

Authoring Dashboards

Building and editing dashboards is referred to as *authoring*. In this section, we focus on authoring interactive PerformancePoint dashboards, which are connected to Analysis Services data sources.

Note **Although it's beyond the scope of this book, PerformancePoint also provides the functionality to connect to other data sources and build reports and filters based on those custom data connections.**

Getting started

PerformancePoint Services is a feature of SharePoint Enterprise Edition. The primary document type in PerformancePoint is a *dashboard,* of which there are two modes of use: authoring (creating and editing dashboards) and viewing (interacting with dashboards). To author dashboards, you must launch the Dashboard Designer.

A PerformancePoint dashboard is made up of several elements: data connections, reports, and (optionally) filters. In the following sections, we walk through each of these in detail.

Launching the Dashboard Designer

SharePoint maintains interface simplicity by showing only those features and options that are applicable based on where you are and what you are doing in that moment.

To open Dashboard Designer, follow these steps:

1. Open SharePoint and click the View All Site Contents link (typically on the left side bar).

2. In the Site Contents page, you will see several libraries. Find and click the Dashboard library.

Note **If you can't find a Dashboard library in your SharePoint environment, ask your SharePoint Administrator or IT department for help setting up a PerformancePoint library for you.**

You're taken to a PerformancePoint site where the SharePoint Ribbon includes a PerformancePoint tab. (See Figure 16-1.)

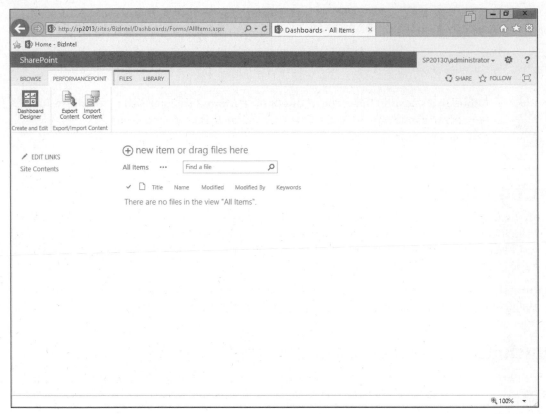

Figure 16-1: Open your PerformancePoint Site and click Dashboard Designer.

3. On the PerformancePoint tab, click the Dashboard Designer icon. If prompted to run initial setup scripts, click Yes.

If it's your first time launching the PerformancePoint Dashboard Designer, it will be installed on your machine. After the installation, you can launch Dashboard Designer from either the PerformancePoint site or your PC (Start ➜ All Programs ➜ SharePoint ➜ PerformancePoint Dashboard Designer).

Whether installing for the first time or simply opening an already installed instance, the Dashboard Designer automatically opens and starts you off with an empty workspace. (See Figure 16-2.)

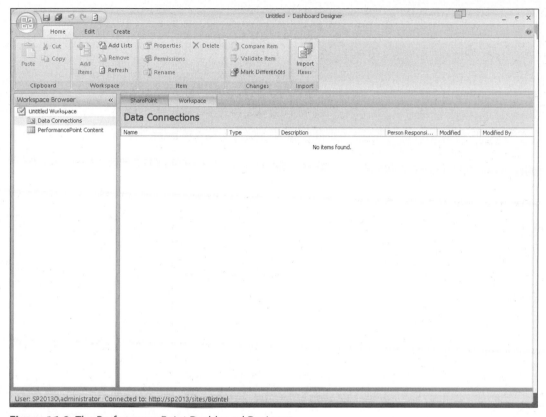

Figure 16-2: The PerformancePoint Dashboard Designer.

Adding a data connection

You can think of PerformancePoint as a user interface layer between the dashboard users and the business intelligence data infrastructure, which is a *data source*.

Note

PerformancePoint is designed to use Analysis Services cubes as data sources in an efficient way, and although this is common, PerformancePoint can also use other types of data sources, including relational databases and Excel documents.

In PerformancePoint, you configure data sources manually in the Dashboard Designer as *data connections*. A PerformancePoint data connection is a small configuration file with information about an underlying data source, making it possible for reports, filters, and other PerformancePoint components to leverage that data source. After they're set up, data connections remain in the PerformancePoint library and you can reuse them across many dashboards.

Follow these steps to configure a new data connection:

1. Right-click Data Connections in the Workspace Browser (the pane on the left side of the window) and select New Data Source.

   The Select a Data Source Template dialog box shown in Figure 16-3 opens.

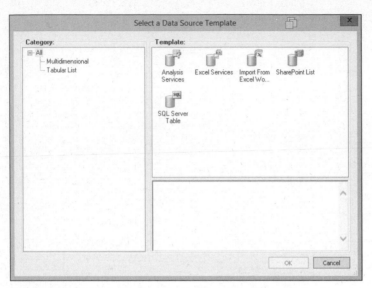

Figure 16-3: The Select a Data Source Template dialog box.

2. Double-click the appropriate template for your data.

   In this example, we select the Analysis Services template.

   The Data Connections Properties window shown in Figure 16-4 appears.

3. Enter the server name, select the database name, and then click the Cube drop-down menu to select the desired cube.

   All other properties are optional (and beyond the scope of this book).

4. Click the Test Data Source button to test the connection.

5. Click the Home tab, and then click Refresh to save your changes to the server.

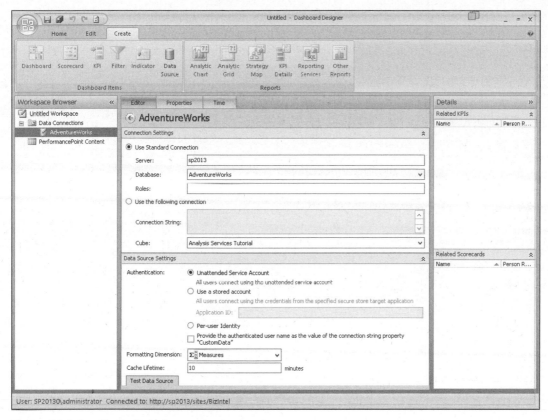

Figure 16-4: Specify the Data Connection properties.

Tip

If you can't select a cube from the Connection Settings dialog box, then either your IT department must resolve a SharePoint configuration issue or you haven't provided the correct values for a server name and database name where a cube actually exists. One way to make sure you're pointing to a valid Analysis Services cube is to connect to the cube in an Excel PivotTable first. If you can connect and browse the cube in an Excel PivotTable but can't connect to that same database and cube in PerformancePoint, then you have a SharePoint configuration issue.

Adding content

After you've created and saved one or more data connections, you can create PerformancePoint content. PerformancePoint content types include KPI, Filter, Report, Dashboard, Indicator, and Scorecard. The following sections focus on Filters, Reports, and Dashboards.

You can add content by right-clicking the PerformancePoint Content folder in the Workspace Browser (the pane on the left side), selecting New, and then selecting one of the available content types. (See Figure 16-5.)

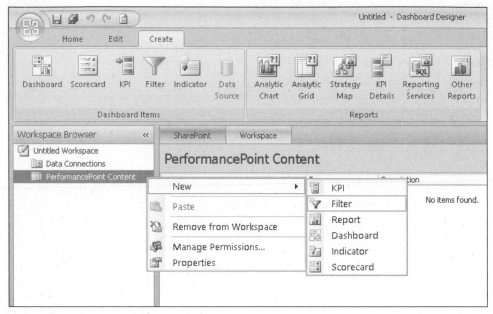

Figure 16-5: Adding content.

Tip

These contents types are also available as icons on the Create tab of the PerformancePoint Ribbon.

Adding a filter

Interaction between dashboard objects is one of the primary features that makes dashboards such powerful tools. One of the most important dashboard objects is the filter, which you can use in a variety of formats based on the type of data. For example, you can use dates in a calendar or use a drill-down tree for an org chart.

PerformancePoint offers a number of Filter templates. If you choose to add a Filter template, you're presented with the Select a Filter Template dialog box shown in Figure 16-6.

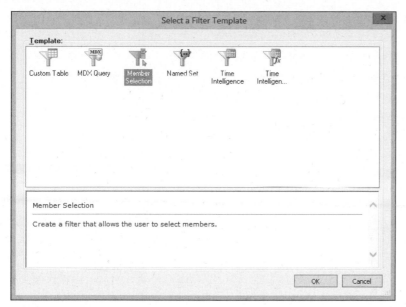

Figure 16-6: Choosing a Filter template.

The Member Selection template is by far the easiest filter template to work with because you're provided with a visual interface that allows you to define the behavior of the filter by clicking and dragging dimension and members. The other filter templates shown in Figure 16-6 require familiarity with MDX or additional SharePoint configurations.

Follow these steps to add a Member Selection filter:

1. In the Select a Filter Template dialog box (refer to Figure 16-6), click Member Selection and then click OK.

   The Create a Filter Wizard appears.

2. Enter a name for your filter in the Name text box and then click Next.

3. Select the data connection you want to use for the filter and then click Next.

4. Click the Select Members option on the left side of the Select Members dialog box, as shown in Figure 16-7.

   The Select Members dialog box shows the list of dimensions based on the underlying data connection. Some dimensions contain multiple hierarchies to choose from. In Figure 16-7, the Calendar Date hierarchy is selected from the Date dimension.

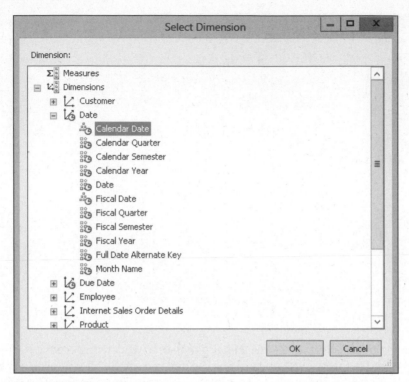

Figure 16-7: Choose the dimension you want to us to populate the filter.

5. Choose the dimension you want to use to populate the filter and then click OK to close the Select Members dialog box.

Tip

While the Select Members dialog box is open, you can right-click a member in your chosen dimension, choose Set as Default Selection, and then click OK. This action sets the member you selected as the default value for the filter.

6. Choose the dimension you want to use to populate the filter and then click OK to close the Select Members dialog box.

   At this point, your Create a Filter Wizard looks similar to the one in Figure 16-8.

7. Click the Next button.

8. Select how you want your filter to be displayed. You have three options:

   - *List:* This option displays your filter as a simple drop-down menu that can be used to select a desired filter item.

   - *Tree:* This option displays your filter as an expandable tree control. Your audience will click to expand the tree control and then select individual items to apply as a filter.

   - *Multi-Select Tree:* This option displays your filter as an expandable tree control with check boxes. Your audience can click to expand the tree control and then select individual items with check boxes.

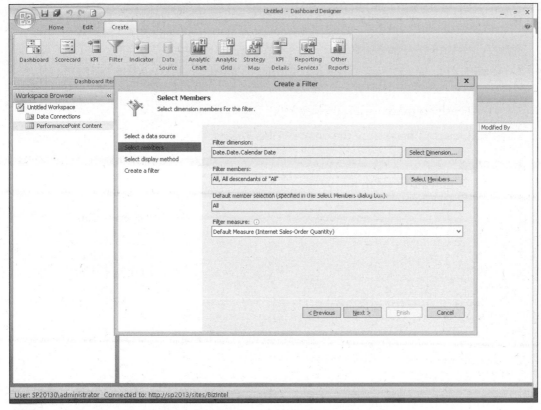

Figure 16-8: The Create a Filter Wizard with selected dimensions and members.

9. Click the Finish button to review the settings.

10. Click the Close button to close the Create a Filter Wizard.

11. Click the Home tab and then click the Publish Item button to save your changes to the server.

Adding a report

Reports are the primary data visualizers in a PerformancePoint dashboard, providing your audience with a friendly platform to view and explore their data. Several types of reports templates are available in PerformancePoint. One of the easiest and most effective is the Analytic grid. The Analytic grid offers your audience a table that you can expand or collapse to see the multiple levels of detail.

Follow these steps to walk through the mechanics of creating an Analytic Grid report:

1. Click the Create tab and then click Analytic Grid.

   The Analytic Grid Report Wizard opens.

2. Enter a name for your report in the Name text box.

3. Click the Select Display Folder to specify where you want your report to be saved on the server. Select an existing folder or create a new one. Click the Next button when you're done.

4. On the Select a Data Source page, select the data connection you want to use as the source data for your report.

5. Click the Finish button to review the settings.

6. Click the Close button to close the Create a Filter Wizard.

7. Click the Home tab and then click the Publish Item button to save your changes to the server.

8. Click the Design tab to get to the window shown in Figure 16-9.

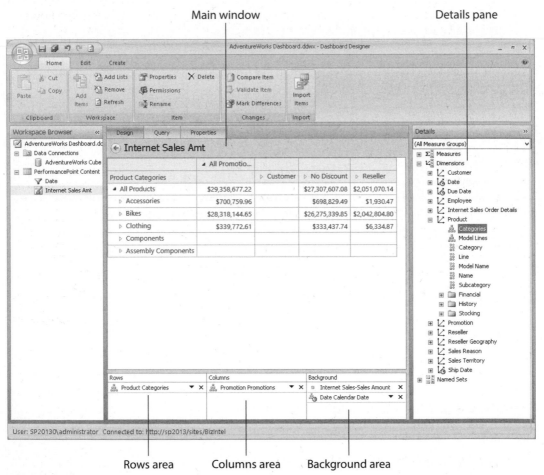

Figure 16-9: Use the Design tab to build out your report.

9. Click and drag the needed dimensions in the Details window to the Rows, Columns, and Background areas (similar to building a Pivot Table in Excel).

10. Click the Home tab, and then click the Publish Item button to save your changes to the server.

The Design tab has five distinct sections:

➤ **The main window:** Here you can see the current layout and results of your report as it will appear in your dashboard. This view updates as you drag and drop cube dimensions or measures onto the cube drop area.

➤ **The Details pane:** This area on the right lets you browse the dimensions and measures of the cube, which are defined based on your data connection. As you identify dimensions and members that you want to use in your report, you can drag and drop them into the Rows, Columns, or Background areas.

➤ **The Rows, Columns, and Background areas:** By dragging dimensions and measures from the Details pane onto these areas, you effectively build a simple MDX query that is used to populate your report. The Rows area corresponds to the horizontal rows of your grid. The Columns area corresponds to the vertical columns of your grid. The Background area contains any hidden filters you want applied to your grid.

Preparing your final dashboard

Dashboards generally have two or more reports, and at least one filter that operates on one or all of the reports in the dashboard simultaneously (called a *global filter*). In the PerformancePoint Content window, to save time you can copy and paste when you want to generate multiple reports, filters, or data connections that might have only slight variations. Figure 16-10 shows an example where the first report (Internet Sales Amt) was copied and pasted into the PerformancePoint Content section, and modified so that it would show Reseller Sales instead of Internet Sales.

The steps to do this are as follows:

1. In the Background zone of the new report, right-click the measure you want to duplicate and select Delete (or click the x on the measure).

   In this case, you right-click the Internet Sales – Sales Amt measure.

2. Drag the measure to the Background zone of the new report.

   In this example, the measure is Reseller Sales – Sales Amt.

3. Rename the new report.

   In this case, the new report is Reseller Sales Amt.

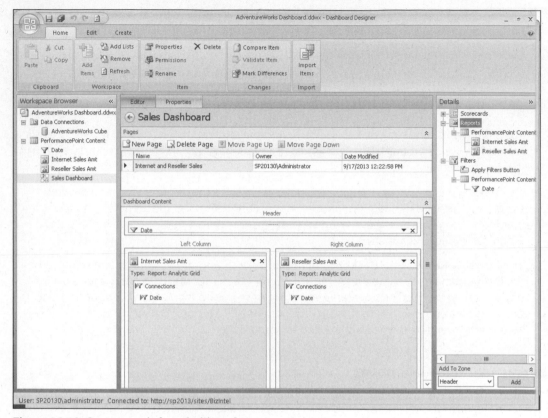

Figure 16-10: Content ready for a dashboard.

Publishing dashboards

After you have created filters and reports, you're ready to combine these widgets into a meaningful dashboard that can be deployed to SharePoint for personal use or shared with others.

To create a dashboard, right-click the PerformancePoint Content folder in the Workspace Browser and select New ➔ Dashboard. Then you can choose a template. The most common template is the Header, 2 Columns template, which allows you to place one or more filters in the header and multiple reports in the columns.

Tip
You can modify the dashboard later to include more rows and columns.

Dashboard authoring takes place in the Dashboard Editor, which works like other authoring interfaces in PerformancePoint. A list of usable content appears in the Details pane (on the right), which you can drag and drop into the Dashboard Content pane in the center. Unlike Reports, this is not a WYSIWYG editor, so you won't actually see your data until you publish your dashboard to SharePoint.

Figure 16-11 shows a dashboard consisting of the Internet Sales and Reseller Sales reports in the left and right columns of the Dashboard Content area and the Date filter in the header.

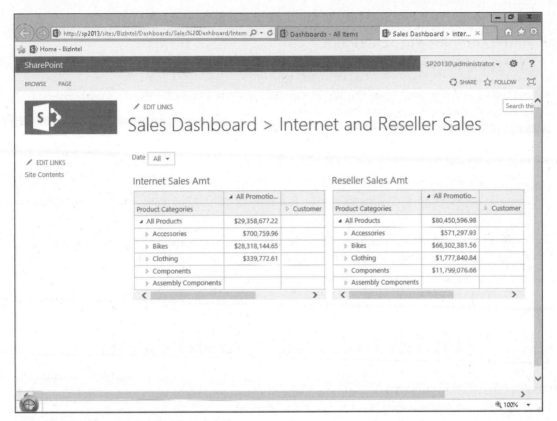

Figure 16-11: A completed dashboard design.

Creating dashboard links

When you add one or more filters to the dashboard, they need to "talk" to the reports. PerformancePoint uses *links* for interaction between objects. Here's how to create a link:

1. Hover your mouse over the filter that you want to use as a source for the link and select Member Unique Name.

   The mouse pointer becomes a cross-hair, indicating drag-and-drop functionality.

2. Drag the filter to the "drop fields" area of a report.

   A dialog box opens.

3. Specify a field for the Connect To value. Click OK when you're done.

   Assuming you used the same dimension in your filter and your report, you see that dimension in the Connect To list; select that one.

You can apply other settings, but the Connect To value is the only one necessary for a functional link between the filter and the report. Do the same for any other reports that you need to update based on selections made in the filter.

Deploying dashboards to SharePoint

Follow these steps when you're ready to deploy your dashboard to SharePoint:

1. In Dashboard Designer, go to the Workspace Browser pane and click the PerformancePoint Content option.

2. Click the Home tab and then click the Refresh button.

3. In the Workspace Browser pane, right-click the target dashboard and then choose Deploy to SharePoint.

   If you're publishing the dashboard for the first time to a SharePoint site, the Deploy To dialog box opens.

4. Select the SharePoint Dashboards library that you want to use and specify a page template for the dashboard. When completed, click OK.

   After your dashboard is deployed, a browser window opens to display your dashboard.

Using PerformancePoint Dashboards

The complexity PerformancePoint dashboards varies greatly depending on who builds them and what they're designed to show. Some PerformancePoint dashboards are simple grids, but others contain highly interactive components that require some training to use.

In this section, you get a few tips for navigating, filtering, and using some of the trickier interactive components found in PerformancePoint Dashboards.

Interacting with filters

A filter exposes a list, sometimes hierarchical, of attributes by which the data can be shown. Attributes displayed in a filter are called *members*. For example, CY 2007 is a member of the Date filter. The currently selected members are displayed at the top of the filter, as shown in Figure 16-12.

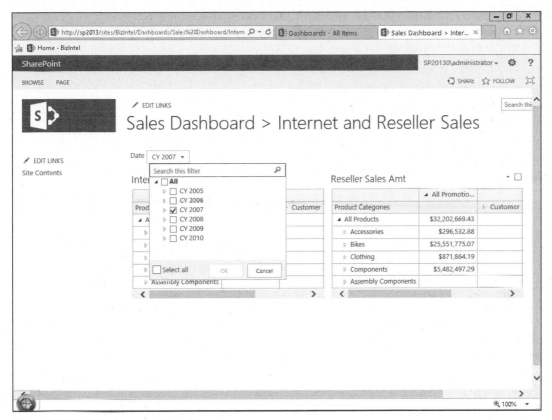

Figure 16-12: A PerformancePoint filter.

A carat in front of a member indicates another level of children members below the member with the plus sign; for example, clicking the carat for CY 2007 drills down to show the semi-annual members for that year.

Filters are used to modify the views on a dashboard page, similar to running a report for a specific set of criteria by selecting one or more report parameters. Although the ways in which a filter interacts with a particular report can vary, most often the effect is to limit the data to whatever selections are made in the filter.

But there are many other ways to use filters. For example, a selection made in a date filter might translate into "retrieve all transactions that occurred on this date or any date since" for purposes of populating the report that is connected to the filter. Because the filter link properties are only visible in Dashboard Designer during the authoring process, the user doesn't always know what is happening and you need to document accordingly.

Though you can place a filter anywhere in a dashboard and configure it to interact with one or more views, which may or may not be located in close proximity to the filter, in a good dashboard design, filters generally appear at the top of the page and interact globally with all views that show data that is relevant to the filter. For example, any chart or grid view that shows data across a date dimension links directly to any date filter in the dashboard. A dashboard user determine whether a filter is linked to a specific view by either changing the selections of the filter while observing the dashboard page to see which views refresh based on the filtering action, or right-clicking the white space of a view (not a cell or data point) and selecting Show Information Bar. If the view is linked, the information bar displays the selections that were applied in the filter.

Searching filters

Integrated into the latest version of PerformancePoint, the filter search feature makes it significantly easier to work with large datasets. Using the filter search, you can perform actions such as the following:

➤ Search through a list of thousands of customers for a specific customer without scrolling. You could find all customers whose names begin with "SMI" or end with "TH".

➤ Select all "Monday" members in a hierarchical Date filter without traversing any hierarchies to check individual boxes (assuming the lowest level has a long date format that includes day of week; for example, "Monday, September 18"). To perform this action, you would search for "Monday" and then select the Select All check box at the bottom of the filter. This causes the report data to be filtered to all Mondays. In the past, doing something like this would have required a separate Day of Week filter.

Ignoring the filter

You cannot remove a filter from the dashboard, but there are other ways to ignore it. The top-most member in a filter is usually a catch-all bucket, appropriately named [All]. If you select the All member of the Date filter, you're viewing data for all available time periods. However, sometimes a filter won't show an All member, and in this case you can click the Select Visible button to select all top-level members. This causes all available data to be retrieved at and below the level of the top-most members in the filter. Similarly, you can click this button twice to clear any selections at the top-most level.

Default and remembered selection, security-limited filters

Filters apply changes to dashboard views after members are selected and Apply is clicked. However, the first time a dashboard page is opened, any filters appearing on that page have one or more members selected by default, causing the views to initialize based on certain predefined conditions. For example, the dashboard design may require that the most recently added data be displayed by default, in which case the date filter would have a default member of the current date, or the current month, and so on. Likewise, a Currency filter may default to USD.

It is also possible that two different users of the same dashboard would see different lists of available members in the same filter, and therefore have different default members. For example, if the business data is segmented by organizational responsibilities, with some users falling into a corporate category and others falling into specific business units, corporate users may see all business units while the rest may only see their business units.

Select and multi-select filter behaviors

Some filters allow more than one member to be selected, making user-defined ranges possible, as when the first six members of the level corresponding to months are selected in the date filter, creating a range of the first-half of the year. Filters that allow multiple selections are called *multi-select filters* and have check boxes to the left of each member (see Figure 16-13).

Figure 16-13: Higher-level selections override lower-level selections.

Multi-select filters differ from single-select in that multiple "buckets" can be selected, which provides greater flexibility for end users to query needed data. However, multi-select filters can be more difficult to navigate:

> ➤ **A user can't clear a selection.** There is no Clear All button, which can cause difficulties when trying to clear selections that have been made several levels deep in a multilevel hierarchy.

> ➤ **A top-most ancestor overrides all other choices.** If a member is selected, but its parent or ancestor is also selected, the top-most ancestor overrides all, as shown in Figure 16-13, where CY 2007 overrides the selections that were made at lower levels of the hierarchy.

The override also applies to the All member, which should be cleared if specific members below it are selected.

Ad hoc filters

PerformancePoint dashboards are enabled for multidimensional analysis. In a given view, dimensions are preconfigured to be located in either the rows, columns, or filter area. However, dimensions can be moved around, and new dimensions can be added based on user interactions.

For example, right-click a member of the Date dimension and select Drill Down By Dimension Location. The Date dimension moves to the filter area (with the member that you right-clicked already selected), and the Location dimension moves to the view where the Date dimension was before.

Dashboard navigation

A dashboard is comprised of links, filters, views, and cells or chart points (collectively called *cells*). User interactions occur either at the page level, as when clicking a link or changing a filter, or within a view, as when drilling down on a cell. Links make it possible to navigate from one dashboard page to another, each with different data and page layouts.

In PerformancePoint, all navigational links appear at the upper-left corner of the dashboard page. When navigating from one page to another, you see the same filter selections if the same filter appears in both pages.

Dashboard interactive capabilities

Many dashboard reports give the user additional capabilities. These features are designed to make the dashboard conform to more of a "self-service" reporting paradigm and allow for data-driven business decisions.

Right-click a chart or grid report — not a data point in a chart — and you find these options to manipulate your data:

➤ **Pivot your data.** Choose Pivot and the X and Y dimensions are swapped in the view. You can often get additional insights in the data.

➤ **Change your report type.** Choose Report Type and then select a different type. Changing the report type allows you to view the same data in different ways, sometimes deriving additional insights into the data as you change the view. For example, you can change a line chart to a bar chart or a grid. Sometimes this spotlights interrelationships in the data more effectively.

➤ **Format your report.** Choose Format Report and then select a new format. In a grid report, you can switch between compact and tabular layouts. In a chart, you can move the legend or remove it completely. Sometimes moving the legend makes a chart more readable.

➤ **Show all available filters.** Choose Show Information Bar and all currently applied filters are displayed at the top of the report, making it easy to see which filters are currently selected in the dashboard. This is especially important if you have a report open in its own window to make it easier to see the data points, and you can no longer view the dashboard filters at a glance without tabbing back to the dashboard Web page.

➤ **Drill through your data.** You can choose Drill Down, Drill Down To, and Drill Up. These navigation commands allow you to explore the current data point by either lower-level detail, or by breaking out the current data point across another dimension. Figure 16-14 shows how one data cell could be broken out by a completely different dimension.

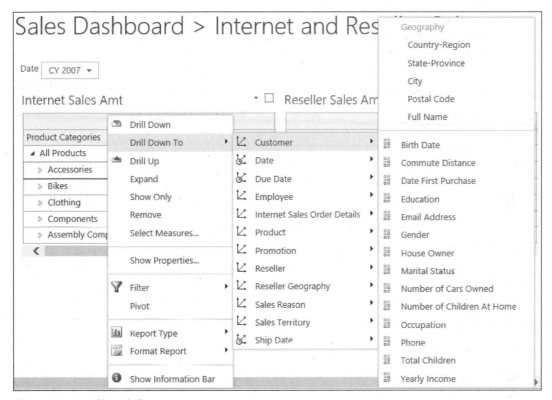

Figure 16-14: Ad hoc drilling.

Appendixes

Understanding the Big Data Toolset

Big data refers to a broad set of tools that are designed to work with large data volumes. These tools are gaining popularity because they solve the limitations of traditional tools by scaling up on hardware and sharing the workload across many linked computers. Using this divide-and-conquer approach allows big data technologies to accomplish tasks that are not feasible otherwise.

When it comes to analytics, there are some special considerations regarding big data. You need an easy way to access and navigate platforms without the need to spend precious time learning new programming languages such as Java. In the past few years several tools have come available that offer a big data SQL solution: a tool that sits on top of a big data platform and allows you to write SQL queries against the big data engine.

In this appendix we review the big data SQL tools on the market now, giving you a sense of the big data landscape. You'll also discover how you can connect to those tools from Excel.

Big Data SQL Offerings

There are several big data offerings that support a relatively easy-to-use SQL engine on top of Hadoop or another similar-style platform.

Note

We cover the talked-about entrants into the market as of this writing. Note, though, that this space is quite new and many companies are jumping into it almost daily.

Most of these technologies have a similar approach to big data SQL. They scale up on hardware and use a divide-and-conquer approach to break big data volumes into small chunks and distribute the processing across multiple nodes. The main differentiator among the various technologies is whether or not they are Hadoop-based. For example, Amazon Redshift does not sit on top of Hadoop, but instead uses a different technology that allows similar scalability as Hadoop. On the other hand, Hortonworks and Cloudera are tools that are installed on top of Hadoop and take advantage of its scalability features.

Amazon Redshift

Provider: Amazon under the Amazon Web Services platform

Web Site: `http://aws.amazon.com/redshift`

Platforms: This tool only runs in the cloud on Amazon Web Services.

Technology Overview: Amazon Redshift is a fully managed cloud-based data warehouse service. You can think of it as a kind of DropBox for databases ranging from a few hundred gigabytes to a petabyte or more. The technology Redshift uses is built to make it easy to scale up on hardware as data needs grow. It also includes compression and a columnar-based design that is best suited for analytics queries and can support very large data volumes.

Pros: Amazon Redshift is a production-grade tool that delivers on its promises. Getting up and running with it is easy, and managing it is even easier.

Cons: It is only available in the cloud with no option for on-site installation. Connecting to the Amazon Redshift via Microsoft tools is a challenge from behind the firewall. Although, most big data SQL tools that are in the cloud have this same challenge.

Hortonworks Hive

Provider: Hortonworks (partners with Microsoft)

Web Site: `http://hortonworks.com`

Platforms: This tool is available on Hadoop and can be cloud- or on-premises–based.

Technology Overview: Hive is the open-source SQL implementation on Hadoop. Up to recently it did not allow real-time SQL queries. However, this has changed with the Stinger initiative, which has the objective of configuring Hive to allow real-time SQL queries.

Pros: On-premises or cloud installation. Allowing on-premises installation is critical if your organization has a no-cloud policy.

Cons: As of this writing, Hive is still relatively new and the real-time engine is in Beta release.

Cloudera Impala

Provider: Cloudera

Web Site: `www.cloudera.com`

Platforms: This tool is a real-time SQL engine that was developed by Cloudera and sits on the Hadoop platform.

Technology Overview: Impala is a proprietary SQL engine that is designed for analytics purposes and high scalability. It can read traditional Hadoop file formats and can span to multiple Hadoop nodes. It uses C++ instead of Java for performance and doesn't translate SQL into MapReduce.

Pros: On-premises or cloud installation. Allowing on-premises installation is critical if your organization has a no-cloud policy.

Defining MapReduce

Many of the big data toolsets offer MapReduce, a software framework originally developed by Google to improve its indexing algorithms and heuristics. The idea behind MapReduce Is that large amounts of unstructured data can be processed in lots of smaller parallel nodes across many proces-sers or stand-alone machines. This effectively distributes the process loads such that it allows pro-grammers to handle massive amounts of data much faster and without communication or server failures. MapReduce is most commonly used for data mining, analysis of large financial systems, and data-intensive scientific simulations.

Cons: Does not allow incremental update of data, forcing a complete rebuild when underlying data changes. This is a pretty big limitation for large datasets as it can take quite a bit of time to reload.

IBM Big SQL

Provider: IBM

Web Site: www.ibm.com/software/data/bigdata

Platforms: This tool is an SQL engine that was developed by IBM and sits on the IBM-variant of the Hadoop platform called BigInsights.

Technology Overview: Big SQL is a proprietary SQL engine that is designed for analytics purposes. According to IBM, Big SQL takes the SQL syntax submitted by the user and translates it to individual MapReduce jobs. Big SQL can also support real-time queries over a single node only.

Pros: On-premises or cloud installation. Allowing on-premises installation is critical if your organization has a no-cloud policy.

Cons: Does not allow real-time SQL queries against multiple nodes because it relies on MapReduce jobs for that.

Google BigQuery

Provider: Google

Web Site: http://cloud.google.com/products/bigquery

Platforms: This tool is a real-time SQL engine that was developed by Google using its proprietary technology.

Technology Overview: Google BigQuery is a proprietary SQL engine that is designed for analytics purposes and high scalability. BigQuery is the public version of Google's own Dremel query service that Google has used for years to track device installation and analyze spam. Dealing in read-only datasets, Google BigQuery allows programmers to use SQL-like queries to extract and analyze billions of rows at a time.

Pros: Is capable and easy to administer.

Cons: Cloud-only installation, which can be limiting for some organizations. Per Google's description, "append-only" implies some limitation on updates of historical data, which could be limiting for analytics datasets.

Facebook Presto SQL

Provider: Facebook

Web Site: http://prestodb.io

Platforms: This tool is an open-source SQL engine that was developed by Facebook and sits on top of the open-source Hadoop platform.

Technology Overview: Presto SQL was developed by Facebook to address the latency limitations of MapReduce jobs and allow interactive queries against large datasets stored in Hadoop.

Pros: On-premises or cloud installation. Allowing on-premises installation is critical if your organization has a no-cloud policy.

Cons: New tool relative to the others in this chapter.

Defining a Big Data Connection

For analytics purposes, your job will mainly involve accessing data from a big data platform. Loading the data into a platform requires specialized skills and assistance from your system administrators. However, after the data is loaded into the platform, you can access it via your analytics tools, including Excel.

Most big data tools allow you to access data via ODBC or JDBC drivers. With Microsoft tools, you use ODBC drivers. The first step in connecting to the platform is to create your ODBC connection.

Note

Before you can connect to your platform, make sure that you have the drivers installed on your machine. Each tool has its own requirements for an ODBC driver. For example, Amazon Redshift requires you to install the PostgreSQL ODBC driver to connect to one of its clusters. You can find the proper driver for each on the tool's Web site.

After you have installed the proper driver, follow these steps to connect to your platform:

1. Open the Data Sources (ODBC) Administrator dialog box and click the System DSN tab (see Figure A-1).

Tip

If you don't know where ODBC is installed on your computer, choose Start ➜ Search, and type ODBC in the search bar.

You may already have data sources defined because of other tools that use ODBC connections. In our case we have two Redshift connections defined.

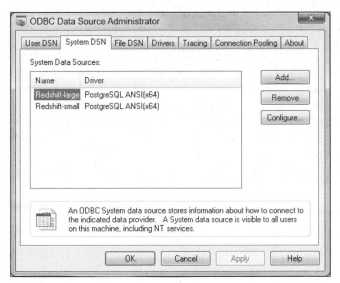

Figure A-1: ODBC Data Source Administrator dialog box.

2. Click the Add button to add a new ODBC connection.

   A window opens with a list of available drivers on your computer, as shown in Figure A-2.

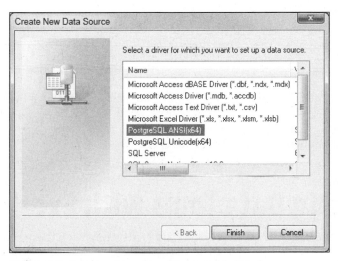

Figure A-2: Select a driver from the available listed.

3. Select the driver you installed.

4. Click Finish.

   The Setup window opens, where you define your connection (see Figure A-3).

   This window is specific to the driver you're using and the tool you're connecting to. You get the connection information from your big data administrator.

Special cloud considerations

When connecting to a cloud installation, you need to be aware of your network's firewall settings. This issue only comes into play when you have long running queries (30 minutes or more) as may be the case with big data queries. By default, firewall settings may kill TCP/IP connections that run long. This causes big data tools to not return the result set to the client tool. Getting around this issue requires you to override this default option by setting the TCP/IP Keep Alive setting to Yes. This option varies by driver and some of them do not allow it (as is the case with the PostgreSQL ODBC driver). Big data tools are still maturing, and most vendors are working on making it easier for you to connect to their platforms.

Figure A-3: Driver Setup window.

5. Enter your connection information, click the Test button to test your connection, and then click Save.

Your connection is now ready to be used in your analytics application.

Connecting to Big Data Tools with Excel

After defining your ODBC connection, you can access your big data tool by following these steps with Excel:

1. From the Data tab, click the Connections button.

   The Excel Workbook Connections dialog box opens.

2. Click the Add button at the top of the window.

   The Existing Connections window opens.

3. Click the Browse for More button.

   The Select Data Source window opens.

4. Click the New Source button.

   The Data Connection Wizard opens (see Figure A-4).

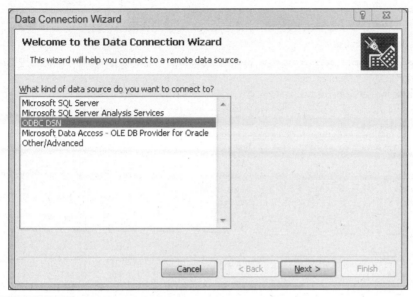

Figure A-4: Data Connection Wizard.

5. Select ODBC DSN and click Next.

   The Connect to ODBS Data Source screen opens, with a list of ODBC connections that have been defined on your computer (see Figure A-5).

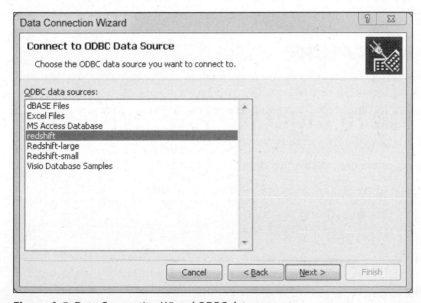

Figure A-5: Data Connection Wizard ODBC data sources.

6. Select your ODBC connection and click Next.

   The Select Database and Table screen opens (see Figure A-6).

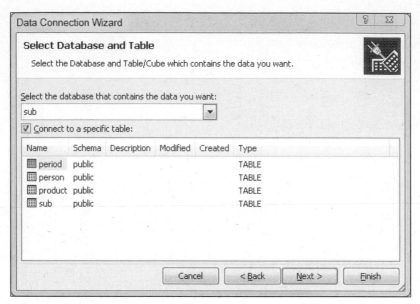

Figure A-6: The Select Database and Table screen.

7. Select a table that you want to access and click Finish.

   The Workbook Connections dialog box opens again with the connection you just defined.

8. Click Close at the bottom of the dialog box to return to the main workbook.

Modifying your connection

With a defined connection, Excel only allows you to connect to a table or a view. You can, however, change the SQL that has been built by the wizard to create a more sophisticated SQL query that would better suit your reporting needs. To accomplish this, follow these steps:

1. On the Data tab, click the Connections button.

   The Workbook Connections dialog box opens.

2. Select your defined connection and click the Properties button.

   The Connection Properties dialog box opens.

3. Click the Definition tab (see Figure A-7).

Figure A-7: The Connection Properties dialog box.

4. Modify the SQL in the Command Text box.

   Figure A-7 shows how we changed the SQL to return the top 10 rows only for that table, but you can get as sophisticated as you want with your query (provided your big data SQL tool supports the syntax you're trying to use).

5. When you're done, click OK to save your changes.

Using your connection

Now that you have defined the connection in Excel, you can start using it.

1. From the Data tab, click the Existing Connections button.

   The Existing Connections window opens.

2. Select your connection and click the Open button.

   The Import Data dialog box opens (see Figure A-8).

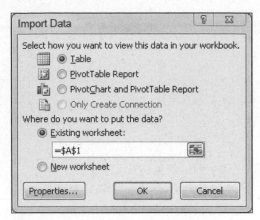

Figure A-8: The Import Data dialog box.

3. Select the type of view you want to create and click OK.

Excel links the table to the query you defined in your connection. You can refresh this data as needed.

Caution

Be careful not to return large amounts of data in your query as your source could have large data volumes.

Considerations for Delivering Mobile BI

A business intelligence platform is not complete without the ability to deliver dashboards and reports via mobile devices. The Microsoft BI platform addresses your mobile access requirements via an array of ever-increasing deployment options. As of this writing, accessing Microsoft BI functionality via mobile devices includes the following deployment scenarios:

> ➤ With **SharePoint 2010** or **2013** and a supported mobile device, you can view sites in the Business Intelligence Center, browse Excel Services reports, interact with PerformancePoint dashboards, and access Reporting Services reports.

> ➤ With **Power View** and a supported mobile device, you can view dashboards and data visualizations in HTML5 (currently in Preview).

> ➤ Using **Office 365** and a supported mobile device, you can deploy Excel Services dashboards and Reporting Services reports. A licensing option called Power BI includes more BI functionality than is available with the standard Office 365 subscription.

> ➤ With **SQL Server 2012 SP1** or later and a supported mobile device, you can view Reporting Services reports, available in the SQL Server Report Manager, using Internet Explorer 10 (or later) or Safari. These reports can be accessed via an iPad, Windows phone, or Windows Surface.

In the following sections, we list each of these deployment scenarios along with caveats and prerequisites.

Note

Check the online Microsoft resources frequently for updates. The list of available technologies for mobile use cases changes frequently, and you want to be aware of the latest options before committing to a deployment plan.

Mobile Deployment Scenarios and Considerations

There are several considerations for addressing mobile use cases, including the type of device (tablet, smartphone, and so on), the operating system running on that device, and the browser. We discuss each of these in the following sections.

In addition to the deployment scenarios that address hardware, software, and settings, there are considerations for offering reports and dashboards to your users via their mobile devices. One of the most important considerations is how the report or dashboard renders on a given device. The same report or dashboard can look completely different depending on whether it is viewed in a desktop browser, a tablet, or a mobile phone. Some planning and testing is required for large-scale deployments to ensure that your dashboards and reports have a professional and consistent look and feel. Though beyond the scope of this book, there are strategies to improve the user experience, such as creating multiple views of the same content so that the optimal user experience can be triggered depending on the device being used.

Mobile devices

The list of supported devices for SharePoint and other Microsoft BI applications is continuously changing. In general, Apple and any manufacturer running Windows Phone or Windows 8 or 8.1 OS are supported. Android is supported for accessing SharePoint 2013 sites using a rendering setting called contemporary view.

➤ **Apple:** Both the iPhone and the iPad are widely used devices. iOS 5 or greater is needed to run most Microsoft BI functionality (some Microsoft BI applications require iOS 6 or greater).

➤ **Microsoft:** In 2012, Microsoft released the Windows 8 operating system, which included many features intended to address mobile use cases. Microsoft's own tablet, Surface Pro 2, runs Windows 8. And as of this writing, there are numerous other manufacturers with tablets running the Windows 8 operating system, including Samsung, Acer, Lenovo, and Asus. Many of the Microsoft BI capabilities are compatible with mobile devices running Windows 8.

The following Windows operating systems are currently supported for Microsoft BI functionality: Windows Phone 7.5 or greater, Windows RT, and Windows 8 or greater.

Note

The list of supported devices, operating systems, and apps is constantly changing. To get the very latest information on what devices and operating systems are supported, use your favorite search engine to look up **Mobile Support Microsoft Business Intelligence Tools.**

Browser-based deployments on mobile devices

There is a wide range of options for viewing SharePoint and Reporting Services content using mobile devices. For example, SharePoint 2013 can be rendered using a setting called *contemporary view,* which optimizes the rendered view for mobile devices and expands the range of supported devices and browsers to include not only the iPhone, iPad, and Windows Phone devices, but also Android devices running Android 4.0 or later. Contemporary view achieves this level of flexibility by rendering Web pages using HTML5.

In addition, Power View, running in SharePoint or Office 365, supports the same level of flexibility by rendering in HTML5.

Running apps on mobile devices

For many mobile devices, native apps can be downloaded and run on the device. These apps are typically developed specifically for the operating system and user controls that are available on the mobile device. Several apps that offer Microsoft BI functionality have been developed for Windows 8 or greater and are available in the Windows Store for downloading on a compatible device. For example, there is a Power BI app that runs on Windows 8.1 if you have an Office 365 Power BI subscription account. The list of apps that provide enhanced Microsoft BI functionality on mobile devices is expected to grow.

Office 365

Launched in 2011, Microsoft Office 365 provides organizations with subscription-based pricing for Microsoft Office, SharePoint, Exchange, and other productivity applications. In addition, Office 365 serves as a cloud-based platform for hosting SharePoint and other business applications. By extension, an organization can license a given number of seats and provide these users with the BI functionality that comes with SharePoint.

In 2013, Microsoft expanded its Office 365 licensing models to include Power BI. This package includes Power Pivot, Power View, Power Map, and SharePoint. There are several key benefits to using Office 365 for mobile deployments. These include subscription-based pricing for SharePoint and reduced setup and maintenance.

To take advantage of the BI capabilities offered by Office 365, users require a compatible device or Web browser. Currently, supported devices include the iPad (running iOS 6 or greater) or any device running Windows 8 or greater. Desktop Web browser access is supported for Safari or Internet Explorer 10 or greater.

SQL Server Reporting Services

Some organizations run SQL Server Reporting Services in *native mode,* meaning that you can access reports via the Web, but outside of SharePoint. This is possible because SQL Server Reporting Services includes a built-in Web server, or alternatively, the option to leverage Internet Information Services, the standard Windows Web server, as a means for deploying reports over the Web. The Report Manager page serves as a catalog of reports that can be browsed by end users.

When viewing Reporting Services reports on a mobile device, you can leverage all the features that have made Reporting Services a popular enterprise tool. For example, you can expand and collapse report areas showing a plus or minus indicator, apply sorts and filters (also called *parameters*), and click hyperlinks. Reports can also be exported to TIFF, PDF, XML, CSV, MHTML, Excel, and Word.

When reports are hosted natively using Reporting Services, users can access them using iPad running iOS 6 or greater, or Windows Phone or Surface running Windows 8 or greater. In addition, SQL Server must be 2012 SP1 or greater.

Note

When using Apple's Safari browser, you cannot view reports in Report Manager, and the only report export options are TIFF and PDF.

SharePoint 2010 and 2013

This book has highlighted many applications that run as part of SharePoint and are intended to provide reporting, data visualization, and other business intelligence functionality for end users. Users with compatible mobile devices can access many of the same SharePoint features that are provided to desktop users. Aside from the ability to open Excel, Word, and PowerPoint documents, SharePoint mobile functionality includes

- ➤ Browsing sites in a SharePoint Business Intelligence Center
- ➤ Interacting with Reporting Services and Excel Services reports
- ➤ Interacting with PerformancePoint dashboards
- ➤ Exporting to PowerPoint or Excel

As of this writing, compatible mobile devices include iPad running iOS 5 or greater, tablets running Windows 8, devices running Windows Phone 7.5 or greater, and Windows Surface running Surface RT. Supported browsers include Safari and Internet Explorer Mobile.

New in SharePoint 2013, contemporary view is a user setting (that is, selected on the device) that causes pages to be rendered in HTML5. Not only does this view optimize the Web content layout for mobile devices, it also allows SharePoint content to be rendered on Android (as well as on the standard supported browsers).

Note

In order to allow users to select contemporary view, the Mobile Browser View feature must be activated for the SharePoint site. This feature ensures that the mobile device is running a compatible browser and OS before rendering pages in HTML5.

The default setting of Classic View causes pages to be rendered in standard HTML format. This format looks exactly like SharePoint 2010.

Using the Full-Screen UI setting causes the content to look exactly like it would on a desktop computer, though more zooming and scrolling is required to see the entire screen.

⊙ Index

StatSlice Systems is a business intelligence technology consulting firm headquartered in Dallas, TX which specializes in data warehousing and business analytics. Founded in 2006 by Bernard Wehbe and Jared Decker, StatSlice provides strategic data services that impart the skills, processes, technologies, applications, and practices needed to achieve better business decision-making. The company emphasizes highly involved client-inter-action combined with a compliance with key business intelligence imple-mentation principles.

The StatSlice team is comprised of high caliber talent nurtured in an environment that encourages resourcefulness, innovation, and creativity. Their forward-thinking philosophy is centered upon the distinct purpose of providing the best data-driven decisions that significantly increase the profit of their clients.

If you are ready to improve your efficiency and launch your business beyond the competition by realizing the potential in your data, contact StatSlice Systems for your strategic data service needs.

www.statslice.com

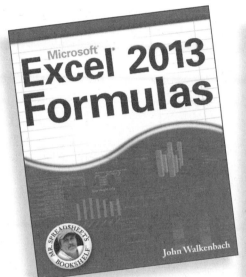

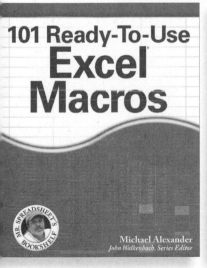
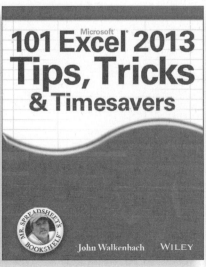
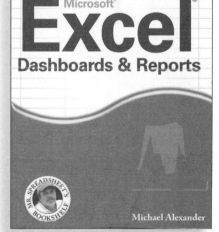